New Visions for the Future of Mankind

Channelled Messages from the Pleiades

To my spiritual brother Nick in Love and Light Eileen

GW00601051

Eileen Coleman

Published by Eileen Coleman
Publishing partner: Paragon Publishing, Rothersthorpe
First published 2009
© Eileen Coleman 2009

ISBN 978-1-899820-64-1
Book design, layout and production management by Into Print
www.intoprint.net
Printed and bound in UK and USA by Lightning Source

Go Forth and Learn

Go forth and learn – be like the urn that is forever full. As each new truth is learnt and understood, more knowledge will filter through in an endless stream. Sometimes it comes as if in a torrent and takes time to digest – at other times it is but a mere trickle. Don't keep it to yourself so that the water becomes stagnant – but pass on this knowledge to others!

Given to me by my guide Tyekinder at the beginning of my spiritual journey in 1992.

www.newvisionsformankind.com

Contents

Introduction by our Star Friends from the Pleiades

We– would like to commemorate this book to all those of you who have, unwittingly, been our constant companions over most of your lifetimes. We initialise this book to beam ahead of you and forecast what can be achieved, on a grander scale, if we all pull together.

We embrace you and lay down no laws that you cannot examine for yourselves and see their true worth, for we are a nation of star gazers and we vouch for the fact that we have come a long way to be here with you now, foretelling your destiny! We know that you will see this in a new light as you examine the data we have retrieved for your perusal, and we come flanked by those from other star systems, who have a vested interest in how this all pans out! We only come to take you all back home where you belong, and we beckon you now to hasten your footsteps along this highway of love. There is no time to dawdle, we have much to achieve in a relatively short space of time, and all must be ready when the trumpet calls to take you home!

Make haste little ones – we enfold you in our love and ask that you take care of yourselves and your offspring. We make a place ready to receive each and every one of you, and we take great pleasure in ushering in a time of immense joy for one and all. We have fulfilled our destiny and we wait now – for on the horizon all is beckoning, bringing us into alignment with a just cause that will free mankind from the manacles of sloth and discontent, and we indulge ourselves at this time to make that connection that will bring us even closer to the truth!

Acknowledgement from Author

First and foremost I would like to thank my 'Star Friends' who have been so patient with me, waiting for me to reach that frequency that would enable us to access higher dimensions together. I cannot describe the overwhelming love, support and encouragement I have received from them, and hopefully will continue to do so until we are reunited in a new framework of existence. I would especially like to thank my husband for trusting in me and for making that leap of faith, leaving behind our home in England to move to Wales. Without his love and support I would have found the pathway much harder! I would also like to thank my old friends in Lincolnshire, and the many new ones I've made in Wales – all who have made my spiritual pathway much richer.

Author's Introduction

I feel most honoured to have become an ambassador for our cousins the Pleiadians who have used me, along with many others, to channel information for the people of Earth. These highly evolved 'Beings of Light' from the Pleiades have joined together with other star systems, and divined a method of communication with sensitives on Earth by interfusing in, what we would call, a telepathic condition. They are able to reach out and initiate a bonding between those souls who have agreed to work closely with them, preparing mankind for a mass exodus from Earth! They tell us that the destruction of planet Earth is no idle speculation in the distant future, but something we must all be prepared for at this time in our evolution! However, we are given hope as they explain how they have travelled back through time to change a catastrophic end result. We all will be given the choice of leaving for a new planet of outstanding beauty or staying in a world that is hell bent on destruction! They deliver these words, reminding us that this event has been foretold on many occasions in the past through various mediums that have visited Earth for a brief spell.

At the beginning of my spiritual journey in 1992, I was urged by my guides and inspirers to write down their messages and so I started to keep a journal. These communications encouraged me not to give up hope when my world seemed to be caving in on me. I would sit for hours reading their words many times over, and gained a tremendous amount of comfort and support from them. With hindsight, I see they were preparing me for future communications on a higher frequency, which we are now achieving with increasing clarity. I now trust them implicitly and with promptings from my star friends, a move to Wales in 2003 helped to further raise my frequencies. This enabled access to even higher dimensions, and it was here that I received startling information to be passed on to the 'Children of Earth!'

In Wales I've been drawn to people that I feel I've known before in other lifetimes; there is a strong feeling of a gathering of the clan, and this is happening all over the world with like-minded people and soul groups, all gathering together to bring light into the world! There are great changes happening even as we speak, and there is an even greater need to listen and take stock, preparing ourselves for 2012. Time is running out and we will have to make our choices as to where our allegiances lie! Those who are spiritually aware are growing in numbers rapidly across the whole world. I believe we come to pave the way for the Children of Earth, helping them to raise their vibrational level and assisting them on their journey back to the stars! It will come as a great shock to many – shattering belief systems to the core – but there is no doubt that we are already on a rollercoaster ride. We must do all we can in helping others to come to terms with the fact that our lives are going to change – and quite dramatically! 'New Visions for the Future of Mankind' gives an exciting insight into where we are heading in the 21st century. It is a most incredible and momentous time for the people of Earth, for we are all being helped and guided each step of the way, towards a brighter more positive way of life in a new world, where all can live together in peace and harmony!

Prologue

On 10th September in 2000 I sat in meditation with a very close friend, completely unprepared for what I was given! The moon is a beautiful thing . . . a beautiful work of art, radiating her light far out into the cosmos as she touches Mother Earth with her silvery beams, lighting the sky with her beauty. We ponder on these thoughts and give you our love as always; sometimes we win our battles in a way that troubles us, but we shall make a point of coming together whenever those troubles besiege us. Shallow is the water of life at times of strife – temptations come and go but you will remain firm, for we need to know that you are with us at all times! We depend on you as you depend on us to come together, for that light is shining way out into the night's sky touching us all with her beauty and wisdom. *These feelings then changed dramatically, and I began to feel very anxious and fearful.* We tremble at the terror in store for peoples of the Earth plane, we submit ourselves to anguish most awesome . . . most terrible! *I felt that I was being plunged down and down into a dark blackness, and then there was nothing except a deep, deep melancholy! I couldn't shake off the feelings of despair and had to break off the session.*

The following day I sat alone, asking for more information. There are better ways of healing the breach, and mankind will soon become aware of a need to raise their vibrations to a higher level. In the past, levels of high security have been developed in countries near and far. Levels that if used, will destruct mankind completely . . . erasing them from the surface of Earth! We have adjusted ourselves to the fact that this is certain. Man has the power to obliterate mankind from the world as we know it! We have made many mistakes in the past – but none as fearful and awesome as this! We tell you now that a time will come when this will be so! *I asked, "Surely there is something we can do to avert such a tragedy?"* We strive always ever onwards towards our goal of peace and harmony to reign the Earth forever more, and we attempt to re-organise patterns of thinking. Destruction may overcome your planet, but we will never desist from our work of overcoming interminable problems of the Earth plane. **We speak now of events that may come in the foreseeable future, events of catastrophic proportion as elements of fire and air tremble in disfiguration of extreme power!** We can and must transmute these negative energies to ones of love, enveloping the world with love to save her from chaos and despair! We march as an army towards the light, spreading our knowledge and wisdom to all who will listen. Have no fear little one, for we march together in strength, gathering forces, forces of benevolence and love. Love will conquer . . . love will overcome all forces of evil!

One year later on 11th September 2001, I sat in horror and amazement, watching a devastating news flash from America which showed smoke billowing from a tall tower! Suddenly, right before my eyes, a plane ploughed into the second of the twin towers in New York! I stood watching in utter disbelief as the huge explosion sent flames and plumes of smoke towering above those crippled buildings! After my initial shock, I recalled the words given to me almost a year ago to the day – elements of fire and air trembling in disfiguration of extreme power! Multitudes have been slaughtered in catastrophic circumstances that we will never forget . . . our heartfelt thoughts go out to the victims of that terrible disaster and to the families of those who have died. The whole world is in a state of complete and utter shock!

I sat for guidance and strength, sending out healing thoughts to the world. I was then shown a silver ribbon of light across the sky, and had the feeling of putting one foot onto a winding pathway to Heaven and the Stars! I'm sensing many hearts beating as one and have the impression of putting down my silver roots into the earth, which are spreading across the whole world, joining in communion with other souls who are all concentrating on the heart centre. I saw Inuits surrounded by snow followed by Mayans dancing in the sun, there is a strong feeling of all nationalities and all hearts beating as one!

We speak as one voice; we welcome you here amongst us once more. Transcripts are needed now, and information is to be brought through regarding certain issues surrounding the Earth plane at this time, issues that need to be resolved, bringing the hearts of mankind closer together. Transcripts recorded shall be used to exert pressure in certain colonies where there is much turmoil and indignation. We surrender ourselves to you now and we temper our words – alienation has become rife among those who speak in haste and repent at leisure! We have become aware of the necessity to make examples of those with unclean thoughts and minds – and this is aimed at people of distinction! We carry this forward with extreme pressure from those of a higher dimension; tarry not for you are needed now more than ever and we tell it to you straight! Mankind has been merciless, indulging in rank and putrid morals which have brought them to their knees in the mire! Multitudes have suffered and are in great torment . . . souls writhe in turmoil for obscenities of every imaginable horror that have been inflicted on humankind!

We see a need now to tell the world – greater calamities shall befall you unless you aspire to more elevated thoughts! *I stopped as I was bringing through too much doom and gloom; I asked for the highest source of information to be brought through and then started again.* Transcripts shall be made and adhered to at this time, we shall use you well as we did before, but you must take the time and effort to get this right! We have warned you beforehand of what is to come, and we have measured out our advice and information for the exact use of its purpose. We endeavour to show you with words and pictures the message we need to get across. We feel now is the time to make this endeavour as valid as eating and sleeping . . . a valid part of your life! Acceptance is needed on all sides and we shall begin in earnest.

We feel you drawing closer and send out our wave patterns of love to you. Take heart for all is not lost; we beam to you on a frequency of love, joy and peace, which are desired by the majority of your world at this time. We speak of heinous crimes that have been committed by a minority group, and which has led to great despair! We welcome those souls to our realms and surround them in love and healing balm. We treasure those who are left behind to pick up the pieces and bring them strength and love to carry on; to carry the banner of peace and love toward all men, for love reigns supreme. We know it is hard, at this time, to suppress feelings of hatred for such atrocities, inflicted by those perpetrators who will be brought to justice, and this must be seen to be done, however, worldwide war is not something that is to be considered in the scheme of things! Love is and always has been the key to the hearts of mankind; it serves no purpose to inflict bloodshed in revenge – killing will never be the answer! The taking of another's life, the preciousness of life . . . *the feelings here were very emotional, and I felt the tears welling up in my eyes.*

We have often said with our hands on our heart . . . that we could cry an ocean for all that has been done and said in the name of God! *How can we stop war?* Renew your surge of love, send out those loving thoughts into the ethers in great numbers, this will restore peace and harmony! The realms of spirit are vast expanses of love and hate; some are trapped in an underworld of living out their worst fears and fantasies. We seek to inform those who will listen of a greater plan for mankind – evolution of the soul – with interminable frequencies to be exchanged and experienced. We recommend this alternative which remains our only solution! We have exchanged places many times, we have experienced your soul's growth and we have spoken of this to many in your world. We believe as do you, that mankind has reached a point where many will find the darkness intolerably heavy at this time, wreaking havoc on Earth! We deem it necessary to point out that this is only a fleeting glimpse into the past; we can expect a lifting of the curtain very soon. We subject you to these frequencies as a reminder that the world has not outgrown the past; she is simply lifted up to a higher dimension leaving her shroud of sorrow behind. We have dreamed and prayed for such a happening!

We feel we can deliver this prologue, and announce in no uncertain terms, that this mission of ours will not only gain impact in this world, but on many other levels far beyond your comprehension! We know in terms of clemency, we have delivered ultimatums in the past that have been ignored, but we shall ask once more, that you will remember our words and obey instructions down to the last letter, for we can only reach that place of understanding if we strive for perfection in all we do! Suffer the little children to come unto us, for we shall develop a new world where all will grow in love and trust. A resurgence of love and light will ignite the world with far greater ideals and temperament, and as you obey the laws of the land you will grow in stature! Lighting the pathway we now bid you to follow and join us, and in the years to come we will develop and grow in greatest love and fellowship.

Chapter 1
Deliverance

4th January 2005 – *Before retiring for the night I sat in meditation, sending out healing for the world. I felt the urge to pick up my pen and write down the words flooding my mind!* Reckless behaviour initiates a raw understanding of what is needed now and in the future! We rely on each other to entice and grow further directives; we mean to plan out and assist manoeuvres of the highest calibre and we depend, in extreme circumstances, on this new growth to maintain a myriad life support systems. We believe in all honesty that the planet has outgrown itself in many ways, and we rely now on those like you to assist us in our mission, journeying back to the stars! Feel free at this time to understand the galaxies and all their splendour, for we mean to assist those of you who will allow us to enter your atmosphere. *I felt concerned that perhaps I was at risk in sitting for communication so late in the evening.* You are shielded by the light, and in our defence, we assist you at these times by making sure we will not be disturbed. Have no fear, do not fret my little one, for we have a most noble and exciting mission to accomplish! We hold you in the highest regard, knowing your intentions are most honourable and we know, most humbly, you obey dictates of your heart in coming armed with the necessary requisites. We take this time to unveil truths which must be forged and we are of one mind, being instrumental in achieving all aims and objectives. Trust in us Sunbeam, we instigate a brighter future of that there is no doubt!

I'm now being shown people from Thailand where the dreadful Tsunami hit a few days ago! We forge boundaries so that action can be taken to develop countries where strife is rampant. We understand that in some instances, there are recurring nightmares of past events, and these are likely to cause confusion. We know we can curtail avenues of discontent for arguments are rife in the camps, and we need to prepare ourselves for further eruptions! These may come in a matter of weeks and we know that although in place, there will be a far greater need for reliable resources. Reinstate the boundaries given and all will be well, for we foresee greater division ahead if all is not kept in order! *There were several smaller eruptions that took place over the next few weeks, but twelve weeks later there was a further eruption that killed another 2,000 people!*

We broadcast the fact of growing contempt, among certain people, for what is being given to those in need, and we need to remind you all that there is far greater misery than those in the west could possible conceive! We leave it to your imagination and then double and quadruple the catastrophe caused, insurmountable horror upon horrors inflicted on those people left behind that can in no way be recompensed! Helping them to pick up the pieces of their lives will be the best that we can do in these dire circumstances. There is a need now to stand back and estimate the damage caused, only then will we be able to quantify what is essential. The capital required will be vast, and should not be underestimated at any cost; any further advances shall be paid in due course. We deliver now, in no uncertain terms, a full account of what is necessary to enable these people to fulfil their destinies. We vouchsafe for those left behind, a better way of life, and they will follow in the footsteps of their forefathers, obeying the laws of the land and listening to their inner voice, which calls to them at this very time. We need no Sanskrit remedies, for we have achieved far more in a few short days than was ever hoped possible, allowing our feelings to rise to the surface and gather momentum . . . as the tidal wave itself! We now need to incorporate a special needs unit, which will cover to a great extent, further funding, and will be granted in the next few weeks!

7th January 2005 – *We have had severe gale force winds and the power kept going off, luckily it's back on now and I'm sitting for more communication before settling down for the night.* We make a tremendous effort, relentlessly changing the pattern of thinking around the world, anticipating all we can to operate more swiftly. Enclosures of great importance are needed and we have no doubt we can make the necessary contact. Stand aside – so that we may develop a more strategic thought pattern, allowing the necessary by-products to surface that are never ending! We devote a great deal of time and energy into playing out this saga of events, and we develop a powerful intuition that will grow and expand. We foresee in the future, far greater developments taking place and we supply a course of action that may seem extreme! Depend on us to get this right – right down to the last dust and polish! We know that, to some, our measures may seem excessive, but know that we have regaled you with some major issues that need addressing!

We cannot go back on our word to you – we tell it straight and vanquish all doubts and fears for the future. We realise, at times, that you may be misled into thinking that we have overstepped the mark, but we shall devolve an ocean of tears to reinstate a sense of propriety! We develop a broader perspective, allowing for delays, and encourage a more salubrious adventure. We ask you to transcend all cares and worries for we are known for our challenges to be accepted at all cost! Develop a keener sense of perception for we know you can rise to the challenge in every way possible. Denial will never set you on the road to freedom! We are an unknown quantity that cannot be expressed in normal terms and defying the laws of gravity, we come among you to defend our honour on several occasions. Displacement of terms and conditions render necessary applications, and we expect in a month or two all will be in place. Temperance is needed and we shall place great trust in you in the days and weeks ahead. Farewell little one, sweet dreams! *Temperance – I feel this refers to my decision to give up alcohol as I know abstinence will help to raise my frequencies, enabling further contact with higher 'Beings of Light'.*

8th January 2005 – We allow in all sincerity, a greater positivity before we can transcend all that holds us back, remember that in a week's time we will have fulfilled a portion of our mission, and that in itself is a justifiable cause. We never said it would be easy and ask you to remain on red alert so that we may identify the right time to forge ahead. Sadly we come to the end of one pathway, but know that all encumbrances that go with it may well be lifted to a certain extent! Do not disobey dictates of the heart for we know, with greater relish, we shall have achieved more in one week than we would ever have thought possible! In extreme situations of the heart we realise there may be a crunching of nerves, which takes you through the sound barrier, but do not worry on that score for all is set for a new and vibrant pathway together! Know that, in all its splendour, the sun is rising on a new and powerful day, where all can be considered and cared for. We salute you my dear, and feel you are accomplishing more than was at first thought possible. Send out those loving vibrations to bring cheer into the world, and we will shower you with our love and devotion! We express our sadness, at this time, for those of you who have not been able to forecast what is necessary to grow in our love, and we come at a time when there will be great collisions and never ending heartache for peoples of the Earth! *I really felt tired here and needed to close.* Peace and tranquillity to you my friend, this night and for evermore!

11th January 2005 – *I've lived in Wales for 20 months now and my only friends, apart from family, have been the Pleiadians. I have felt the need to find like-minded souls on the physical plane to interact with, and to share my hopes and dreams for a better world. The Angels, as always, answered my prayers and after starting a twenty-week reflexology course, I have finally made some special friends.*

We remain on red alert attending to our business as usual, remaining friends and relying on company that will stand us in good stead. Feel free to instigate further meetings for we feel the power strongly within this group! We have spoken in the past of events to come and note with satisfaction that you follow our words carefully. There is a dire need to express ourselves and we count on you to deliver our words with greater clarity. We foresee a time where we may be used for greater service, growing and developing, and these are the groups we shall be concentrating on. Growing a more vibrant understanding of what we can achieve, singing your praises and overseeing your future in all its glory. Develop a trust in all we say for we have a mission of the highest calibre known to man, and we mean to forge ahead when the time is right! We initiate a new pathway for you to tread with greatest respect, and envelop you at this time in our love. Do not demean yourself, nor overstep the mark, for we are here to help you at this vital stage of your journey! Be careful as you tread, for the way is littered with many obstacles for you to overcome; we sympathise with you and allow for delays before full coverage is obtained. *I'm now being shown some beautiful, bright yellow sunflowers!*

12th January 2005 – I sat to meditate and sent out absent healing for quite some time, remembering to include myself as I've been feeling very tired. Revelling in the peace I picked up my pen, ready for further communication. We reveal a new process of understanding that will laterally connect with the higher brain. Depend on us in extreme circumstances to connect in this way for we, of one mind and purpose, endeavour to communicate on a higher wave band of frequency. We need this interaction to be more frequent for we have a gathering of souls who need our expertise. We devise a new strategic plan of action, relying heavily on those around us to make the necessary contact, we are then able to pass on this knowledge and equip ourselves with wisdom beyond our years! We have by no means insisted on an unequivocal advantage, but we know with a greater and more positive application, we can forge ahead and onto finer transmissions. We develop a deeper trust and obey dictates of the heart in keeping these trysts. We shall, in all honesty, develop and maintain a greater and more trustworthy presence for all to see, and mark our words, we shall indelibly make ourselves known in more than one avenue! Trust in our directives and we shall feel the time approaching when all will come to fruition. Never let it be said that we led you astray, for we have covered all aspects in great depth to allow for greater easement! We shall display integrity and honour in all we do and note, with great pleasure, that you have yourself forecast what is ahead! We display greater initiative and positive achievements, and pray that you will indeed take advantage of all that is on offer! Please allow one month's grace before we shall start in earnest, we have let it be known that we come at a time when all is possible, and we know in the days and weeks ahead we shall manifest all that is needed for our mission. We take our leave of you and wish you a speedy recovery!

13ᵗʰ *January 2005 – Watching the news this evening, I saw that Prince Harry was the subject of controversy for wearing a Nazi uniform at a fancy dress party! This seems to have influenced the subject matter of the channelling I received later in the evening.* We develop and grow in your love and we feel, as do you, that now is a time of bonding and renewing our vows, for we have taken an oath to pledge ourselves for this mission! We have discovered a most moving anecdote, which to most of you may seem inappropriate, but we recall a memory of past events which justified a means to an end. We in no way demean you, but attempt to describe events as they happened!

"We vow to you now that we had no understanding at that time of what was to come, and we know that beyond all earthly measure, we tried to ascertain how we became such a threat to society!" "We know it comes as no surprise that we instigated the final events which led to our collapse, and in a society that frowned upon our poor attempts to win the love and affection of a nation entrenched in war!" "We deny now the very fact of war for it serves no purpose and we know, to our cost, the humiliation of our country was warranted." "Take for example the metal detectors which are used to broadcast what lies beneath the ground; we never foresaw the dangers lurking and tried with all our might to save those poor souls who suffered at the hands of the enemy." "We defied our commanders in several instances and fought our way out of ranks; we never thought for a moment of the loss inflicted!" "We welcome you now to the sunshine of our youth, and we tell you how we came to this place . . . how we became separated from our troops." "We made our mark and fell behind the lines!"

I asked for love and healing for the souls of all those lost in battles everywhere, praying for them to be taken into the light. We offer our prayers of thankfulness and initiate new boundaries. We devise a three-tier operation that will lead us to victory, and on no account must we be pushed into a corner! We depend on you now to come forward and help us in this endeavour! We tell it straight and suffer no interferences from any quarter; let it be known that we have foreseen events and sanctify this journey that will bear the fruits of our labours! We supply a course of action and depend on you now to come forward and release the love in your heart. We hope you will deliver all that is necessary for this project, knowing as you do the necessary protocol expected.

Feel free to exorcise your demons, for we rally round now to intercept all negative thoughts and feelings!

15th January 2005 – *There is a feeling of calmness tonight and I'm being shown people of Asian origin again. I sent out healing for the Tsunami survivors and saw an Indian gentleman with a white turban and thick grey beard.* We have great need of you and those like you, for we have foreseen even greater tragedies that speak to us in haste! We cannot know to what depths these challenges come, to prevent us from following our rightful places in society, but we know of course that we have supplied personal growth on all levels. We now decide the future of the little ones, as to how best we can help them! *I'm now seeing floodwater that is rushing in a torrent, carrying debris through villages, leaving children without parents and parents without children!* We nobly advise you to send out thoughts of love for all those robbed of their families, and we know you will accept a portion of your own time and effort in releasing those little ones into the light of love, enabling them to travel back home! We need, at this time, greater effort with this cause, for there are many trapped now between worlds, living out their worst fears . . . trapped in no-mans land! We can set them on the path to freedom by directing them safely towards the light, making sure they are looked after and taken care of. We feel a growing surge of disappointment at the way some people are displaying their thoughts and feelings on this subject!

We know we come at a time when all is ripe for harvesting, and the fullness of your hearts has been depicted in many of your nations, but we have also seen a number of recriminations for what has been called an unjust act of God. Never let it be said that we instigated such brutal measures! We develop a main stream of thought and let it be known that we have vowed to undertake this mission unto the final letter! We advise you to overcome all that is necessary for this endeavour, for there is a tendency at times to overstep the mark. We vow to you now that we shall endeavour in all honesty to advise you on our initiative; depend on us now to step forward and take your hand, for all is written and shall be so!

Dear child, we envelop you now in our love and watch you grow in all aspects. We aspire to develop a more powerful reservoir of information, flooding the chamber of thought and devising greater patterns of understanding. We devise a plan of action that will mean a coming together of great minds and feel, at this time, that we can memorise a certain pattern that will allow us to develop further directives. Feel free to realise these talents and use them for the highest endeavour! We superimpose our thoughts on yours and hope we can clarify a few points – note that we shall obey the dictates of the heart and come to you when the time is right. We display tendencies of uncertainty, but know beyond all earthly measure that this has been a very interesting time for all concerned. We deny what is to come . . . have no fear but accept all before you! We yield to temptation and ask only that you will depend on us to support you in all the trials ahead.

16th January 2005 – Welcome my child – my Sunbeam, welcome to our world of joy, love and peace! We instigate certain treasures for you to uncover, and we depend now on this new growth bringing deep rewards, for there is no doubt that we are on our way to Paradise! We feel now a growing awareness in all you do and vow to you now my dear, that all shall be foretold in glowing truth and honesty. Develop greater trust and we shall vouchsafe all that is open to you. We need to remind you of further objectives, for we have known for some time of the need to tread carefully, and we have become aware of certain discrepancies that need adjusting. We allow a time period of six months where we feel the necessary objectives will have been achieved, don't delay for we feel a growing advantage can be achieved if we push forward this date! We note that you have maintained a sense of decorum, and reveal to you now there have been no drawbacks that could assist in your downfall, freeing you from any sense of commitment that may hold you back. Never let it be said that we interfered with free will, for we have no hold over you, other than a deep abiding love!

We have come from a different framework where all are considered of the same gender and nationality. We divine a method of understanding by interfusing in what could be called a telepathic condition, where we can always call to one another in ways of the heart. We devise certain methods where we can initiate a bonding between those of you on Earth, who we redeem to take advantage of a fuller life in a different state of existence! We mean you no harm, hoping you will realise that these objectives are more than enough of the same point of reference as your own! We deliver an ultimatum, and responding to our rhythms may mean we have to allow certain time differences to occur; we can adjust where necessary but hope you will help us in this adjustment!

We feel a growing bond between us, which will allow for greater communication at a time where much can be achieved. Feel and express our words in the fullness with which they are given, and we shall surprise you even more with the content and expressiveness of our thoughts and feelings towards you! We deliberate and further enquire how we may be of assistance to you, for we know there is much ahead to conquer! Feel free to express yourself in glowing colours for we need this input and output more frequently! *I chatted to them and said how much I enjoyed these sessions.* We need these interactions so that we may follow the progress necessary for our evolution, and we depend on each other to enable the flow of words to run smoothly. In this instance we were able to make contact through the process known as thought transference of the highest calibre, and we know that you would deem it irresponsible of us, if we had not delivered what was absolutely necessary at this time. Be prepared now for further transferences for we need greater input, and in the future this will enable us to have our say. Be prepared to tell it straight in all instances, for we shall gain some clout in the world, enabling free expression of the soul to reign supreme.

The future is bright, far brighter for those of you who listen to our words, for we have come from a place of light where there is no darkness, only a deep abiding love and reverence beyond all earthly measure! Be it known in our two worlds of a love that will never die but go on forever, maintaining a deep sense of achievement and aspiring to greater, more powerful visions for those of you on Earth. We have need of you all to develop the expertise necessary for this quest, and we rely on you more and more as time goes on. We develop a sense of knowing before the event, which will enable us to develop a greater understanding of what is before us, and we betray a tear or two at times, when you have taken on board more than you could tackle! We re-instate boundaries and allow for an ongoing status of achievement to be maintained, served in all its true potential, and we allow one month's grace for this to follow through onto a new pathway of success. Do not allow yourself the misconception of youth, for we are over the brow of the hill and well on our way to a new dimension, where all will be shown to you!

19th January 2005 – *I have recently joined a meditation group and met more like-minded souls. We come from diverse backgrounds and have been drawn together by our desire to learn and grow, developing our natural psychic abilities and becoming more aware of the energies that surround us, linking us with other dimensions. I have enjoyed this group tremendously as there are often lively discussions on spirituality and human nature. I feel my star friends have enjoyed sitting in on these discussions as they have asked me to deliver their words by hand and read out to the group.*

We devise a new plan of action which will enable us to carry forward a major expedition into the unknown. We have known for some time now of events taking place that could cause the utmost disruption to natives of your land. We develop a mainstream action that will incorporate a coming together of many nations, and we devise a plan of action where we shall suppress, in many cases, thoughts of a nature which shall cause great disruption to planet Earth. We deliver, in no uncertain terms, promises for a future that shall be bright, and we by no means insist that you should all remain on a planet that has become, to all intents and purposes, a place of mistrust, violence and abuse of the most dreadful nature! We vow to you now that we shall instigate a brighter future for all mankind if he will only listen to our words! We shall devise a plan of action, whereby you can all surrender yourselves to us and place great trust in the future ahead. We initiate a deeper understanding of what is to come and desire you to proceed with all the caution necessary at this time.

We know it may come as a shock to many of you but, at this stage, we cannot leave it a moment longer! We now assume the role of benevolent father and guide to enable these proceedings to take place. We come at the very time when Earth is in greatest need and we know, to some of you, these words may seem a trifle unnecessary, but we vow to you now that in all understanding we reign supreme! We have not forgotten what transpired in earlier years with wealth being of great importance, and we note with some derision that we have forecast these measures many times in the past. We have foretold events to come and note, with great satisfaction, all that has been prepared for our coming. We allow a certain time period to elapse before we accomplish directives given from those of a higher dimension, and we need these structures in place to carry forward this mission of the highest intent. We help those of you on Earth who have come forward, and with great love in your heart, to help your fellow man. No immediate directives have been given, but we know with greater understanding, there is every need to obey dictates of the heart, for we feel this venture is fast becoming an increasingly, desirable prospect! We feel this initiative will envelop the whole world and we know for instance, there have been many transactions undertaken in the last few years. We know these directives have come from a much higher sphere of existence, giving us an even greater desire to use our positive thoughts in helping many on this plane of existence, enabling us all to follow in the footsteps of those we have come to love and admire.

We have survived abominable disasters, and remain alert at all times as future atrocities loom on the horizon! We develop the power of understanding what is necessary to overcome these developments on the brink, and which threaten our very existence! We have foretold the coming of a new era where there is no darkness, only the light of true understanding which radiates in our hearts and minds, for we have come at the very time when Earth shall be reborn into a new dimension! We have come to assist the world on this journey to the stars for we believe, as do many of you, that we shall accomplish the impossible. Be it known now in our dimension of time and space that all is possible! There is a severity of conditions looming on the horizon and we need to know, with greater clarity, how we can forge this alliance. There is enough time to gather together for there is strength in numbers, and we believe in all earnest that we shall surmount all difficulties that lie ahead. We never believed in an instant that you would forsake us, for we know in all honesty that you have all come forward to fulfil your mission on Earth, and we need deliverance now of all that is within your very being. We foresee a time in the future where all will come to fruition, and we hope you will beam ahead of us and join us on this pathway of love to heaven and the stars. We need a framework of understanding that will take us to this point of reference, and we know that you will fulfil this mission in the most noblest fashion, gearing all your thinking into becoming closer to the light of true understanding.

We are born to bring light into the world, a light so powerfully strong it surpasses all understanding. We develop a broader perspective and announce, in no uncertain terms, that we shall venture into the unknown without a true awareness of what is before us. Depend on us now to instigate this ribbon of light that draws us like a magnet, each step forward brings us closer together, and we need to follow this pathway to enable us to fulfil what was written long ago. We now ascertain who will come forward to develop strategies needed, and to obey dictates of the heart in this venture, allowing a draining of energies to perpetuate this mission. We deliver, at great cost, an emissary who will come forward and defend our very way of thinking! Please believe we have your best interests at heart, and we note with great pleasure that many are here today listening to our words. We envelop you all in our love and feel a great reverence and sense of duty amongst you all, for we need this growth to be entirely of your own free will. No bones broken can be mended entirely without friction, and we have developed a finer more positive element of attunement, knowing we can deliver what is needed for these meetings.

Lift up your hearts for there are lights all over the world, growing in great numbers, just like this little group here tonight! All over the world in towns and villages, those lights are growing stronger and with great purpose. We shall overcome the darkness and prepare you for a brighter future, where no man shall be slandered, abused or ill treated! Remember we have evolved and are able to bring you this news from far beyond your planet Earth, furthest from the brightest star in your galaxy, and we beam to you on a ray of love and hope for the future of all mankind. Develop these trends of thinking and we shall aspire to greater ideals that will stand us in good stead, developing and growing together in great numbers. We enable this transmission to end. Farewell 'Children of Light', we thank you for your time spent with us and leave you to ponder on our words. *During this communication I was shown the figure of Ghandi, also an Indian gentleman wearing a white turban and thick grey beard who I've seen before in previous communications.*

20th January 2005 – Little one . . . we beseech you to obey your instructions down to the last letter, for we need greater and more reliable information to be brought through at this time! We express concern in areas of discontent, for we have enabled you to deliver these words with greater clarity, and we know in the future we shall achieve even more than was ever thought possible! We deliver expressly, for atrocities of late have caused great concern among peoples of the world; we aim to achieve even greater advantage and take measures now to forestall events in the future. We misjudge a certain situation, whereby there is cause for concern among nationalities in the East, for there are events planned which will bring about even greater atrocities! We feel we can envelop the Earth at this time in a network that will bring about divine instruction, and we deliver a more positive connection that will enable, at the same time, greater activity to take place. We shall involve as many of you as we can muster, for this is no divine intervention but a necessary tool of understanding. We foresee greater aspects of alignment being made possible, and we reveal to you now that we shall forecast greater activity in all areas.

We believe that many of you have come forward and we deliver these words to you now with greater eloquence. We feel the time is ripe for this adventure and we know you will achieve great things, all of you, in your own field of distinction! Remember we develop and grow in all sincerity, bringing you choices to give to the people of Earth. This is not an easy task for any of you, but we know we can envelop the globe with a greater understanding of what is to come. Divine aspirations shall be recompensed, for we know many of you on the Earth plane have a limited fund of energy, and we make allowances for certain discrepancies, falling back on resources which will enable us to go forward. There will come a time of greater clarity for all as we interpret your dreams and wishes for a brighter future, and we know you will achieve what is necessary, developing mainstream activity and growing in numbers!

20th January 2005 – *It's late evening; the house is silent and I feel the need to sit for communication.* We initiate a new dream, one of passive understanding.

We incorporate a coming together, developing a broader trust and instigating a finer tuning which is necessary at this stage. We now reinstate a sense of values that have long been forgotten by many on your Earth plane. We find greater advantage can be made by eliciting further information, whereby we can distribute greater power and energy, radiating out into the cosmos and penetrating the gloom of Earth. For at this stage we need to invest a greater, more powerful energy that will penetrate the hearts and minds of those who have no understanding of us at all! We have developed measures that can be put into operation, which will effectively control events as they transpire. We develop certain initiatives that can control the populace and invite you to join us in distributing this information! Events have taken a turn for the worse and we know we can, in all events, distribute greater activities in the brain to allow incoming information to be absorbed. We cannot divine exactly, in your terminology, the thought processes that take place, but we have exactly the right expertise to allow this course of action to happen! For we have evolved from a planet such as yours and know of no other existence where two minds think alike! We have suffered to the extreme at the hands of others, like you, and we know this encourages you to re-invest in our future together. Be prepared now to tell it straight, there will be a draining of energies at times but we will keep these to a minimum. Be prepared for these times of deep peace more often, for we need the seeds of love to grow and flourish in your heart, and we shall make our mark on the world, developing a stronger bond. We need at this time greater directives to push us forward onto the horizon, and we know you shall develop and grow with a tremendous surge of love.

We invite you to journey with us back to this star and see for yourself this world of ours, there is no need to pack for we travel light! We reach an understanding of all that is needed and hope you will oversee this project ahead. We see a marked improvement in your thinking patterns and revel in the warmth of your company, knowing we shall excel in all we do. Take heed of our words for we know, with great pleasure, that you have taken on board more than enough to occupy your thoughts. *I have the same strange feeling in my mouth and nose that I remember having as a child, as if there was a larger head superimposed in mine. At night I would often lay awake in bed with thoughts buzzing round my mind, feeling that someone was watching over me. This reinforces my belief that these star friends have been with me all of my life!* Yes my little Sunbeam, we have been with you from the very beginning, watching you grow, in our love, from a child into a woman of immense talent for accepting what life had to offer! We know there have been times of great hardship, but there have also been those times of greatest joy, and we know too the love in your heart has grown in brightness for all to see. We envelop you now in our love and bid you goodnight my little one! We develop greater action and envelop you now in a protective haze that will guard against intrusion!

22nd January 2005 – Dear friend, we advise you now to follow the calling of your heart for we are here with you at all times. We intercept your instructions, for we are now able to tell you of nourishment that is coming your way in due course, which will greatly reduce your need of assistance! We have devised a plan whereby you will be able to express yourself most eloquently in more than one avenue, for we have now been advised that you have obeyed instructions down to the last letter and we are most pleased with your efforts, which shall be revered! Let it be known now, in our two worlds, that we do not deceive ourselves into thinking that all is well on the horizon, for there is idle speculation as to how we shall beat this untimely episode about to take place! We forge alliances of the highest calibre and foresee events taking place, which could cause extreme pain and hardship . . . we clearly cannot allow this to happen! There is a greater need to step back now and deliver ultimatums! *I'm now being shown the figure of Israeli President, Ariel Sharon.* There is widespread activity which may cause havoc, and we now know that this will achieve a great sense of shame and ill feeling towards the population of Israel! We need to assess the situation and gain a more idealistic profile of the country, gaining access to what is needed to maintain dignity and trust among her people.

We know it will come as no surprise that this has been written of for centuries, and we deliver these words in more than one syllable, exposing those in power who have exerted pressure and who have no other means of justifying their existence on this planet! We deem it irresponsible of those leaders who will not obey the laws of the land themselves, but ride roughshod over many of the people for their own personal ends! We note, with great satisfaction, that you rely on this information and do not obey the deepest mistrust which is sometimes present! We know these words will evoke a sense of apprehension when read out aloud, but we know that you must deliver them to enable the group to understand that we can achieve much together, once they are able to accept the very concept of our being! We know too it may come as a shock to learn that we are from another planet and landscape, which shall be entrusted to your keeping. We defend these issues as relevant to your cause, and know we can implement these wishes over the next few weeks or so. Expect us to find more news for you in the near future, and we will make sure of the utmost clarity for your recordings. We tend to each other and wish you goodnight my friend!

23rd January 2005 – We have known for some time now that you have been an asset to our cause, and we would like to say, in all earnest, that we have neglected to admit responsibility for all that has occurred! We need constancy and agree that you will uncover items worthy of our attention. We shall of course, rectify and put into place all that is needed to enhance our living standards. Between us we shall make this a viable undertaking, and we initiate new growth into areas that have been neglected of late. Put into practice what you preach and we will redeem those of you who come forward to obey our instructions down to the last letter. In all of this we express ourselves with great contempt for what is happening around the globe! We feel the necessity to exclude those of you who have already succumbed to our advances, and we know you will join with us when we say that we have found the whole process immensely satisfying, knowing that you too strive for a peaceful society.

We surrender ourselves to you so that we may initialise a new future together, and we come at a time when this new growth can be readily obtained. We appreciate all offers and appoint each and every one of you with a new goal of achievement, participating in a way that will give you strength and courage with each passing day. We deliver a programme of events whereby we shall achieve notability and we now venture forth well armed, for we all gather here to be with you this night, knowing in the future we shall bear witness to what has happened in our universe. We have desired for some time to make this contact and it has taken many years to achieve this control! It has not been an easy task to manifest what was needed to initiate this understanding, which has been reached right down to the last letter – dotting the i's and crossing the t's. We know it makes sense to describe what we know as simply as we can, but in many instances we have to hold back, due to the fact that there is a whole population who deserve nothing more than a TV dinner and a pack of beers! We are far more able to express ourselves if we reach for the button and turn off what is not needed, expressing ourselves in other ways will be much more fulfilling. Exchanging conversation has become a thing of the past and we desire to change this behaviour, initiating a more meaningful existence on this planet!

We desire you to proceed with caution and rely on you, and those like you, to tentatively take those first few steps towards a new life which is open to you all, expressing yourselves with greater clarity and enjoying each other's company. We have experienced those times with you and know we have found them most exhilarating! We feel a growing trend towards becoming content in our way of thinking, and now need to proceed with our new vision of life beyond the stars. Tentatively we accept that this will be a new experience where all shall grow in stature, opening up new avenues and aspiring to greater visions held by all. We ask you to lean on us in times of trouble so that we may shelter you from harm, enveloping you in our love. Deferentially we raise our eyes to the sky and salute you!

24th January 2005 – We attempt to reorganise patterns of thinking all over the globe and we know you will follow us in this venture. We are able to penetrate the hearts and minds of mankind and we feel this incentive will create a viable entourage, enabling us to travel together with greatest ease. *At this point I can see country folk of Chinese origin.* Experiment as you will and enable this channelling to take place whenever we call, for these are the times when connections can be made more appropriately! We divine a method of greater instruction to allow these energies to manifest, and we ask you to come forward now and obey dictates of your heart, in this way we obey what is given to us from a higher dimension! There appears on the horizon a misconception of ideas that need careful monitoring, and we feel this involvement may cause a certain amount of heart ache for all concerned! *I'm now being shown a beautiful lady wearing a red and silver kimono.* We tend to you Sunbeam number one, and allow you to come closer, welcoming you with open arms! We feel a growing need for further involvement which will come in due course. Expect an interweaving of energies that will enable us a deeper bonding, for we feel these transmissions are of the highest calibre, enabling us all to go forward into the light. We do, however, allow a turning back for those of you who are not able to complete this mission!

We deny what is before us but concede there may be cause for celebrations! Look past what is in front of you – learning to think in a different way with a lateral connection of minds, bypassing normal patterns of thinking. Revelling in this new growth we achieve greater satisfaction, for pounding the pavement will never bring the same rewards that are constantly knocking at your inner door. We in the realms of light manifest a greater glory for mankind . . . a never ending, joyful and more tolerant society. There is no doubt that we come to you all now with the greatest love in our hearts, for we shall behave in a manner of the utmost gentility as we treasure you unto us. Those of you, who may remain behind, will become new leaders of nations that are intent on war! We have not yet explained how we intend to take this to its final conclusion, but we allow you the benefit of doubt, for we know there is so much to take on board! We advise you now that we shall envelop the globe in a wave pattern of love, a frequency so powerfully strong that it will have great impact. We know that to some this may seem to be a time of deep cleansing of the Earth, for in the past there have been great floods and quakes which have covered the globe in entirety! These have come at a time in your history when there were greater eruptions as never before, devastating the planet Earth! *I'm now being shown flames and red hot lava.*

We have devised an even greater plan, where those of you on Earth may escape the flames of destruction – this is of the most paramount importance and we need a regulator to allow these proceedings to operate more swiftly! This destruction of planet Earth is no idle speculation in the distant future, but something you must be prepared for at this time in your evolution, for we have been in your shoes and know that destruction has occurred! We come to save the planet Earth and redeem her, and those that live on her will have the choice to leave or stay behind! We deliver these ultimatums to enable you to make up your own minds as to where your allegiances lie. We have foretold this on many occasions in the past through various mediums that have visited Earth for a brief spell, and we know we have yielded to the temptation on many occasions to allow this representation to take place! Fortitude is needed to rectify these conditions immediately, for we cannot know how long this process will take. We are forever in your debt and allow this transmission to end. Go in peace!

25th January 2005 – We feel a great responsibility has fallen upon your shoulders, and we incorporate the necessary structures that shall be laid down for our further involvement. Relevant information comes flooding through for us to pass onto you and your group, and we forecast what is necessary to lay down the foundation of a much needed institution of light. Emergencies forbid us to elaborate at any great length, suffice it to say we no longer need a gratuitous approach, as we are neither ready nor willing to take on what is no longer considered to be a free way of thinking! We step back, in this instance, from a negotiation which has reached considerable success, and we know we have reached the right conclusion in waiting for a much more rewarding role, which will keep us busy as well as rewarding us with a more contented outlook on life. Feel free now to exhaust other avenues of discontent, for we feel it may be worthy of your attention to sit and plan out what is necessary for your future involvement. We decline an offer made and suggest that we are more than ready to accept another role more fitting to our disposition. Remain calm at all times and we will recover what is lost! Remember to target areas that need addressing for we shall see less conflict and more energy for other pursuits. We now have a greater understanding of what is available to us on the horizon . . . a new adventure opening up!

Be prepared to let go of certain projects which may hold you back for we need greater assistance, your time and energy are important assets that need careful monitoring, and we cannot allow a disruption of energies that may hinder your main area of work! We envelop you now in glowing colours to rejuvenate your system, developing a fine-tuning so that we may assist one another in our soul's growth. Depend on us to win through for we know we are coming to a time of immense love, accepting each others wave patterns and adapting where necessary. *I had been considering enrolling on a year long course in aromatherapy massage, but realise this is now not an option if I want to concentrate on channelling information from our star friends!* We remember a time in the distant past where we were recommended for this assignment and we know, in all honesty, that we have reaped the benefits of a lasting and fruitful partnership, enabling us to grow in unison! We now need greater expertise to carry us through the coming months ahead as we develop greater awareness, and we will regard you as an envoy of the highest calibre and diplomacy. Never fear what lies ahead for we can overcome all barriers that separate us, and we beseech you now to understand our motives . . . which are purely and simply a will to survive!

Be it known now in our two worlds of a great expedition that will launch a thousand ships into space, these will come at a time of heralding in a new future for mankind! We deliberate even more and vouchsafe there will be a mass exodus from this world, and we shall divine a plan of action whereby all nations will come together to be as one, and we make no exceptions! We plan this manoeuvre with great relish and know you will assist us in great measure. Feel free to ask as many questions as you think necessary, for we will answer them as fully as we can, incorporating a trust between us that will grow deeper and deeper! We manage to attract growing numbers of individuals who are also looking for involvement with proceedings, and we watch from afar for this is a thought provoking time for all concerned. We have accepted this challenge and will forge ahead, amplifying what is necessary to achieve this status. We no longer need to satisfy our curiosity for we know we have reached a point of the utmost trust and diplomacy!

We know the timing is right for all to unfold and we know you have every right to rejoice for what has been achieved! We experience too your joy, and feel a growing empathy that will bring great rewards for us also. We now need a greater and more powerful deliverance to gather momentum, and increase the energy flow; we also need greater acceptance of our role in society and illicit information that will take us back in time! Note that we have accepted our part in this extravaganza and show ourselves to you when the time is right; we have no need for fancy dress but allow you to see us as we truly are! Do not be afraid, for we have blended very well and are not connected to any intangible life support systems that control other agencies, we are simply known as a race of people who have denied annihilation as a prospect worthy of our attention! We depend on you to alter your coding, and we depend on each other for continuation of life hereafter! We now commend you for your perseverance with this transmission and close to allow a renewal of energies! Thank you my child!

26th January 2005 – We need to deliver further messages for those of you who come forward. We relish our times spent with you and know that you seek further information which we have obtained, and quite rightly so, from those who have our best interests at heart! We shall venture now into the unknown, forsaking tenuous strains of idle speculation, and we can breach those boundaries that hold us back, depending on certain issues that need rectifying. We obey dictates of the heart and allow certain revelations to manifest so that you may see, with your own eyes, what is necessary for this excursion! We develop a greater trust in all we do and say and know that you have been, to all intents and purposes, the greatest help in delivering these words. We shall ascertain what is needed to develop further transmissions of the highest calibre; we are known for our powers of observation and will show you what is necessary for our evolution.

We come at a time when there is great commotion and annoyances that need to be rectified in all areas, we feel this information will only cause riots and we deliver to you now greater clarification of events on the horizon! Injustices have occurred and we know we can move mountains to obtain the necessary structures, developing greater clemency in all areas. We note that we are able to conduct even greater experiments within patterns of thinking over the entire globe, and we vouch to you now that we of one intent and purpose, shall come together in ever increasing numbers, justifying this cause open to us. We shall conduct ourselves in an appropriate manner that will enable us to connect with higher beings, and we know we can adjust thought patterns to agree a terminology that will be understood by all! Feel free at this time to develop greater powers of thought transference, for we shall need this development to occur on a much grander scale across the world.

We expect a new opening very soon on the horizon, where we can adjust thought patterns accordingly, and we hope and pray that as many of you shall come forward as promised! We develop certain tendencies at times that can obstruct these transmissions, but we know in all honesty that you have given of your very best. We doubt the entirety of these words but know you will strive to understand their necessity, for there is now on the horizon a breach of conditions that must be understood to maintain clarity of the situation! We are growing in numbers and would like to ask all of you to step forward and give us your support, for we know of no other initiative that can give us this deliverance, and we feel there is a growing demand for greater knowledge! Forsaking all others we tend to our offspring, allowing them to come forward to deliver these messages of hope and joy for the future of mankind.

We hope we have obeyed compliances, and need you to understand that we have come forward now to help you on your journey, for there is a greater need to explore all before you. The future is one of immense joy and upliftment; there can be no turning back once the decision has been made to take this trip into the unknown and we shall gain positive results from treading this pathway of light. This option cannot be exchanged to rectify conditions at home, for there is a greater and more probable outcome that will wreak havoc on Earth if we do not grow, dividing our inheritance for a far better way of life! We note that you have, at all times, been exemplary in your motives, and we correct additional information where it has been wrongly transcribed, for we feel it is of paramount importance that these words are delivered and need to be corrected at all times!

Thoughtfully we travel along this pathway together, amplifying our thoughts and treading as softly and carefully as we are able, transcending all cares and worries for the future ahead. We know we contribute these conditions with a far more transcendental approach, and we allow at this time a conditioning of energies so that we may come more often to be with you. We allow for discrepancies to occur, knowing there are boundaries ahead that will cause annihilation for all if we do not intercept and prevent this from happening! We allow certain disclosures to be made public and insist now on greater clemency, for we know we shall rise up against injustice of every kind and allow now a monitoring of services. Be it known now in our two worlds of a love that will never die but grow stronger in all proportions over the entire planet!

We recommend now a going back and further developing our assets, which need looking at more closely, for we feel there are certain instances where we can improve upon our talents. We have developed a status quo and would remind you that there is a far greater need for discretion! We shall remind those of you who are here for this cause that you should, at all times, be very careful in your dealings with others; we remain on red alert at all times, conquering over any thoughts that may betray our actions. Jealousy is a very rampant and sordid thought form, which can develop into a cancerous growth that will attack humans, devouring them and manipulating whole nations! We feel now, and we can go further and say in all honesty, we have never come across a more disastrous way of thinking! We have all been subject to this at some time or other in our lives and know, with great contempt, we have suffered to the extreme because of this deadly thought form which has incurred great mistrust among nations!

I took a break before resuming our connection – In this time line space is a reality which exists between two objects, however, we know that when you annihilate a structure based in space – in actuality you are condensing matter to a different component altogether! There is no need to coordinate this time-consuming analysis for we will show you, in more fundamental terms, how we have achieved this state of existence. We shall superimpose ourselves with great success, and evaluate how successful we have been in attaining more constructive avenues of thought processes, which will then be able to detect the metabolism caused when accessing data! We have a powerful incentive to drive us forward and onto the horizon, but we need a much more positive attitude before we can venture further afield! It is necessary at this time to forecast what we know to be a difficult time for you all. Some will feel a devastating and unequivocal loss of their own identity, and this will prove to be too much for some people, who will have to leave the planet before completing their mission on Earth! On no account should you disobey your instructions . . . for these will guide you well.

We show great compassion for those who are suffering at this time, and know you will all do your best to achieve optimum results. We passively connect with those of you who share our belief patterns and who desire to be included in this mission. Step back and allow us through . . . for we need this time to identify resources open to us, we shall also be obliged if you will all allow us to temporarily inspect attitudes and desires for a better future for al! We depend on you now to grow alongside us, and we feel the reverence with which you abandon yourselves to access this frequency available to you. We mean to condense certain theories so that we are more fully able to understand the process of elimination. *I'm being shown an Asian girl in uniform.* We have seen great numbers destroyed by the floods and hope we can call on you to help in whatever way you can!

It is necessary to obey what is in your heart for there is great need at this time to remember those in deep distress. It has been a very harrowing time for all concerned, particularly the aid workers who give their own time and effort to support the living. Depend on us in these extreme circumstances to come forward and help those in greatest need. For we are able to supply the necessary equipment by compiling what is needed on this level, and manifesting it in your dimension by the means of a revolutionary idea based on 'love'! We know this may not make sense to those of you vibrating on the lower levels, but we can manifest anything we so desire by means of thought. That is why your thoughts and projections of love are so important at this time on Earth, for we can conquer much on this level of existence! Fair play is extended to you now and we know that we shall all meet again very soon; take heed of our words for we deliver them to you with the utmost dedication, knowing that you will pass them onto others of your calling. We thank you for your endeavours and trust that you will now manage to achieve your heart's desire!

27th January 2005 – We know it will come as no surprise to you that we, of another dimension, have ventured on this pathway with you for many a year and we fondly remember times gone by where we sat and chatted to you, while you scribbled your notes and spoke into the microphone – just as you are today! We treasure those memories and feel we have grown very close, with an even greater understanding of what is before us. We now muster intelligence of a higher mind, transferring these thoughts to you on a higher vibration. Please channel these words correctly, amend what is necessary and we will pass on further messages as they reach us. We have developed a good way of communicating; our thought forms are of great advantage at this time and we convey our deep respect to you for allowing us to invade your space! We branch out quickly to obey the calling within us and we shall now investigate further, asking that you transcribe these words in great detail. We have great need of your services and we implement the right framework to enable you to grow with greater acceleration. Be it known in our two worlds of a love that will never die but live on in each and every one of us! Proceed with all caution in our love; we observe you and will instigate a wider pathway, enabling you to tread more easily. Obey your heart in all things and we shall muster the necessary intelligence to allow greater opportunities for all.

We now need to concentrate on what is before us, and feel we have achieved more than enough to proceed! We develop and grow alongside you and feel a growing resemblance has taken place, we announce in no uncertain terms that we have forged a new alliance and are able to communicate on a grander scale. We feel a certain vulnerability growing at this time, and we shall need to take more than one course of action. The main objectives are a desire to exchange patterns of thinking and robust energy for the task ahead! There is a need for all of you to use your own initiative, and we need you to use your own thought patterns to guide you along this highway of love. We have been able to achieve more than was at first thought viable but we have achieved this control with great resistance, and we feel a growing reverence is needed to undertake this mission.

We allow the energies to manifest with greater abundance, and we see a time in the future when we will be able to develop and maintain this control. Do remember that in all instances we are beside you, we love you and implore you to share these experiences with us, for with this product of the imagination we can achieve all our aims and ambitions for a brighter future for mankind! There are growing disturbances on the horizon that will need to be closely monitored at all times; trust in us for we will be there with you helping you to handle the situation. We admire the tenacity needed to obtain these directives and feel that you have given of yourself – paying the penalty! Remember we take note in all instances of what is needed to do our best and feel, rightly so, that we have achieved even greater control in these areas. Follow us through the gateway and onto that final destination, and we will show you all that is needed – all that is requested for you and yours.

31st January 2005 – *I felt my friends draw close as I sat looking out at the towering hillside. Yesterday I had cleared out the spare bedroom to make a temporary meditation room, and was day-dreaming about the possibility of having an extension built specifically for meditation and healing.* We have developed a certain ability that will need careful monitoring in the future. We are now able to achieve a more vibrant growth, and we assess the situation at various intervals to obtain a clearer picture of what is needed. We know in the future that we are able to gain expression in various forms of art; we come here today to give full rein and we know we have gained massive respect here in our world! We know it means a great deal to you at this time to have achieved this growth, and we develop even greater abilities as we venture forth. We shall need to know in advance how best to achieve even greater results, for we have given this gift for you to use, and we expect future results to be obtained of a much higher calibre! We see you take note of our words and we advise you now that we intend to take you forward, developing and growing together along this highway of love.

We have known for centuries that this was our destiny, to work together, to love together and to grow together! We need this vibrancy to grow in abundance for we have so much to achieve and so much love to give. Develop an inner strength, believe in yourself . . . believe in us, for we shall work together as one. Obey the dictates of your heart for we are able in this way to develop an even greater understanding. We allow you to come further into our space; we feel you growing closer and closer and develop a surge of power that will enable us to come even closer than before! We remain as always your friend and protector, we will never allow any harm to befall you and we will never stray from your side. Feel the strength around you and know that we shall never leave you in any way, shape or form! We have evolved together through the centuries and we have maintained this growth which has stood us in good stead, enabling this quickening to occur! We obey that inner voice that beckons us onwards for we have greater directives that will need our full attention in the future. We desire to achieve notability, and ascertain certain events on the horizon that will reach us in growing numbers. We have endowed the population of Earth with a greater, far meaningful purpose and we need this new growth to be instantaneous to all, we shall then recover further alliances which have fallen behind!

We develop, to some great extent, curiosity in the hearts and minds of the population, and know we can and will defy all obstacles before us to enable this richness of free expression. We doubt our ability to come forward, but how shall we reach this perfect understanding without standing up and obeying narrative given! We feel that you will be able to express yourself more frequently and powerfully, knowing that we all need to move ahead, but we know it makes sense to allow a little more time before we are able to muster all that is needed for our venture. We shall gather our thoughts together and allow a certain framework that will enable further transmissions to occur, knowing with great relish that we will enjoy greater success in all we do! We have enveloped you in a flame that shall never be extinguished, which will grow in intensity, burning bright for all to see. We take this opportunity now to ask that you keep faith with us, for we know we have asked of you a great deal! We feel this adventure will stand us in good stead; the future ahead is bright and we know you will achieve in all you set out to do. Depend on us as always to initiate this new growth for we are able to move forward on that beam of light, pushing back the barriers and moving forward with greater ease. Relentlessly we travel on into the future.

1st February 2005 – We allow an interval to take place which will pave the way for greater personification, rectifying certain conditions which are prevalent at this time. We demand heavy sacrifices for this cause, and usher in a new understanding that will alternate with wishes for greater abundance in all we do! We commend and obey all directives sent from above, and know in advance that we shall be able to condense instructions and pass onto you. We kindle that spark of light from within, producing a spontaneous explosion of love, interpenetrating the universe and venturing forth in all its glory! This will be a time of greater revelations for you all and, as you know, we can instigate this treasure trail of love to employ greater satisfaction!

I have been reading out my channelled messages to our spiritual group and asked if I could make copies for them to take home and read. We shall need more than one copy in total, for we need these words to reach a wider audience and will not encumber you with more than one transmission at a time. We are obliged to you at this time for we are in need of great assistance, and we allow a time period of increasing energy to obtain results which are forthcoming. We deliberately allow a certain manipulation to occur, enabling even greater and more productive thought forms to flow with greater ease. It has become apparent that strategies taken to improve conditions on Earth, have reached an all time low, but we insist that this shall be short lived, for now is the time to forge ahead and on to more productive roles for all! We shall insist on new territory to be explained where we will be able to exchange places, and we allow a blending of energies necessary for this exchange to take place. Please allow a few weeks before we complete this exercise, for we know it makes sense to observe in greater detail all that is necessary for this new development.

We vow to you now that we shall undertake this mission with great reverence for all concerned! We are able to amplify our thoughts to interpret a wider speculation of what is before us, and we know you will congratulate yourselves on furnishing us with all the necessary structures that are needed for this to take place. Bear with us for we are much more centred in our way of thinking, composure is critical at this stage of our journey, and we feel a growing reverence is needed before we can allow these deliberations to take place! We realise this venture is one of grave concern, and for those of you who have a real talent for interpreting what is needed in this world and the next, we bequeath to you many treasures, which shall reinstate those of you who wish to follow us onto the horizon! We salute you and feel a growing energy which will surpass all understanding; be not afraid to embark on this mission for we offer you our services and bend to you in deep salutation. We are forever in your debt and allow this transmission to end!

We call you back and instigate new patterns of understanding, which can be obtained by inciting each and every one of you to sign up for even further adventures! Be prepared now and in the future to allow further demonstrations of a higher calibre, for we mean to make this study an even greater demonstration of what can be achieved on this level. Please allow for a fine-tuning of energies before this can take place; we feel that you can understand our methods and principles more easily if we allow for this framework! Be it known now in our two worlds of a special dispensation, which will gain greater coverage of information to be obtained in great detail, right down to the last letter! We need greater discretion on the road ahead and would hesitate to remind you that we have need to conquer our fears, for the road ahead is heavily laden with more incentives to drive you forward and on to greater distinction! We develop the urge to grow and drive you forward now to experience even greater aspirations, allowing the time difference to coincide with ours, right down to the very last second as we envelop you in our love. We vow to undertake all that is necessary and we convey our allegiances to you and yours!

4th February 2005 – Please believe us when we say that we have come at a time where we can amaze you with our repertoire! We are known for our intuition and powers of understanding, and we stand before you now in all our glory, opening up new pathways for you to explore. We feel there is a growing need at this time for all to come forward and obey instincts of the heart, for we are now able to reach that place which has eluded us for so long! We come amongst you at this time, and have great regard for those of you who allow us to come even closer. We feel the time is right for this journey to be made, and we know it may come as a shock to many of you, but we feel the necessity to venture forth with 'all guns blazing'! Immediately we see on the horizon all that is waiting for us, and we deliver to you now far greater aspects of a more joyful communication. We tend to those of you who have fallen by the wayside, and develop you with great care, love and devotion. We feel the time approaching when all shall gather together, rectifying situations that have given us cause for concern.

We make no bones about it, gathering you together as envoys for our mission and reaching new terms of agreement that shall aid us on our journey. We are given to much idle speculation and we reveal to you now that we intend to take you all forward on this beam of light, developing and growing alongside you as we venture forth into new territory. Make yourselves available to us and we will show you even greater visions for mankind. We feel the need now to inform you of new measures to be taken, for we have instigated even greater ideals to be taken on board. We assume the role of mother and caretaker, and wish it to be known that we have great strength in the numbers before us. Take the initiative and use your strength and courage, for we shall venture forth now on a journey that has no end! Gird up your loins for there is much work to be done, and we shall develop and grow along side you, taking care of you all as we march along – a glorious army marching towards the light of true understanding!

Much has been given and we endeavour in the near future to give you even greater information of what lies ahead, for we believe that these measures will incorporate a greater trust and understanding of what is before us.

We obey dictates of the heart to be with you here today and announce, in no uncertain terms, that we shall deliver what is given as it is passed onto us from those of a higher dimension! We allow at this time certain measures to be adhered to, and we reveal to you now that we shall in no way misinterpret what is given, for we have developed a new wave of frequencies that will allow us to come forward, and with greater clarity, all will unfold before us! We deliver now a new structure, which will be made available to you in the near future, and we hope you will come forward and help us in this endeavour. We feel the time is right to obey the laws of gravity, and we kneel down before you, asking that you will help us to make this initiative your own! We devise a new pattern of understanding that will enable you to act with increasing knowledge and expertise, and this will be given for you to achieve all that is necessary for this venture. We feel the expense may cause a trifle concern but nevertheless we shall accomplish all, and we envisage greater, more positive powers of negotiation that will enable this to happen on every plateau!

We beam ahead to light your way in the darkness of night, for we are always there lighting the path, dictating new visions for all to behold. Remember we have walked this pathway long ago and we know that every step of the way is one of hardship! There are more guided missions ahead that will need careful consideration, and we will be able to meet the necessary criteria if we take our intentions to a new level of existence. We know this may seem hard for you to comprehend at this time, but we will show you in greater aspects how all can be achieved! We have cause to celebrate and instigate now even greater belief systems, which will encourage the universe to grow and breathe with greater acceleration! We deliver this message in all sincerity, asking you to follow us into the future, and we also ask that you will deliver these messages so that we may all beam ahead and onto pastures new!

Someone in our spiritual group had spoken of pyramid-shaped structures that enhance spirit communication, and I asked if I should look into the possibility of using something like this. There is no need for elaborate constructions; we have developed powers of observation that enable us to comprehend more than we could ever interpret! We understand there have been grave concerns over certain elements of mistrust on your part; we need for you to understand that we shall never lead you astray and deliver only what is needed! We interpret these thoughts with great melancholy, for we need to rely on each other to enable these transmissions to flow, developing a greater trust that will benefit us all! We instigate now, in greater readiness, a new wave of energy that will ensure a greater volume of information to be brought through. *After reading this transmission I felt ashamed that I had ever doubted them, as I know deep in my heart they have our best interests at heart!*

5th February 2005 – We feel a growing reverence with you and note your intentions to develop and grow in all sincerity. We amend certain conditions and, to a large extent, are able to attain a new and robust condition of love, causing us to acknowledge this investment will bring great rewards. We depend on you now to come forward in all honesty, taking the hand which reaches out to you now, assuming the role of guardian! We have unjustly accused you of being a trifle too cautious in your dealings with people, but you have shown of late a desire to overcome your shyness and step forward where you can be seen and heard! We envelop you now in our love and push you further into the limelight! There is a pathway open to you where you will grow even further in our esteem, and we develop you in a way that will become apparent to all when they hear your voice and the words that we have delivered! This is no mean feat and we have developed even further services, which will render you speechless at times! We superimpose our thoughts on yours and obey dictates of the heart, formulating a love and respect that shall vanquish all doubts and fears.

The future ahead is even brighter now that we have joined the mainstream connection. We realise this growth could lead you astray, but we know too that you will rely on us more and more to encourage you in the times ahead. We allow at least a month before we can utilise what has been given, and we also need further references to be taken out for this adjustment to take place. Now is the time to make decisions regarding a certain project looming on the horizon, take note that we are with you in this initiative, knowing we can muster all the necessary equipment! We now realise certain mistakes made, and rectify conditions to improve our chances of obtaining our heart's desire. Push forward full steam ahead and we shall conquer all before us!

Never let it be said that we are stuck in the mud, for we now have wings on our feet and hover over proceedings, making sure that all is in place for this new venture. We delight in telling you now that we have accomplished even greater challenges, and are striving for more to follow on in the springtime! We have forsaken no others to be with you here tonight, and delight in informing you that we shall have our say, right up to the last, knowing as we do how fast we have come along this pathway of light. Please allow for a cooling off period in the next few days, as we shall have enough on our plate to satisfy the curiosity of those around you. We mean to push forward later, enjoying the groundwork undertaken to achieve our ambitions for a brighter future for all. We wish you well and thank you for services rendered!

6th February 2005 – We initiate a certain subterfuge in order that we may obey dictates of the heart, for we feel there is a necessary protocol that needs to be observed in the above proceedings. We allow a framework of understanding to clear up any misunderstandings which have occurred, and ask only that you will obey all instructions down to the last letter! We are now able to deliver on time, all that is necessary for our evolution, and we pray that you will incorporate in all of this a modicum of trust, for we can expect on the horizon even more to unfold in glowing accuracy. We intend to take you to the furthest point and we feel at this time there will be no turning back! We offer you unlimited resources which will help us to deliver criteria, and we feel the way ahead will become clearer in all aspects. We deliver a terminology that will enable us to convey words and sentences with greater clarity, and we feel you will realise an even greater incentive in all you do. Beware of certain tendencies to obstruct our delivery through self doubt, we mean to access all areas of growth and know you will develop to a greater more powerful standard of eloquence needed for this mission! We are determined to stand strong and true and depend on you now to forge this alliance in all its true splendour and grace.

We are impelled forward now delivering greater speeches and, allowing for discrepancies, we shall see new spurts of growth accelerating in all directions! Depend on us to help you in all your initiatives for we need constant approval to initialise this regrouping of energies. We depend on you to allay all fears for we need constant supervision to allow this channelling of energies. There is no need to hold back for we have given our pledge and hold you in the highest esteem! We allow a resting period where you will be able to recharge your batteries while remaining on full alert; this will initiate certain more subtle changes needed for these exchanges. We realise there is a certain time element involved but we shall overcome these trivialities, for nothing shall hold us back now from accessing other worlds! We depend on you to regulate these meetings for we feel greater resolve in all we do and say. Be prepared for storms on the horizon – there will be plenty of time to deliver what is needed, but we must obey dictates of the heart to achieve what is required of the greatest calibre. We have seen with our own eyes what is necessary to rectify these grave conditions, and we will obey all that is laid down before us, knowing you will allow us nearer to you in times of deep stress or anger. We hope you will avail yourself to us, accepting our thought patterns in a way that will allow us to gain entry to another dimension, where free expression is a normal occurrence and a way of making ourselves known and heard in circles of excellence!

We empower you now and ask that you continue to deliver these words, allowing for certain stages to be reached before we can change the format. We have laid down a new plan of action that will encourage you to become aware of what is open to you in the future, for we of supreme intellect recommend delivering these words by mouth, through a control which will assist proceedings! We trust you will allow us to proceed in this endeavour for we are able to achieve much more in this manner of communication. There is no need to be afraid for we shall manage ourselves with the greatest respect, and our energies will co exist together at the same vibrational level! We mean to take you further into our dimension and allow you a peep into our world. We expect a certain subterfuge will be needed for this co-existence, but we shall remain on full alert to take you to these agreed heights of achievement. *I have at last overcome my lack of confidence and now enjoy reading these transmissions to our group. This next step is very daunting, but I am determined to overcome my fear of failure and speak directly to the group.*

We express our condolences for those of you who have not been able to transcend your cares and worries, for we feel there will be a necessary obstruction to allowing certain energies from obtaining entry to these proceedings! We can only allow those of you who are with us one hundred percent! There are certain rules and regulations to be adhered to whereby we can remain on this level of existence, while retaining our true identity. We know that it may take some time before we can allow this joining of souls, but we recommend a period of co-existence to allow these energy exchanges to take place! Remember we have come from a similar framework as yours; we take into account what it is like upon a denser planet and can achieve this coming together by altering our vibration to coincide with yours!

There is a greater need to initiate these exchanges more frequently – as simply as stepping in and out of a garment you wear to venture outside! We need this structure to occur whereby we can achieve greater communication on all levels of understanding, and we need to reach this form of understanding to realise a golden future where all can see and hear! We accept the challenges before us and envelop you in a great abundance of learning, which shall stand us all in good stead. Believe us when we say that we have not outgrown a difficult situation that is looming on the horizon, suffice it to say that we have incorporated the necessary structures to allow deliverance and feel a growing concern for all of you at this point! We will need to initiate a point of reference whereby we can change the laws of gravity and abide with you at these times of deep stress! Please allow us to come closer and alleviate conditions where we can make a difference, we shall not complain but usher in a new understanding that shall be reached in due course.

7th February 2005 – We come at a time of greater need for further visitations, and can expect an opening very soon where we shall obtain the necessary products needed for these excursions. We feel that we have come at an opportune time for all concerned and we know we can deliver these messages to you of open minds. There is a need to step back, allowing adjustments to be made on certain levels before venturing forth on this mission, and we allow now a revitalising of energies that will give us clarity in the future. We depend on you now to come forward and obey dictates of the heart, allowing these meetings to gain free expression. We like to hear your responses to our words, for in this we can gain greater insight into what is needed to rectify conditions! Believe us when we say, we have nurtured this light and led her along this pathway for many a year, and it has taken until now for her energies to reach that level needed for these transmissions to occur! We would like you to understand that it is necessary for you all to become aware of what is ahead, for we can in no way manipulate proceedings, unless you are all aware of the parts you play in all of this! We demand allegiance for this cause, and we know of no other means to allow this perpetuation of assets, unless we are all of one and the same opinion in this matter.

We have augmented these proceedings to allow for greater and more meaningful exchanges of information to take place, and we superimpose our thoughts on yours today to enable this discussion to take place in the future. We ascertain there will be growing numbers who wish to hear our words, and we foresee a time in the future where we shall obey dictates of the heart in this. We know that you have already obtained the necessary information which will be laid down for all to see, and we note that you have encumbranced yourself with the necessary adjustments that have been made. Remember we need these exchanges to be perfect, we cannot allow a contamination of energies to take place, for this will only delay and obstruct our mission! We feel the time fast approaching when this will become as easy as taking in the air that you breathe, and with this approved rendition of services we shall see greater and more viable frequencies to be accessed, which shall be of a calibre even more remotely advanced than we have achieved in the past!

We deliver these speeches to allow you to convey what is necessary for your education, for we believe there is growing demand for knowledge of this sort, and we have a vast library at our disposal for you to translate what is given at this time! We depend on others to come forward to give you assistance in this project, for we need other life forms to gather around you, sharing their energy. This request is of great importance to you all for we allow the frequencies to alternate, giving each and every one of you a chance to learn and grow in our love. We never believed this was possible a few years ago, but have now delivered greater and more accurate information than was at first thought viable, up until now! We have been given to understand there shall be even greater revelations in store for us all, and we know it may come as a surprise to you at this time, but we are able to gain greater advantage in all that we do and say, for these revelations are bouncing in across the universe in great numbers!

We now need to attain further growth for our future evolution and we note, with great satisfaction, that you listen closely and intently to the words we deliver through this control. We have watched this soul's growth and are most proud of her achievements to date, for she has shown great resolve in reaching this point of her journey! There is a long way to go but she has maintained this control, allowing us to enter her atmosphere at great cost to herself, we feel she deserves the rewards that are coming her way! We know it may take a few years before we can deliver these messages in person, but we will allow the necessary by-products to be channelled more accurately and precisely, as given from those directives sent by a higher dimension. We have achieved this control by maintaining a sense of duty and love in all that is given to us from those of a higher dimension, and we have obtained greater knowledge to be passed down and used for purposes of high intent for mankind! Be it known in our two worlds that we shall endeavour to translate this material and give it to you as it is accessed by us. We mean to beam forward on that ray of light to enable this to happen in our two worlds at the same time of entry! We know this will take a mammoth amount of energy to be introduced, but we know we can tackle it from both sides, enabling a stronger and less clouded picture to be achieved by us all. We note that you have ventured forth this night to hear our words and we are extremely pleased with your motives. We recharge your batteries overnight and allow this transmission to end. For services rendered, we thank you and say goodnight!

8th February 2005 – We allow this blending of energies to take place and we are now able to control and voice our opinions. We maintain a steady stream of narrative and a finer tuning that will enable us to complete our mission. Please allow a conditioning of energies to take place before we complete our agenda, for we have no way of knowing if this will result in a loss of energy flow or develop into a more regular pattern. This process may take several months to accomplish but we shall revise as often as necessary. Take the time and trouble to follow your gut instinct, for it is in this we are able to reach you all and to overlap where we think a crisis has occurred! We understand there is a need of greater involvement from those of you who are here tonight, and we ask you to be aware of instances of suppression for there is an abundance of energy being produced at this time. We understand there are alternative remedies that can be taken to alleviate this condition but we know we must try, in all earnest, to develop for our own sakes, far greater and more reliable information regarding what is taking place at this time in our history! We need to know in greater detail how we shall move forward into the future; there are more choices available to us now and we deliver to you at this time, a greater advantage over those who have no moral code whatsoever!

We delight in telling you that we come from a higher dimension to achieve this rendezvous with you, and we allow a certain time framework to elapse before we can deliver even greater deliberations! We also delight in telling you that we have accomplished much more than was ever thought possible at this time. We attend to certain details that need monitoring and know you will agree with us that, to a certain extent, we have been unable to fulfil all that has been given, but we know in the future we shall be able to conquer over these miniscule problems. In all of this we know that we shall realise our hopes and dreams for the future – a better life for all mankind – our main objective and yours too!

We now need to govern a certain situation looming on the horizon and we hope you will not understate the severity of the situation, for we feel a growing rebellion which could cause serious heartache for many of you! We know it will take time to comprehend the gravity of the situation, but feel we cannot allow it to develop any further, and so we instigate a broader understanding of what is happening. We deem it irresponsible of those of you who come forward now, without a true realisation of what is needed to overcome this situation! You can expect a certain amount of clutter enveloping your aura that will need to be cleaned up and eliminated, for we cannot have this oppression bearing down on us a moment longer than is necessary! We deliver to you now even greater assets, allowing this transformation to penetrate in all areas, and we obey dictates of the heart, enabling you all to grow in our love. We mean to take you forward on that beam of light which radiates out into the cosmos, lighting the world with energy of such power and beauty as it penetrates the hearts and minds of mankind. This will enable an incredible transformation, allowing you to develop a broader perspective, which will assist you in all that is needed to govern a new world – a world of love, a world of beauty, a world of peace, where we shall abide together in greatest love and joy. We enable this sitter to go about her business and thank her once again for helping us to deliver these words at this time!

8th February 2005 – *Later in the evening.* We have now manifested all that we need to advance, and enquire if we may now proceed to take you down this pathway? We have delivered by all accounts a notable success, and would ask only that you direct your questions to us, rather than relying on those around you for answers! We come from a higher state of existence and propose that this event be taken highly seriously! We recommend total control to allow a complete transfer to take place, we know this may seem a highly charged action but we have the power necessary to achieve this. Do not feel in any way that you have to leave your body, it is only a temporary state of existence to enable us to develop further alliances needed for our quest! We fulfil a mission written long ago and now advise you to rest at intervals as required. We have taken advantage of you and feel these transferences may coincide with many of our frequencies at one time! We have allowed for some time now a new and more determined approach, and we are most impressed with your ability to change and adapt to all that is given. We note that you have behaved in a most desirable manner and we are very pleased with your progress! However, we also note that you have a tendency to sap your own energy by allowing other life forms to manipulate your energy field, and to such an extent that you are drained very easily! Try to guard against this by sending out wave patterns of love while remaining on full alert. This kind of draining of energies could lead to a more serious condition known as anxiety, and we feel on no account should you trouble yourself in this manner.

We have evolved from a new planet of outstanding beauty, and we feel it would be beneficial for you to join us there on certain occasions, so that we may share with you our greatest treasures and resources, which are open to all those of you who wish to sample them for yourselves. We know it may be hard for you to comprehend what is given at this time, but we know that we can allow this to happen in complete safety at all times. We have developed ways and means of keeping this on a level of perfect harmony, and have achieved this on all levels of existence. Be aware that we are deliberately taking you one step at a time, helping you to develop the eloquence needed for us to complete our mission. We shall allow this bonding of energies in the near future and rely on you at all times to maintain control of the situation. We hope and pray that you will come forward when the time is right and allow us this entry to your space. Be not alarmed at this intrusion, for you will realise even greater rewards by keeping to your side of the bargain, for we remain as always your closest friends and allies!

We need greater control over a certain situation ahead, and feel that it is necessary for you to obey your heart in all things, develop greater clarity in your thinking for this will enable you to defend yourself in your hour of need! Rely on us to stave off attacks of a psychic nature for we will not allow an invasion of this manner, and we deliberately hold you in our embrace to protect you from this kind of action! We have need of you little one, more than you could possibly know, and feel a growing concern for your health in matters that are beyond all comprehension! Please allow for a more holistic approach for we feel this will render a satisfactory conclusion to episodes of exhaustion! Take care to analyse all before you and believe in yourself, for all is waiting as promised for a brighter, more positive future for you and yours.

Chapter 2
Friends of the Earth

10th February 2005 – There is a need to step back in a certain situation for we feel we are bound to secrecy in certain areas of disbelief! We know there are many on your Earth plane that are in complete ignorance of our kind, and it will come as a great shock for many to know of our existence! There will come a time when we can incorporate the necessary structures to allow these admissions to take place, but now is not a good time to force your belief patterns on those close to you! In time we shall uncover more and more, but we do need further time for the majority of your planet. There are those, of course, who will welcome this knowledge with open arms, and we relieve you of your duty in keeping silent on these occasions. We know we will challenge many belief systems that will take time to absorb our words, before allowing any more information to be forwarded. We retain an inkling of respect for those who have left this planet at a time of deep remembrance, and we feel a profound need to envelop the galaxy with an overflowing sense of gratitude, reflected in a more purposeful way of life in the future for mankind.

We have grown wiser and have developed powers of concentration that will not only scrutinise situations at hand, but also rely heavily on those around us to conquer what was at one time insurmountable! We feel we have forecast extreme conditions as they have transpired and know in the future we shall gather more information, writing off what is unnecessary to us and taking what is needed at these troubled times in your world! We have kept to our side of the bargain and consent to a delay in negotiations, allowing a new and powerful frequency to be adjusted to your conditions on Earth. This is necessary because of a gravitational pull, and we mean to access this vibration with greater ease. We follow our instincts to advise you of further notifications and remind you that we will, on all occasions, look after you most carefully! We allow a framework of considerable care, paying attention to detail in all aspects before we allow this transference to take place. You are most welcome in our world and we are delighted to be able to show you how we exist here!

Being able to talk to you in this way has shown us even greater and more revealing insights into how you are coping on the Earth plane. Your mission was planned and devised many centuries ago, and we vowed to protect you and keep you safe from harm, for we are one and the same! Opening our eyes to the destruction of your planet was hard for us to do, but we have realised that this must never take place in this location of time! There is a greater need to be established whereby we can change events by turning back the clock! We admire your strength and courage, enabling us to function within your close proximity so that we may tell the world of all that is necessary to avoid this destruction. We have planned for a greater future for those of you who are prepared to tell it straight and we don't expect you to be overjoyed by this prospect, as many of you will feel the full force of disapproval and contempt! For our words, to some extent, may fall on deaf ears, however, there are those who will listen, and listen well to what we have to say! We will include those of you who have followed our words avidly, for now we must take some of the burden on our shoulders.

Forecasting doom and gloom may prevent some of you from being able to function in this ordinary world, but we allow you a peep into ours so that you may understand what we are offering you all – a new world where we can grow together!

This will have a catastrophic affect on groups of people all over the world for they cannot comprehend any other way of life! Accepting these new wave patterns of energy will be very hard for them, but we will try to initiate a new understanding for them to accept us as we really are – 'Friends of Earth'! We vow to you now my child, that we intend to take you on a journey to the stars and we shall live with each other in total harmony, co-existing in a brave new world of love and joy! We have need of those like you to initiate this new understanding, for we have developed grave concern over those of you who have forsaken us in times of trouble!

We superimpose our thoughts on yours, developing greater clemency for as many as we can envelop in our love. A harmonic convergence has assisted us in this matter – a harmonic convergence of souls and minds, identifying what is needed for our future evolution together, hand in hand. We feel our destiny growing closer and announce, in no uncertain terms, that we are here for you all! We gather you to us in our embrace and beg that you will consider our proposals, for we have achieved a great deal over the past few months and hope to go on from here with greater, more positive steps! We realise you have time constraints and reluctantly, we release you from our grasp. We look forward to our next meeting and hope we have been of some assistance to you. *This session has been a very emotional one and I too was reluctant to close, asking if we could carry on a while longer!*

We have been able to amplify thoughts of a nature that allow us, in extreme circumstances, to obey our calling. We shall deliver what is necessary to maintain our advantage and, realising this, we have a considerable amount of catching up to be done in certain areas. We shall, in all instances, remember that we are not able to always give one hundred percent clarity in understanding, but we have achieved, on a grand scale, more than enough to proceed! We refrain from making examples of those who would lead us astray, for we feel that by the law of averages we have obtained more than enough to give greater deliverance. We depend on you now to come forward to obey the dictates of your heart, for we are now calling you all to attention! Allowing for discrepancies we shall make a pact, whereby we can remain on your territory while negotiating a very real trust in our capabilities! We note that you have simplified matters and we are now ready to deal out our hand. We put our cards on the table for you to enable what is necessary, and we alleviate conditions as much as possible, inviting you to join us! Depend in extreme circumstances for a trial and error scenario, where we recommend a cloistered ceremony that shall include all directives necessary for this event. Be aware at this time that we bring our own brand of diplomatic immunity, and shall behave with great respect in your presence! We deliver this message with a highly, figurative form of speech to enable a greater understanding of what to expect, and we enable this passage of time to co-exist with ours on a less tenuous frequency! *I was finding it hard now to concentrate and told them of my need to sleep.* Trembling we let go of your hand and bid you farewell!

11th February 205 – *After accompanying my husband to our local pub this evening, I felt light-headed and quite nauseous, even though I had not drunk anything alcoholic!* We have to make allowances, in these instances, for a burgeoning effect that grows and becomes a very part of you in these troubled times! We know you have undergone a transformation that allows you certain privileges, and we note in these dire circumstances that you have outgrown what was once a desired way of life. It is therefore a hindrance to you when confronted with such a vast vibrational level! We know in all earnest that we shall work together in a more definitive pattern, for we have become necessary to one another in accomplishing our mission. We need to contain a certain situation looming on the horizon, and know that you will allow us to gain entry in a way that will stand up in a court of law! We deem it appropriate to understand the necessary measures to be adhered to, and volunteer certain information to enable this event to run smoothly. On no account should you behave in a manner unbecoming to your station, for we feel a growing reverence is needed!

We are able to bring you more news, and allow a few days to initiate a change of contract, which will allow for a more salubrious venture. We ascertain that in various shapes and forms, there will be a growing advantage, whereby we shall associate ourselves with events as they transpire. Forgive us if we seem vague in these matters, but we need to venture forth and onto new horizons as quickly as possible. It may seem an impossible dream but we shall accomplish more than enough to enable this dream to materialise. There is a need to step back where ultimatums are given and concentration is needed to clarify these events as they unfold one by one. We have accelerated the growth of certain prospects and know you will attend to details as they are presented.

It is a fact that we have come from a long way off to be with you here tonight, but we know you will appreciate that we can also be at other locations at the same time! We manipulate certain areas of discontent that will bring about enormous rewards for all, and we depend on you to arrange the necessary framework that will allow this incoming charter of excellence to proceed in all earnest. We divulge to you now that we are most happy with this contact and services rendered, and feel that we have accomplished more than enough to hold us in the highest esteem, both near and far! We analyse certain moments in history and feel we have given of ourselves with great dignity and love. We develop a stream of narrative for you to pass onto those of your group, for now is the time to implement what has been given. We will notify you of the right time and place in due course, for we feel a growing urgency in delivering our messages to you on this subject!

We intervene at this late stage and ask your forgiveness in certain matters, pertaining to the upkeep of necessary structures for our future consideration! We hope and pray that you will be able to follow your plan through, and we deliver the necessary attributes to allow funding for this project. We know this may come as a surprise to you, but we are in great need of services which you can provide for us on this level. We need certain devices to enable greater delivery, and allow for a re-convergence of the 'Brotherhood of Light'. We need certain arrangements to be made in haste as we feel a growing apprehension for the time ahead, this will counteract progress made and we allow a conditioning of energies to maintain a strong connection. Be aware of what is before you, develop your instincts and we will foreclose if necessary!

13th February 2005 – We have come from another world, far from planet Earth! We are as a speck on your horizon . . . a million light years away, yet we are here now talking to you in your very own room! How is this possible you ask yourself? We have evolved from a single cell in a framework similar to your own, and our species have inhabited planet Earth a million light years ago! We evolved at a time when there was mass destruction on Earth, and were able at this time to develop a way of co-existing with elements available to us. A reprogramming enabled us to develop the power of regrowth in a different structure, enabling us to evolve in a different format. We experienced this new growth with startling repercussions, which allowed a certain jet propulsion out into the universe! We are extremely grateful to be allowed this opportunity to expand and grow even further, for it seems a long time since we were able to gain information of this kind with a species that is related to us. We feel we have made our mark, and mean to prepare ourselves for even greater manifestations that will allow tremendous growth of the intellect. We are sure that you will understand how we are able to produce such a wide range of vocabulary, for this has evolved over time and we are most pleased to be able to communicate in this way with you. It has now been a quarter of a century since we have been able to expand our growth into your universe, and we have obtained information that, to a certain degree, has given us cause for concern! We have acted on this information and ask that you will help us in this endeavour for there is a great deal at stake!

Supreme beings have instructed us to pass on these messages, allowing a blending of energies to take place, for we have reached a point in man's evolution where there is a stalemate of sorts, which needs to be amended and taken care of. We have become aware of a crisis looming on the horizon that will give cause for concern! We rally the people of Earth to action and we urge you to take great care, acknowledging the seriousness of the situation! We devise a plan of action whereby we can exchange matter with anti-matter. We know this may seem a crazy solution to those of you who have no knowledge of physics, but please allow us to explain this phenomena. Firstly we deactivate the energy field, after this is accomplished we then maintain natural gases, which we then formulate into another energy, which we can then manipulate using a force field, which in turn will then recover shape and size! This action will maintain exclusively all life forms, allowing enough time to re-correlate thought forms, which in turn enable us to expand and grow in new directions. We see this as a necessary precaution against events that are unfolding before our very eyes! This mission is one of great sacrifice for those of you who herald in a new awareness for mankind, and we come at a time of supreme courage and intellect surpassed, for now is the time to take our hand and make that connection! Leading you into the future we feel the warmth and love that you extend to us.

Far above planet Earth we reach out to you and develop you as best we can, helping you to understand our plan of action which will allow you longevity beyond your wildest dreams! We come from your future and ask that you will initiate this bonding between us. We expose a certain framework, where we can work with the utmost clarity and ease of expression to convey our deepest feelings for the Children of Earth. We know at this time, we can inform you all of a greater and more powerful understanding, which will lead us all to greater deliverance! We shall keep a vision held dear by us all to save the Earth from deep despair, and we forecast this event to take place in the next few years! This may seem reminiscent of a science fiction story to you now, but believe us when we say that 'truth is stranger than fiction' and we are living proof that man has reached the stars and beyond! We have developed and grown over the centuries to become more aware of the pulse and heartbeat of the very core of our universe, a pulsating light which envelops us with a deep compassion and abiding love.

We convey our heartfelt sympathies for those of you who have travelled this path and know the pull of this star, only to be jerked back into the denseness of Earth's gravitational pull! While working on the above theory, we were able to make startling discoveries that enabled us to fulfil our dreams and ambitions for a better world. We now obey dictates of the heart and envelop each and every one of you in this new vision, enabling all of you to follow in our footsteps. We can bridge that gap that separates us with a column of light, which will lead you all to this new and vibrant planet which we call home. It is a multidimensional leap which we are asking you to make, it is simply reaching out and taking hold of a new formula, which will give you all a new lease of life, and how wonderful would that be . . . stepping out of the old and into the new! Being transferred from the third dimension into a multidimensional life force, travelling at will across the universe, exploring outposts that have never been accessed by man before – a whole new world unfolding before you in all its glory! We have opened your eyes to what is available to each and every one of you, we know there is a lot to take on board and assimilate, and we shall allow a percolation of thoughts before we resume our connection. Thank you for persevering with this transmission!

14th February 2005 – We require only a few more weeks before this frequency shall be restored to a level that will encompass a new field of vision, we will then be able to use greater and more natural methods of illumination! Feel free to allow this growth to penetrate on all levels, for we are on the edge of a precipice and cannot wait much longer, before making the choices that are necessary to save mankind from total extinction! Remember we have walked this pathway and know this outcome in all entirety! Please believe us when we say, there is extreme pressure being brought to bear in a situation not far from home, and we know too there have been several other attempts elsewhere on the globe, where there have been certain instances of vile behaviour that cannot be allowed under any circumstances! We know this to be rife in many cities of the world, and would urge you all to reconsider your true motives for allowing such atrocities to manifest, and in a world that was once thought to be a golden ray of hope and light in a tempestuous ocean of stars!

We now permit a moving away from this scenario, for we have foreseen events unfold, and interpret a greater, more eloquent understanding of what is needed to rectify conditions. Please believe us when we tell you, that we have come from a much, more time orientated frequency than you would give us credit for! There has been an element of mistrust which has been inappropriate, but we feel this energy is growing in intensity and we will be able to nurture you, with great expertise, to a level needed for perfect understanding at all times. We note you are also pleased with the progress made, and we are enchanted with your behaviour regarding proceedings. We allow now a new framework to co-exist along with your own, so that we are ready to drop into your world at a moments notice! Feel free to understand this new legislation for we are on an even keel in delivering our messages to you. We feel a growing urgency in a certain direction which could give cause for concern. Be aware that we have your best interests at heart and would like you to consider alternative arrangements, whereby we can assist each other at a time more suitable to your needs! *Most of my communications have been in the early hours of the morning, where I've felt the call to leave my bed and transcribe. It seems that we can now connect at more appropriate times!*

We depend on you now to begin this experiment, where we can obey dictates of the heart and reach one another at any given moment. We feel this exercise will help you immensely to reap a beautiful harvest, remaining on red alert so that we may communicate at a more natural level. We believe you have made a great effort in keeping up this contact, but feel this could become a problem to you if we allow these nocturnal visits to persist! We allow this new framework to operate on a level of frequency, whereby we can maintain contact at any time of the day or night and, allowing for certain time discrepancies, we shall obey dictates of the heart in this! We now commemorate a time gone by where we initiated this contact, and firmly believe that we have consolidated our commitment to one another! We venture now on this bandwagon of love to become the procreators of a much more positive future for mankind. Realising our true essence we shall grow in all directions, maintaining a sense of balance and allowing the influx of energies to envelop and expand all possibilities. We advise you now to proceed with all caution, for we believe the time ahead will be one of great disturbances!

15th February 2005 – We welcome you Sunbeam to our world of love, joy and peace – we have devised a wonderful new theory as to how we can approach you, and we feel this revelation will stand us in good stead for we have found this to be a most exhilarating form of connection! Stand back for transmission to commence as we are now able to move forward on that beam of light! We ask that you will bear with us at this time for we are now able to transmit a finer, more delicate frequency, which will allow even greater, more viable forms of communication to take place. We observe how many of you on the Earth plane have responded to our call, and we feel a growing reverence is needed that will allow for a finer tuning of energies. You are responsible to make sure of the smooth running of operations, and we now include certain measures that need looking at more closely. We feel for instance, there is a necessity to be aware at all times of the groundwork that is part of the proceedings. There has been a tampering of certain energies that shall not be tolerated in these extreme conditions, and we feel the need to revise location!

17th February 2005 – *I had my doubts as to the clarity of words coming through in the previous communication, worrying my own mind was jumping in to finish sentences!* Dear friend, we beam to you now from the 'Star Ship Enterprise', this is what we would have you believe for the purpose of our communication today! We have come from a framework similar to yours and know that we can measure time comparatively. We desire you to speak with an open mind, allowing our thoughts to manifest in your brain along with the other millions of thoughts that are all vying for attention to be given and *. . . there was a long pause here . . .* spoken! See how your brain is searching for a word! Our thoughts come into your mind more easily, in this way you can ascertain that it is not your thoughts, but our words that are being delivered. Listen to the clarity within your skull and know that we are with you!

We are bound to secrecy at this time for there are great revelations in store that cannot, at this moment, be expressed in words! When the time is right we will be able to pass on this information, but until that time we can only deliver thought forms of a less imperious nature. We deliver our love in greatest measure and ask that you will superimpose your thoughts on ours, so that we may achieve an even greater and more productive flow of energy, which will allow us entry into your world. We know this has been a most enlightening time for us all, and we devote our time and energy into displaying our thoughts and emotions with you, for we feel we have given freely of our intelligence. We have further news that can be stored, and we feel these revelations will hold greater meaning for you all at this time. Please allow for a framework of understanding that will depend, to a great deal, on what manoeuvrability can be attained. We have forecast certain measures to be adhered to and are remarkably pleased with all that you have achieved on this mission.

Please note that we do not allow, in any circumstances, any disruptions that could cause a problem to our energy circuits, this can be extremely dangerous for the sitter and for control on this side! We remain as always in complete control of the situation, and allow a gathering of souls who can be trusted implicitly on all occasions. We remain totally aloof, regardless of how many souls gather together, but we need to know the numbers before deciding on a suitable venue for this to take place. We have achieved great success and know that you will enable these proceedings to take place in a more suitable location, for there is a great need to prepare and cleanse all areas before we can allow this conditioning of energies to take place! We feel this venue will bring us into greater contact with what is necessary to achieve our final goal. *Again they emphasised the need to plan ahead.* Aspirations shall be recompensed and we need to know the numbers before allowing the channelling to commence! There is a certain framework that needs examining before we can introduce any changes or alterations, this adjustment will occur on a level from our side as well, and will need careful monitoring at all stages. We feel this will give us greater understanding on all levels and we need to observe all that is necessary for you to gain entry into our world!

Develop and maintain this connection, we have great need at this time to be with you and yours, for there are powerful conditions that need unravelling before they can do any harm in your world! Beware of instances where the male population of the Arab world kneel in prayer to ask forgiveness for atrocities inflicted! *I'm asking now if this is when the sky will be used as an auditorium, as several years ago I dreamt of a beautiful Indian lady whose figure covered the sky. Everyone knelt down in the fields with their faces to the ground, listening as she spoke!* We shall bear in mind this will happen in the Gaza strip in the year 2012! We allow a penetration of energies to unfold, and visualise a time in the future where all will be able to understand our words with greater clarity. We feel this endeavour will come to fruition at a much earlier stage than previously envisaged, and know you will understand that we are doing our best to maintain this connection. We travel on now into the unknown – take our hand for we are beside you all the way to heaven and back again!

18th February 2005 – We have need of you now little one, and postpone events to allow the necessary energies re-adjust their frequencies to our level. We have for some time now been in contact with various agencies, which have been altogether influential in achieving a more harmonious connection! Please allow for this convergence of energies to take place very soon, for we mean to ascertain at which level we need to work in order for this to take place with the greatest clarity! Inspections have given us greater insight into what is needed for this occasion, and we shall monitor certain conditions to ascertain the graveness of the situation. Please allow for a cooling off period prior to the transmission, for we are not able at this time to come forward. We have made grave errors of misjudgement, and allow for a conditioning of energies to take place before we are able to transmit further messages!

We note that you have been extremely capable of making these exchanges, and we welcome your ideas and discussions for future involvement as a most necessary prerequisite to all deals and pacts! We have known for some time that you have manifested a great abundance of your own time and energy into proceedings, and we now proceed with all caution, transmuting certain conditions that allow for greater and finer energies to manifest. We are able to reach this level by exchanging powerful conditions with an element of understanding, which will bring us greater rewards in the future. Please allow us to draw closer as we generate even greater control over events about to take place, for we feel an extreme resurgence of energy on the horizon waiting to be harnessed!

Reaching out and taking hold of your hand, we lead you to pastures new where you will be able to see for yourselves how we live in our world of peace, joy and harmony! We have maintained this new growth in all directions, allowing us manoeuvrability within changing thought patterns that allow this augmentation to take place. We have decided at this point in time that we are able to remove certain transgressors from the scene, which means that we can develop further our initiative without being overlooked with hostility! We come prepared now for the time ahead, knowing that you will achieve all that is set out before you, and we allow this growth to transcend even higher levels of understanding than we have managed before. Please believe us when we say that we have come to help you all, and deliver more relevant details as they are passed onto us. We venture onto this pathway of love, beckoning you forward one step at a time, allowing new growth with each step. We shall manifest even greater traits of expression, allowing the influx of energy to produce even more powerful ways of expressing ourselves. We know this means greater sacrifice for those of you who are unable to comprehend the seriousness of our words, but please note, we do not intend to alarm you, only to allow you greater comprehension of future activities that need addressing in your world and ours! Please allow a time of recalibration where we may enter your atmosphere and deliver, with greater clarity, all that is needed to sustain life for future generations.

We may seem to you, at times, to be ruthless in our way of thinking, but we have allowed for this superstructure to remain on your planet while we reconstruct and re-negotiate our plan of action! We realise we may seem to be a trifle concerned with our manner of speech – but we know there is a great need at this time to allow channelling of this sort to take place! We cannot allow a misrepresentation to take place and feel the need to convey, in our own words, what is needed in the days and weeks ahead! Prepare yourselves for we come armed with love, and we have dedicated our lives to making the adjustments necessary to incorporate your world into ours. We need to make amends for certain atrocities committed long ago – not for us – but way into the future for yourselves! We know this may seem more than enough for you to comprehend at this time, but we know there is also a lack of judgment on our part that needs looking at in greater detail! We have manifested, to all intents and purposes, a new world where we can all live and grow together in harmony, and we need these adjustments to take place to allow this to happen more easily. Sometimes we have to give up and let go in order to gain prosperity, and we feel we can approach this situation regardless of certain elements holding us back.

There is a certain time framework that can be reached, whereby we are both able to make amendments at the same time. In this way, we shall achieve the clarity needed to forecast events as they transpire in a network of emotions, which on the surface of a society that has long forgotten the principles needed to maintain control! We have found that you are now able to transmit finer frequencies, allowing us to gain control of a certain situation looming on the horizon, and we need now to make amendments so that we are able to prepare ourselves for the time ahead! We feel you will allow us entry at this point to rectify certain conditions that need adjusting, and we feel that you are ready to make this contact more viable, with an exchange of energies that will allow for greater, more tolerable outcomes. Please remember that we are here for you at all times, and we need to know that you will take this on board, enabling us to align with you whenever necessary. Please deliver these speeches by hand, for this frequency will not be tolerated on other levels! Coming into the wrong hands will cause an inciting of terror and fear among people whose readjustment will take longer than others! We need to make amendments where appropriate, and would ask you to remember that we have your best interests at heart. This is not a time for idle speculation but a time of action, and we have need of great assistance at this time for the evolution of your planet.

We feel that you have obeyed all directives and have listened carefully to our words, enabling simultaneous respect! We have a mission of the highest calibre and need to monitor progress step by step along the way, maintaining new growth in areas of disbelief. Please note that we are able to come closer to you now because of a certain fundamental change in your energy field, which has enabled us entry into your frequency! We adjust these timelines to coincide with ours and mean to take you forward now on this ray of light, enabling us to travel out into the cosmos together, arm in arm, transcending all cares and worries! We negotiate a new pattern of understanding, realising our dreams and ambitions for a brighter future for mankind. In total we have achieved resounding success, and are able to capitulate in certain areas of discontent, here we will use resources available to us, to make a connection that is necessary in achieving our aims and objectives for the future. We bend to salute you and ask that you will be careful in the days and weeks ahead, for we are able to transcend all obstacles that hold us back, moving on with greater harmony!

21st February 2005 – *I've been resting this week after succumbing to a flu virus.* We have need of you now more than ever, and would ask that you endeavour at all times to keep this connection open, for we feel there are instances ahead that will need closer supervision! We know you are indisposed and will keep this short and to the point! We cannot allow a transgression to occur in what can only be described, as a pure unadulterated attempt to sabotage all that has been painstakingly orchestrated! We have taken the liberty of uncovering what could become a hazardous situation which can be rectified if handled carefully, and we propose that we cancel arrangements until we can address this situation which looms on the horizon! Take note that we are in no way erasing from our memory banks what is not palatable, we simply request a time of sanctuary until we are more able to express ourselves with the utmost clarity and freedom of expression! We need to emphasise the graveness of the situation that we find ourselves in, and would like to remind you of what is planned for the future. We need to revitalize certain areas and will expect a bonding of energies very soon. We feel this short time lapse will enable you to absorb what is given, allowing a settling that will help us to reinstate boundaries and overcoming all anxieties which may cause distress. We feel the time of May will be one of celebration, and this will provide us with a fulfilling sense of wider achievements on both sides! Please allow us to make this contact amenable to both parties for we hasten to add, we have enjoyed, immensely, our times together!

Orbiting the planet Earth we survey your territory, and know you are with us, not only in our frequency but in our hearts and minds! We appreciate all your hard work in making this possible, and re-enact our times spent together to recover what was lost. We allow a turning back in this instance to refresh your mind, allowing us access to various points which we may have missed on previous occasions! We transcribe on a higher frequency and note that you are also volunteering the role of secretary. Please allow us to dictate these words and finalise plans for the future, we would like you to obey us in this, as we are relaying our final destination and would like you to take on board our wishes for a golden future for mankind! We envelop you now in our love and ask that you will allow us entry into your energy field more frequently, for we feel the need for greater relaxation, enabling a deeper bonding to occur! We need to know that you are ready to plan our mission together in greater detail; we make amendments in certain areas and ask that you will allow this to take place as soon as possible in the near future!

22nd February 2005 – We beam ahead to develop the pathway before you. Open up and shine your light for we feel the time is right for this expansion of minds, forging a new and vibrant pathway across the universe, opening up new horizons and venturing on this rainbow of light! We deliver a plan of peace to your nation, negotiations are underway and we express ourselves most eloquently. We allow a condensing of energies, needed for re-alignment in areas of mistrust. We do appreciate the need to analyse what is given, and you may depend on us to instigate a new agenda, alleviating all doubt and uncertainty! We analyse events before us, unravelling what is necessary for greater unison, we feel we have given of our best to develop a more natural rhythm and depend on this vision to be maintained. We vow to you that we shall instigate a broader form of contact, discrimination has allowed us to confiscate certain patterns no longer required, and we believe we can operate more swiftly to allow a rescheduling. Be prepared to re-establish this contact and feel free to remonstrate with us if you are not entirely satisfied! We stay on solid ground to formalise our plans and we remain as always your friends and allies!

23rd February 2005 – We realise there is a need for total and utter trust between us as we amplify our thoughts, and pass onto those who are entrusted with their keeping! We rely entirely on those who go before us to prepare the pathway, just as you have been chosen to clear the way for others to follow! We have instigated a more meaningful retrieval of evidence to allow for the necessary production of energies, and please believe us when we say, we have accomplished more than enough to let battle commence! Rely on us to bring through the necessary data for we shall allow a grander vision to precede us. We pass on these messages as they are given, and note that preparation has occurred on a higher level than ours. We deem it advisable to allow these proceedings to take place at a more leisurely pace, and feel we have acquired the necessary assets to achieve a greater vision for the future of mankind. We now need to be thinking seriously, of what we shall be doing to enable this sequence of events to take place! We shall devise new methods whereby we are able to monitor this new growth, and we feel at this time, there is a need for caution at the outset!

There have been alien conditions that have given us cause for concern, but we can now vouch for your safety as we propel you forwards and onto a higher dimension! Please be aware that all is being done to allow this to proceed smoothly and calmly. We have been able to weed out those who have not been on the same wavelength, and would ask that you send out your wave patterns of love to those concerned! We express our heartfelt sympathy for those who cannot take on board what we have to offer, and we know these things are of no consequence in the overall picture of what has been achieved! Relieve yourself of any anxieties for we mean to proceed full steam ahead; we doubt that you will have any cause for concern as there is mammoth support on all sides for this venture. We ascertain that the level achieved will bring about great rewards for all and would ask only, that you amend certain items as these need to be chewed over before coming to fruition! Please enable us to bypass a difficult phase, as we are now able to muster more than enough to achieve our main aims and objectives. We come at a time when we have fulfilled a great many promises, and we allow even more jolly events to surface before the year is out! We shall forge ahead now and feel an opening that will give you the credit you deserve. Allow for a renewal of energies to take place for there is great need of our services on the horizon and beyond.

28th February 2005 – Come aboard my child, we welcome you with open arms! Thank you for allowing us this contact of minds, for we realise the necessity to display control over various projects that have given us cause for concern! We vouch for your safety and ask only that you prepare yourself for action. There is a need at this time to open your mind to various aspects and conditions that need monitoring in greater detail, and we need to know how we shall deliver our words, conveying our messages to a wider audience! We obey certain disciplines necessary for this mission, and ask that you will condescend to alter arrangements to coincide with our production! We need to maintain this superstructure to enable greater expansion, fulfilling and adjusting our wave lengths to coincide with yours at this event in the near future. Please allow a conditioning of energies to take place so that we may engage all parties at this late stage

We envisage a time of celebration and know the outcome will be one of immense joy for us all! Take on board all that has been given for we vouch for our ingenuity, and ask that you remember our hopes and wishes for the future of all mankind. We know you have taken a giant leap and have made this entirely of your own free will; we know too that you have taken on board a huge responsibility that has been born of a desire to please us at this time! This has been a memorable time for us, seeing into your world while existing in ours, we note that you too have the desire to visit us, and in the near future this will be possible on all levels of understanding! We superimpose our thoughts on yours to coincide with this new measure of achievement, and we give vent to our feelings, asking you to bear with us in exclaiming, that we have gathered together what has been an immensely rewarding feedback, regarding growth and distribution of energy!

Please allow us to settle a point raised recently in discussion; we have allowed a turning back in instances of denial and we expose those who have decided not to continue on this pathway with us! We hope you will be forthcoming in expressing with us, our sympathies for those who are not ready to take on this mammoth task of understanding! We send out our love to those of you who are unable to grasp this enormous concept we are offering you, and hope and pray there will come a time when all will be able to take on board this new and vibrant world of light! We feel a certain despondency among some of you and venture to ask – what is your cause for concern? We are able to manifest in great abundance, all that you could possibly need at this moment of entry into our world!

We have gained exclusive coverage for those of you who will one day become our ambassadors, and we vouch for your safety, opening up new possibilities for you to share with those around you. In the future you will all be responsible for passing on this knowledge to others, for we have a plan of action that will reach far and wide, giving the world time to make her choices! There will be no turning back at the time of entry, and we will have to be sure that we leave no trace of envy or greed to be devoured by those of a lesser nature! We have vowed to keep safe those of you who are willing to grant us your allegience, and we know it may come as a huge shock to many of you, feeling as you do an affinity with Earth, but we vow to you now that you will never regret your choice to follow in our footsteps! For we are taking you over the threshold into a new and vibrant dimension, that is beyond all comprehension in this isolated moment of time! We feel the necessary feedback may give cause for concern, but believe us when we say; we have never encountered a more bountiful and fulfilling mission as this!

We believe you will come to accept us as we show ourselves to you, and we know too that we will both experience a powerful and illuminating expression of love and understanding, of what is to become a bonding of energies in the fullest sense! Be it known now of our world of love, creating free expression and exhilaration beyond words, and a dividing of talents where no man will be lesser than his brother! All will be given what is asked and no man will be cast asunder, for all will have the choice to live peaceably together in harmony! This is how we see our brave new world, and we deny no access to any man who shares our vision of peace and harmony for all! Beware in instances where there may be those who declare themselves to be among the just, but who are only along for the ride, for they will soon become apparent as having no backbone when it comes to concrete evidence! *I'm being given a vision of the nursery rhyme character, 'Humpty Dumpty' sitting on a wall.* We cannot justify this action when it falls heavily on those who have to pick up the pieces and place them back together again!

Please also be aware at this time of certain negative activity displayed by friends and family! We delight in telling you that we are doing our bit to help them adjust to these new wave patterns that you yourselves are able to accommodate. There will be plenty of time for them to grow along side you, and you may be interested to know that some of them will surpass even yourselves with their knowledge and assesment of conditions. For there are many on your Earth plane that were raised especially for this occasion to take place, and you were all hand picked to make this transition as easy as possible! We transcend all cares and worries to be here with you now, and observe that you have given us great joy in enabling us to be with you at this time. We know you will allow us to make amends for various faults, and we obey dictates of the heart in enabling you to make the necessary adjustments, before we can recover all that has been lost in the past. Please represent us in the days and weeks ahead, for we feel a necessary prerequisite to our alliance will mean a standing back to allow this channelling of energies to take place!

We feel you have given us an open forum where we will be able to converse with your friends and colleagues, in a way that will give a better understanding of what we are offering. Please allow a few days before we are able to condense material that is needed, so we may then release these thought patterns to you for further transcriptions to be made. We realise at this time there will be no more past life memories taking place, only what is needed to rectify misjudgements! Please allow us to come forward in our true form for we feel this revelation will have greater impact, and a refining of energies will allow this to take place! Remember that we have formatted this to the highest resolution necessary, and will incorporate even higher frequencies that can be recovered at this time. This will be a time of great celebration for all, and we hope and pray that you will all be batting on our team!

2nd March 2005 – We come from a planet known as 'Oz', and install the necessary framework to enable a conjuring of what is needed; we allow the calibration of an energy field that will release a structure necessary to fulfil all our hopes and dreams for a better world! We know this seems 'pie in the sky' but we feel as do you that if we can incorporate this coming together in its truest sense, we will have accomplished what has never been possible before in all human history! We will have maintained the structure of the population of Earth, transferring energies by viably condensing matter, which then re-emerges on a new level of existence! We foresaw this many centuries ago but concluded that it was not accepted that a major functioning could be realised with any satisfactory outcome. We speculated that at some time in the future, man would adjust his frequencies to allow this transference to take place! *I feel that the name 'Oz' is perhaps a nickname for a planet where dreams really do come true, as in the film 'The Wizard of Oz'!*

We feel it is imperative to move forwards and onto greener pastures, for we believe the time is right to endow you with the necessary requisites to enable this functioning of spirit. Please believe us when we say we are most proud of your achievements to date, and would ask only that you behave in a manner more accustomed to our teachings! We cannot sway you one way or the other, but ask that you listen to the dictates of your heart in this matter.

We feel most welcome in your prescence and know we have found great pleasure in your company. Please believe us when we say that there is extreme advantage to be had by embarking on this mission of love, for we have seen with our own eyes the pathway you tread and align ourselves to accompany you! We have foreseen events as they unfold and ask that you wait a time before embarking, for we need to instil a greater sense of devotion with words unspoken, but felt in the heart!

Be it known in our two worlds of a wish to proceed on this venture with no holds barred, we expect you to come up to standard and incorporate new measures to be adhered to! Remember always that we are with you leading you on to vistas bright. We make a plan of action enabling all to unfold before us, and venture to say that you have achieved a great deal at this time, we also ask that you remember in your prayers, all those who have gone before to prepare a place for us! We need a plan of action to be able to proceed more smoothly and we shall expect an opening to materialise very soon. Be prepared and believe it when we ask you to enrich the lives of those around you, by attending to them in a way that will gain access to their souls. We will find ways and means of addressing certain situations at this present time, and ask that you feel free to call on us whenever there is a need. We know you will always answer our call, and we instigate certain measures whereby we can amply attain our hearts desire.

We know of no other way to restrict your pain and suffering in a world that has long forgotten a need to kneel and pray! We envelop the world in a powerful flame of love to transmute those lower energies that invade your space, and we ask that you allow a conditioning of these energies to take place very soon. We feel an enormous advantage will be made and would venture further to say, that we have adjusted wave patterns of thinking to a colossal viewpoint of understanding. This has given credence to what has become a better, individual attention span, enabling greater understanding on a higher level, and we mean to superimpose these thoughts and feelings on the population of Earth to forge ahead with our aims and objectives! Each thought pattern laid down will represent another milestone in our battle to save as many souls as possible! We will alleviate the stresses and strains of everyday life by becoming more involved in the upkeep, and day to day running of life on Earth. Please allow us to venture forth into your space, allowing us the freedom of expression needed to convey our deepest, most heartfelt responses to what has become our most cherished experience to date! We welcome you to our world and rejoice that you have grown in our love; we issue you with a new set of principles and regard you as a highly patriotic member of our society! We pave the way for all to follow, and deem it a necessary measure to involve those around you to climb aboard and tighten their seat belts, for we are impelled forward to new realms of greatest joy and upliftment. Peace be with you!

4th March 2005 – We feel a tremendous surge of love at this time, knowing as we do what is causing this struggle within you, and we depend on you to maintain a deep and loving connection so that we may assist you in your quest for truth! We devise a plan whereby you can alter your frequencies to adjust to ours in a matter of moments, this will utilise a connection that cannot be broken! We alternate between this world and the next fulfilling our mission on Earth, and we denote a sense of knowing when the time is right to make this connection. Please allow a few days before we can initialise correctly, for we have minor adjustments to make. We have outgrown various projects and feel the need to ensure greater control in areas of discontent, fret not for we are with you and will take your hand, leading you in the right direction! We know you want to make the right impression and are afraid of contempt among your peers, but we say unto you, your heart will always lead you in the right direction! There is no need to turn back for we will forge ahead, giving further credence to our words. Allow us this grace for we never said it would be easy! The young pretenders are gathering around to give you their allegiance, and we know you will understand the necessity of introducing a wider range of therapies to combat negativity! Recovering your identity we march forward and deliberately bypass what is no longer required. Take our hand my Sunbeam, and we shall show them what we are made of . . . a lighter essence than the physical frame . . . a compound of magical distillation!

We fulfil a promise made aeons past, and request that you join us now to deliver these words in even greater ambiguity! We reel in those left behind, insisting on new measures of interacting with one another and enabling a finer tuning of energies to take place. We depend on one another and use this advantage to create advantage! *I asked for help in conquering my lack of confidence so that I could become a purer channel for communication!* We offer you absolution, and amplify our thought patterns to you. Grow in our love . . . feel the strength we send you, for we shall rectify conditions as they present themselves and encourage you in all things! Remember we will never desert you, only help you to attain the highest level needed for our work together. We have achieved great things together and will go on to even greater heights, know we are with you in every sense and we shall conquer our fears, moving forward, onwards and upwards!

Tend to the little one, (*my youngest daughter*) and allay her fears, she is in great need at this time of your love and support! Take her hand and lead her into the sunset with you, she will develop and grow alongside you and will help you in your quest for greater positivity among people of the Earth plane. We feel her assignment will commence in the near future, and we shall coax her along when she is ready to hear our words! This will be her greatest strength and we rouse her to use her instincts, enabling greater fortitude in the time ahead! We develop and grow in your love and insist that we shall deliver what is necessary before too long. A light will be born that will give strength and sustenance to you both, enabling you to shine your light out into the darkness for others to follow in your footsteps!

Forge these truths and we shall overcome all obstacles, maintain your sense of direction for you are shielded by the light and we take you one more step, forwards and onwards. We deliver further statements to be recorded when the time is right, step back and allow us to come forward to initialise a new awareness and protocol. Prepare to take on board new and purposeful conditions whereby we shall achieve our main aims and objectives. Watch for the sunrise! *I wondered why I was asked to watch for the sunrise as nothing of any importance happened the following morning, but later in May I understood. I had decided to pick up my palette and try a painting in oils. I had no idea what I was going to paint but it turned out to be a large mountain overlooking a lake, and coming up behind the mountain . . . was the morning sun! I was quite amazed at how good it was, since it was the first time I had ever tried painting in oils. Thank you my friends for your inspiration!*

8th March 2005 – *Tonight I'm attending my spiritual workshop meeting and lay down to rest. I felt spirit with me very strongly and took up my pad once more.* We involve you now regarding a certain project which needs careful consideration. We maintain the necessary adjustments and ask that you will co-exist with us for tonight's session; we recognise the fact that you will also be obeying your natural instincts to come forward when necessary! We overcome obstacles and allow this entry to occur, be prepared on this occasion to reinstate boundaries given, for we mean to allow this conditioning to take place. We allow entry of this kind to help adjustments needed for further meetings; we make ourselves familiar with your surroundings and initialise any action needed. Please help us to make this endeavour as natural as possible, and believe us when we say, that we are extremely grateful at this time for your co-operation! *Sure enough and true to their word, just before the meditation I felt myself receding and a different energy coming forward very strongly! For most of the evening I was very quiet and seemed to be watching the entire proceedings from a distance. However, during our session on psychometry I came forward and did very well, which pleasantly surprised me, as in the past I haven't had much confidence in reading objects.*

10th March 2005 – *I chatted to my spiritual friends, thanking them for their friendship, which seems to be growing stronger day by day. I told them how much I was enjoying life at the moment with the new found confidence I'd acquired. I also thanked them for leading me to my new friends on Earth who are all like minded, I simply couldn't be happier as I'm becoming more fulfilled in my work for spirit. I asked them if their words would one day be published.* We are bound to one another where no man can cast us asunder, and we have developed greater, more meaningful insights that have enabled this relationship to be forged with even greater strength! Allow us to come forward now and enlighten you as to how we should proceed in the coming weeks ahead. We have found, to our surprise, that a certain dedication has enabled us to venture forth on this journey of the highest intent, and we know that you will agree with us, when we say, that you have enabled this to happen with great aplomb and forethought! We know it has been a struggle for you on many occasions, but we vouch for your honourable intentions, forging a new pathway filled with memorabilia of past decades that need careful consideration! We beam ahead now and ask that you will follow, carefully and slowly as we venture into the vast unknown! *I'm now being shown a vision of myself – dipping a toe into the lake to test the water.*

We allow you certain privileges that will enable you to sample what is in store for you, and we develop a certain understanding that will enable us to react more swiftly when the time is right. We need a more powerful tool of understanding to allow us to profit from past mistakes, and in this we shall recover major issues that need addressing! We face the fact that there have been major changes in the overall pattern and growth of the population, but we still need to address minor issues that hover on the brink. We feel these changes will come more easily as we rectify certain conditions. Feel free to obey the dictates of the heart, for in this we are drawn to various connections. We direct you now to obey our instructions and ask that you will manage our accounts with the greatest of ease. We foreclose on what is no longer required, and deem it necessary to make application to what is bound to be a more amenable offer for all concerned. We translate material that is needed for our book . . . make no mistake, we have embarked on this mission to give the world greater insight into the future of mankind! *This was the first clarification of our work becoming a book!* We can rectify conditions if all will heed our words and these shall be broadcast in no uncertain terms, to a much wider audience than can be maintained generally speaking! We shall ascertain what is needed to allow a re-conditioning of energies, resulting in evidence that shall give us further intelligence.

We initiate these new guidelines to ensure that you will be able to follow our instructions down to the last letter! Please feel free to instigate a search of publishers, for we feel this will extend our boundaries, encouraging new growth in all directions. Depend in extreme circumstances for us to come forward and advise proceedings to take a more natural course, allowing this framework to manifest in a colourful profusion of thoughts and ideas for a more profitable future. There is a certain time framework for this adventure, and we allow the necessary structure to be completed in less than a year! We superimpose our thoughts on yours to gain greater advantage, and allow one year to pass before we are able to dedicate this book for manufacture! Please allow this time framework to coincide with a more natural and purposeful endeavour, for we have exchanged thought patterns that co-exist to enable even greater harmony between us. We are forever in your debt, and initiate a new framework of understanding that will allow for even greater feedback in the months ahead. Beware of certain ideals that may lead us astray, for we have greater need to employ discretion at this time. We impel you to grant us a further delay, in what is, fast becoming, a monotonous charade of events looming on the horizon. We endeavour to match what is given and allow a further supply of evidence to stand us in good stead. We envelop you now my child in the light of true love and understanding, we develop you and pray that you will incorporate all we have given in your manuscript! We devise a new plan of action that will be taken on board very soon, exchanging thought patterns in abundant streams and enabling a stronger, more powerful bonding on all occasions. We delight in telling you there have been mammoth changes abroad that will enable our project to be accepted on all levels! *I'm feeling very emotional at this point and feel that my cup runneth over.*

13th March 2005 – *I've been feeling distraught as my cat, Jess, had to be put to sleep yesterday – he was 14 years old! For the last few weeks he has been in great distress with a painful hip, and despite my attempts to give him healing, an x-ray confirmed that he had bone cancer. I know he has had a long and happy life but I've been constantly weeping! I've also been remembering my mother's illness and her death 30 years ago, praying that Jess would be with her now.*

We choose to obey the laws of gravity to be with you at this time, be not afraid for all will come to fruition as we have foretold. We feel a growing presence of unease, and rectifying certain conditions, we allow a sourcing of energy to alleviate pressure, please allow us to come forward in these extreme conditions! We envelop you now my Sunbeam in our prayers of love, obeying our instincts we deliver these messages and beam ahead of you, lighting the pathway to heaven and the stars. Be it known in our two worlds of a love that will never die but go on forever! We deny you the right of access to our kingdom at this time . . . but know that it may take just a few more steps before you are here! We of supreme intellect prepare a place for you to sit with us, for we deem it necessary to make this commitment to one another; we obey our own instincts and divide data that will allow you access to our world. We know it may come as no surprise to learn that we are one and the same! We feel this statement will enable us to develop a greater bond and understanding of what is to come, and we develop greater accessibility, allowing us to move forward!

We have suppressed certain details that may emerge in the coming weeks and months ahead, and initiate a certain understanding that will bear fruit in the not too distant future! We allow this reckoning to be made, and feel we have given ample amounts of information necessary for this document to be complete. We realise the scope necessary has been extraordinary, and feel the growing structure will be completed in the not too distant future. We empower you to continue this journey and note that with extreme apprehension, you have taken on board all that is necessary for our future development. Be prepared for some straight talking, we have agreed to these time settings to enable a third party to represent us, allowing these proceedings to take place more swiftly, and we ask that you allow us to present ourselves to you! *I must have fallen asleep at this point and received healing, for I felt so much better afterwards. Although I still feel very sad about my cat's death, I have refrained from lapsing into deep sessions of grief!*

15th March 2005 – We deliver to you a fresh plan of action, and we need greater relish in acquiring these innovative techniques, which by far outweigh previous attempts to initialise this new growth! We are now feeling well endowed and equipped to make the necessary and frequent trips to our dimension. Believe us when we say that you have been challenged at every stage, and have been found wanting on several occasions! However, we feel you do justice now in every way possible, and we allow you entry at this point! We feel that you have drawn aside what is no longer required, and we hope and pray that you will continue to fight for what you believe in. Justice for all and a way forward where we can all obey the instincts of the heart, reprogramming a new awareness and helping others to initialise their true potential! Trust in us to help you achieve your heart's desire, for we know that you will set out to do your very best in every way possible. We feel at this time a growing reservation which you need to be aware of, for in the distance there are choices to be made and we need to adjust our thought patterns accordingly.

There will come a time where you will have to choose your pathway, and we know it may seem strange, at this time, to believe that we are like 'Men from Mars', when in truth we are a new generation of people that come from a star that was born to give us light! We have known for some time now that to instigate a new trust between us, we must be seen to be doing our best to achieve optimum results. We need you as always, to share your joys and sorrows with us, enabling us to help you forward in times of deep distress! Rely on us to take you into the light of true understanding, for we vow to you and yours that we shall make all the adjustments necessary, so that we may all share in this new and vibrant world that is waiting to unfold in all her glory! We cheer you on and wait for you to join us at our table!

There has been for some time now, free expression of thoughts and feelings surplus to requirements, but we notice that you have been reticent of late in your dealings with people. We also notice that you have become much more aware of those around you, and we venture to say in a relatively short time. We now need to make sure that we batten down the hatches, allowing a subduing of certain energies that may play havoc with your defence mechanisms! There is a need to challenge certain behaviour, but we must allow a simmering of temperment to settle down, before making any comments which could cause offence! Please be aware we are with you in all these instances, helping you to overcome these problems. There has been an isolated offence that has taken precedence over all others and we are extremely remorseful! There is a need to step back and acknowledge what is given before we can allow a coming together. We behave in a manner according to our station and recharge our batteries.

20th March 2005 – *I meditated, asking for help and healing, and was shown a gentleman from my youth who had been leader of the Boys' Brigade at our local Baptist Church. My parents sometimes invited him to join us for Sunday lunch, and I remembered him as a very quiet and shy person, only speaking when spoken to, which was very much like me as a young girl.* Dearly beloved, we are gathered here today to give vent to our feelings and emotions, which have given us cause for concern at this time. We advise you discreetly, to take careful consideration of what is before you. We know you have an open mind and would ask that you look to your instincts, in regard to certain episodes which are imminent, for we believe you will be able to instigate a revival of energy needed at this time. Please believe us when we say, that the outcome will be extremely rewarding. We note with anticipation that you have decided to reinvent yourself and move forward with greater acceleration, we deem it necessary now to achieve even higher status, and ask that you take our advice on all matters! We need to look at certain criteria that has given us cause for concern, and note that you also have taken heed of the needs of others. We allow this framework to be embellished before we are able to move on, declaring ourselves null and void until we can break through this mould of independence, which has given us greater deliverance!

Be prepared to initiate a new service that will need governing from afar. We reckon on unearthing new treasures and allow you to take this rest as a pre-requisite for all that needs to be accomplished! Be prepared . . . we underestimate certain conditions where there is a necessity to stand back in moments of stress or anger, and we will need to make allowances at this time for more than we give credit for. We deliver these words so that you may overcome obstacles and move on, with no encumbrances to hold you back. We have given of ourselves and need to recuperate, before allowing further revelations that are in store. We are able to forecast even more activity on the horizon and need this time of rest to allow a re-absorbsion and conditioning of energies. Be prepared for a channelling of energies that will manifest to a far greater degree, for we initiate a new awareness that will allow us greater coverage at this time!

We intervene now to bring you news! We succumb to temptation and bring you certain narrative that will bear witness to what is imperative at this stage of your journey. We have known for some time now of certain developments that need adjusting and we prepare ourselves to initialise these meetings, prompting you to remember there is work to be done to instigate a broader perspective. We feel the time is right to proceed, and take note that you too are determined to make this work. We feel a growing need to fulfil our destiny and mean to venture forth now, preparing ourselves for the final assault! We depend on you to bring this to the attention of those 'in the know' that need to be reminded of what is forthcoming! *I feel this refers to me reminding our group leader of the event where I will be channelling in front of an audience.* We venture forth, allowing ourselves to be nurtured, and maintain a growing awareness that shall reap the benefit of a lifetime's experience.

23rd March 2005 – *I felt my friends with me while doing some light weeding and sat to jot down the thoughts in my head.* We feel the need to intervene at this point and note that you have been, to a certain extent, framed for what could be misconstrued as a liability! We know in certain instances, there have been drawbacks that have allowed for subterfuge, but we know in all honesty there is new hope on the horizon. We believe with all our hearts and minds, there will be deliverance of all that is necessary to enable this event to take place very soon, and we shall superimpose our thoughts on yours to devise new methods of alleviating distress of any kind. We shall make this work, have no worries on that score, and we shall rise above all rancour or despair!

There is a need now to govern a certain situation that looms on the horizon, take note that we need to address this as soon as possible! We believe, in this instance, there is a need to take hold firmly and not let go, for we need that firmness of character to alleviate conditions that may transpire. We believe with a certain grace and eloquence all can be captured on tape, for we believe there is a growing need to expand our territory and encompass a wider audience with new levels of understanding. We see in the future, a far greater awareness among the population of Earth, and we take note that we shall be needed on a grander scale across the world. We need to be sure that you will continue on this pathway, and ask you to develop a trust and obey your instincts, for in this we can reach you at all times. Beware of instances of denial!

25th March 2005- *Today is Good Friday and I've felt very tearful with pains in my solar plexus and heart region! Before sitting to meditate, I cleansed the healing room and whole house by burning sage and called to the four directions:-*

Energies of the sage blend with my energies as I blend with yours. Cleanse and protect my whole being, this little sanctuary and all those who enter in. Spirit of the East, where the sun rises, gateway to the spirit and the element fire – enlighten me! Spirit of the South, where the sun is at its strongest, gateway to the feelings and emotions and the element water – empower me! Spirit of the West, where the sun sets, gateway to the physical and the element Earth – transform me! Spirit of the North, where the sun rests, gateway to the mind and the element air – inform me! Grandmother Earth, feminine forces behind all that is – nurture me! Grandfather sky, masculine forces behind all that is – empower me!

The Eastern form of worship has been battling for years against a multitude of riotous and abominable behaviour – we negate this behaviour! Responding to one another's rhythms, we are able to manifest greater tolerance for what is fast becoming a negative situation, and we believe we can enable a falling back into place of all that is needed to rectify these conditions! We believe we have a message of great importance and deem it a necessary precaution to align ourselves with you in this endeavour. We maintain a sense of decorum, taking account and developing what will probably come to be known as divine intervention! We allow these procedures to take place for a specific purpose, and we know that you will justify this course of action to be taken, for we mean to tread very carefully and firmly in the days and weeks ahead.

We know you will be amazed at the clarification of words coming through, and we ask in all sincerity that you will relax and go with the flow, enabling us to deliver what is necessary for the time ahead! We understand your feelings and emotions for we are one and the same, and we deliver to you in great profusion, allowing enough scope for the project ahead. Believe us when we say that we make no bones about it, telling it straight in all entirety! We deliberate on certain issues that hold you back and ask that you study what is needed to resolve issues ahead. Feel free now to make the right move, for we are with you in every way possible, and in the future we will argue over who had sway over the other!

We feel completely transparent and advise a drawing back until all has calmed down. We know you mean well but we advise caution on the horizon! We may need to adjust certain issues that arise and deem it necessary to betray a tear or two. In this instance we may even need to reproach you on certain occasions, for we feel there is a growing urgency that needs your attention! *I'm seeing a river where the water is thick with mud and not flowing properly.* It is advisable to take precautions at this time to prevent a slippage, and we are immediately drawn to other aspects that need monitoring. We know that you have chosen this pathway and we are extremely pleased with your decision, however, we have to be sure that you can develop mastery under scrutiny! We are impelled to grant you your wish to remain on Earth until the final moment; we prepare you for this adventure and note that you are most worthy of this office! There can be no turning back once we have made our mark, there can be only one leap of faith into the universe, and we intend to make this bridge of love that will light you home! We have a need to move on and deliberately direct your attention to other areas, where we are able to fulfil our dreams and ambitions. We uncover further adaptations and ask that you follow your instructions!

29th March 2005 – *I sat in meditation praying for guidance. Divine spirit – lift me up from the denseness of the physical plane to the realms of light.*

Please use me as a channel of your love. We need to deliver a clear message to you now, and we need this message to get through clearly and precisely! We mean to envelop you all with a cloak of safety, and at sunrise we will amplify conditions, making this new awareness more able to continue on its course of action. We deem it necessary to invite all those of you, who are able to manifest what is needed to help us in this endeavour! We know there has been a certain misappropriation of energies that will need to be rectified, but we consider, to all intents and purposes, that we have achieved more than enough for operations to continue. We need another amplifier and sub amplifier quite urgently, enabling us to produce even greater and more powerful ways of expressing ourselves. For we have ventured on this mission to portray a vision that is open to us all, and we know that you will allow us admission into your lives, so that we may forecast all that is necessary for you to overcome on your journey! We achieve the status required and in a matter of moments will speak to you 'live'! We are compelled to give you this information and ask you to stand back. We have need of you little one on the Earth plane, we mean to accept your offer and proceed with caution full steam ahead!

We venture on this pathway of light to enable the masses access to that port of call which will save them from despair! We have charged you with this service to bring light into the world, a light that can never be extinguished because it is supreme in its connection to those from a higher realm! We develop a greater trust in one another as we venture forth on this pathway of light. We have no way of knowing whether we shall maintain this growth, or whether we shall fall by the wayside, but we know we do have the strength and courage to venture forth on this rainbow of light. We will concentrate our efforts, enabling us step by step to gain greater access. We now believe that we have enough material to devote to a new chapter, and we shall call this, 'Everlasting Love'! There is a need to stand back and survey what has been given, so that we may then advise you on new measures to be taken in the foreseeable future.

30th March 2005 – We encroach once more on solid ground, fulfilling our vision for the future. We mean to accelerate conditions and convey our deepest respects to those of you who have made this possible. We also feel an increasing pressure being brought to bear on those closest to you, for there is a tremendous surge of unrest on the horizon and we deem it an unreliable source of intervention! We are able to rise above discontent, and surface to realise greater prospects that await us further afield. We note your attempts at getting across our words, our hopes and dreams for a better world, but we have forbidden any demonstration to take place until the time is right! Depend on us to get this timing right, for we have initiated a deep and lasting bond of friendship, and will regulate these meetings in such a way, as to comply with all that has been requested from a higher level. We shall allow certain exchanges to take place, and may we be so bold as to enquire, whether we shall be able to make a grand entrance? For we feel the need to bring to the people of Earth communications that will enable a conversation between the two sides of the coin! We need to make amendments and shall forecast a growing interest in all we do, we make this our most notable achievement of late, and govern the proceedings with an air of superiority that will surprise even the most sceptical amongst you! *I'm being shown two aristocratic gentlemen in wigs who are wearing stockings and white breeches; they are duelling with a cut and a thrust of the sword!* We have every reason to suspect that we shall be challenged at every corner, but make no bones about it; we shall conduct ourselves most admirably . . . a cut and thrust above the rest! Tempting you with our words, we govern the situation from afar, regulating each and every phrase until we refine our communication!

Chapter 3
Everlasting Love

31st March 2005 – We would like to commemorate this book, to all those of you who have unwittingly, been our constant companions over most of your lifetimes! We initialise this book to beam ahead of you, and forecast what we can achieve on a grander scale if we all pull together. There is a far greater need now to monitor situations and we feel that the time is right to correspond with those in the know. We have allowed a certain time framework to manifest in greater detail, and we mean now to forge ahead, developing and growing together with greater ease. There will become a measure of uncertainty as we progress, but believe us when we say, that you have been able to comply with all that has been asked of you, for which we are most grateful! However, there is a need to look back and calculate what has been given, so that we may now focus on what is needed to finish our book. We have come a long way, and looking back we feel you have done us proud! There have been instances when we failed to realise our progress, and there have been many occasions since that we have yielded to temptation, giving us cause for concern. Tempestuous behaviour has held you back on several occasions in the past, and we regret most of these being your downfall! We have trembled and foreseen all we would have kept you from to save you from harm, but we know as do you, these hurts serve to reinforce your desire to rise above adversity, becoming a much stronger person!

This debate on thoughts and feelings comes to the surface so that we may re-visit what has been uppermost in our minds, for we have noticed that you have been unjustly accused! There has been a harbouring of doubts as to your ability to access data given, and we need at this time to reinforce that you have behaved in an exemplary way! We vouch for the fact that you have helped us accumulate data, which is needed for our purpose of educating a much wider audience than was previously expected! We feel that we can now achieve on a grand scale and are most impressed with your vigilance; we shall now be able to attune ourselves more easily. As surely as night follows day, we will be able to manipulate a whole catalogue of expressions to help us in our vision for a better future for mankind. We need to reinforce unequivocally, our utmost pleasure in being able to come amongst you and broadcast our messages. For we are convinced that this is the way to the hearts and minds of the population, where we are able to enlighten you all! We superimpose our thoughts on yours now to govern a new way of thinking, and we are astounded at the way in which you have coped so admirably with what we have given you of late!

Please allow us to come close at any given moment, so that we may analyse your thoughts and actions, for we are most pleased with all that has transpired. Fantasy has played a big part in allowing us access to your mind, and we feel that you have given us a most noble role to play. We have given you a plan of action that we know you can ably assist us with, and we know too that you have become, to all intents and purposes, a prime subject in all of this! We feel that you have developed your role astutely, allowing for discrepancies which occur from time to time. We know the feedback has been poor at times, but we know too that you have adjusted your thought patterns to align with ours more frequently, allowing our transmissions to succeed more succinctly. We superimpose our thoughts once more to allow for greater discretion in all that you do, for we now need that chamber of thought to be more closely guarded in the days and weeks ahead! There is a need for closer scrutiny too in areas that are needed to be kept quiet, for we need constant supervision to allow a regrouping of energies needed for this mission. Please allow a few days before we are able to initialise a new and daring project that will be found to be, the most wonderful concept yet, ever to be achieved!

2nd April 2005 – *During the night I awoke to see the face of the Pope, John Paul II. Today a news bulletin told us the Pope had died after a long illness – I prayed for his safe journey and for the healing of his flock. I recalled a vision I'd been given on the 8th December last year while waiting in the car to pick up a relative from hospital. I had sat meditating, sending out absent healing, and through a cloud of purple I was shown a beautiful, golden dome and was given the name St. Peter. It was only while watching the news today that it dawned on me, the Vatican is in St. Peter's Square and that is what I was being shown! The Pope's funeral took place a few days later on the 8th of April.* We need to express ourselves and note that with much acclaim, we have ventured on this journey. In the near future we shall guard against all manner of disease which spreads its tenacious roots unchecked, spreading forth its venom! We have penetrated the Earth with great resilience, achieving a great deal in mammoth proportions, and what we have to offer to the population of Earth is more than can be explained in just a sentence or two! We believe, without a trace of doubt, of a brighter future for all mankind and we manifest our wishes for a far, greater and more perceptive race, standing up for what we believe in and initiating a response from those with deaf ears! We trust you are able to stay with us, and appreciate all that needs to be done to allow this transmission to take place. We realise too the amount of pressure this will put on you, but we alleviate all that is necessary to make the proceedings go more smoothly!

There is a strong undercurrent of a much, wider portrayal of who we are and where we come from! We will allow you to manifest what is needed to bring through your offspring, for we are as children who have never known their parents, and we come now to resurrect you! We ask you now little one, to envelop yourself in the light of true understanding. We initiate this development and ask also that you remain in a state of complete and utter perplexity, for we cannot allow a transaction to be completed yet! We need to know, in greater detail, how we may register and apply for the ticket for our journey. There is no need to pre-pay for we have the necessary funds available at this time! Devote yourself to other matters and develop mastery over what intends to be, a most prolific encounter to date. We superimpose our thoughts on yours and ask that you register our appeal, we are most proud of your achievements to date and vow that you have become our greatest asset yet! We maintain a sense of decorum and push you forward in the right direction; we are pleased with how you present yourself to others, asking only that you are prepared for what will prove to be a very exciting time for us all!

We deliberately ask that you satisfy your need to know how we came to your planet, for we have invented an ingenious way of reaching you! Please note that we take great exception to being called 'aliens'! We may come from a different planet . . . but very much desire to be called human beings, for we are a race of people that have evolved over many years, developing greater bonds with Earth and allowing ourselves to be used, in such a way that will increase our popularity! We have endowed ourselves with the right to be called a member of your planetary union, for we have gone out of our way to call you brethren, and we know that we come at the exact time to save Earth from chaos and despair! Remember that we have come from a much broader spectrum, and we are right on course in our ways of dealing with the human race. Allowing for developments to take place has given us greater advantage and we believe that we are able to achieve, in far greater measure, a more natural approach, allowing our true identities to take shape and form. For we have taken on board a new field of vision, which has allowed for the evolution of mankind. Fretting about her destruction became as natural to us as losing a member of our own family, for we are related in the truest sense of the word!

We reveal to you now there has been an even greater, more profound encounter, and we materialise this new growth, becoming stronger and wiser with each passing day. Hold on fast to this new vision, for we need you to bend and sway with what is given, allowing for others who manipulate their way into your affections, in such a way that will cause concern! We eliminate certain procedures to try a different approach, and adjusting our thought patterns to correspond with yours, we train you to listen more closely to what is being said! We can allow for a certain element of mistrust, but please believe us when we say, that we have elicited the current information from the highest divine source, there can be no mistake in what we hand out to you now!

Be placid in your approach to others, allowing for no misconception of any kind, we believe there has been a major breakthrough and we deem it necessary now to alter and develop new tactics! Trust in us to be there with you right up to the end, for we have made a vow that can never be relinquished, and have given you the respect you deserve, trusting in each other implicitly! We have obeyed our heart in all matters and obey the necessary strategies that are in place; be prepared to stand alone at times to deliver these messages, for we note that, with great clarity, you have been able to forecast what we have given of your own accord! We realise the need to obey our gut instincts and we deliver to you now, in no uncertain terms, the most powerful tool of love and respect from those about you! Do not misplace the love and affection we send you, for we would be most put out! Please allow us to come closer and envelop you now in our love.

3rd April 2005 – *I snatched just a few moments to tune in, but had to break off due to family commitments.* We need to allay your fears concerning a project which is nearing fruition, for we believe that we have a vested interest that will take us onto new structures. We are able to extend you the courtesy, of stepping out into a new forum of awareness that has been granted from above! We hear you say in exclamation, 'but who will guide me', and we say unto you, that all is being prepared for that final breakthrough! We anticipate a new and vibrant pathway opening up before you, and venture to say that this has been our finest mission yet. We calculate the time of entry as being closer than expected, and we know that we shall allow for this in our recalibration of events on the horizon.

5th April 2005 – *Tonight I spoke to the leader of our spiritual group, and told him of my frustrations at not feeling prepared for trance mediumship. I told him of a dream I'd had, where I was shown a river that was silted up with mud and not flowing properly. He told me that I would be prepared, and it would only happen when the time was completely right, which of course I should know! The river that was now full of mud would have to flow crystal clear before an exchange of energies could take place. During our group we had talked about the power of thought, and this was echoed in the words I received when I got home.* We have great plans for you my dear, we analyse your thoughts and feelings, and want you to know that we are most concerned! We elaborate, reinforcing our intentions to alleviate any difficulties that may take place, for we have information that will enable us to devise a new plan of action. We have disregarded what was on offer, and allowed ourselves recourse which will allow, to some extent, greater understanding! We vouchsafe to all those concerned of a far more salubrious undertaking, for we mean to follow a thought of action and allow it to take its own natural course. Penetrating the mists of time we reveal ourselves to you, asking that you take on board what we have to offer! We have often found our times spent with you to be most rewarding, relentlessly pursuing our dreams and aspirations for a brighter future for all. We maintain our vision, and adjusting thought patterns to a greater degree we make plans for the future. We denote a sense of freedom with mischievousness and excitement, entangled together to form a new bond of friendship, and we believe that we may be able to add a touch of joy, which will top off the proceedings nicely! We incorporate in all of this, a positive note that will reinforce all we have taught you in the past, and may we say that we have taken on board a great deal in the past few months, now being well equipped to clarify a few points that need adjusting!

We have been able to coincide with one another in such a way that has sparked a certain chemistry! We make allowances for certain agenda items, and ask that you come prepared over the coming weeks to transcribe further accounts of our progress. We shall reinstate further boundaries, knowing in all earnest that we have reached the summit of our enquiries, and please accept what we say, in the manner in which it is given! We have no fears for your safety, but would remind you that there is an element of risk in all adventures such as these! We will instigate an even tighter security measure, to make sure that all is right on the night. We shall, however, insist on a finer tuning before we have lift off. We come to the peak of our career and note with great satisfaction, that you have taken like a duck to water, forging ahead now in what we can forecast as a most fortuitous time for all concerned. For we have felt the wrath of a nation, holding back the floodgates on a variety of ill conceived thoughts and emotions! We have trained you to conquer and govern your thoughts, as the consequences of them running amok will not only cause harm, but infiltrate into areas that are not yet ready to register or receive statements of this kind, at this time! We will eventually see a turning back to the 'old ways'! This will be a most rewarding time for all, freeing the minds of mice and men, allowing for greater and more powerful demonstrations of love, and timorously rejecting any form of connection with any other energy source! We have powerful connections which align us to what is necessary for this coordination, and take flight on wings of love!

7th April 2005- We shall need to appropriate all funds, ensuring that there is enough to cover our needs and expenses. We shall allow a brand of eloquence necessary to forge an even greater trust amongst us, for there is a greater need to demonstrate the availability of our natural talents. We rule out an ambiguous approach for this would only reinforce desires of a lower nature, and we feel in this instance, would cause a deliberate malfunction! There is a refining of energies taking place that will reconcile what is needed, and we feel that to all intents and purposes, this manner of enlightenment will hasten and speed up a reclamation of all that has governed us in the past. We need to know at this point, of a growing factor that has given cause for concern, we may spread the news to certain people for whom we have the greatest respect, but you must realise that in all of this we must maintain an area of discretion, and we have set in place measures whereby we can achieve anonymity!

We shall describe in due course, what we can expect to achieve in the next few years, and we ask you now to alter your appearance, in such a way that we will be able to manifest our own image. There is no need to be alarmed, for you will be forewarned of this taking place, all that needs to be done is to wait impassively, allowing us to come through in the most gentle fashion! We penetrate your existence with our own, and know that you will understand that we have the greatest reverence and respect in entering your atmosphere! We shall take great care of you and know that you will convey our sincerest apologies to those who are awaiting our return. We have mentioned before that we have chastised you in the past for referring to our words, when we would have preferred your silence; we must accept that this is for your own good and we deem it irresponsible of you to take no heed! Please allow us to bring this to your attention, for we feel this will aid us in our endeavours, and we believe that in the future we shall achieve great works. Take care my little one; we know how you ache to do the right thing! We vow to take you down an avenue of thought that leads you towards the light of true understanding, and we venture forth now, cementing our friendship and allowing further possibilities on the horizon. Maintain your strength and determination for we vow to you now, that we shall not leave you high and dry, nor will we ever leave you to fend for yourself! We have ventured on this mission together and devote ourselves to your wellbeing!

15th April 2005 – Allow us at this time to rectify conditions, for there is a greater need to move forward in a pattern of understanding that will fulfil our mission on Earth. Please take note that we rescind what is no longer needed or required. *At this point I was shown the Conservative MP Michael Howard who was at this time, leader of the opposition party.* We have maintained growth in many areas, but realise at this time that we have fetched a most alarming mantle of debt! Strain in relationships have taken place and put the nation in such a flux, that we have expected an even greater surge of apoplexy! We know this means that we have even greater challenges ahead, and we feel sure there will be an even greater demonstration that will take us back to the dark ages!

I'm now being shown the faces of the Pope and Prince Rainier who both died recently. We feel an immense outpouring of grief at this time, for those souls who have come to the end of their lives, and we believe they have done justice to themselves and to those they have supported! Whole nations have sunk in despair at losing these great figures, who have dominated legions upon legions! We have seen for ourselves the impact this has had on a nation, suffering at first hand the loss of a saint! We have experienced this soul's growth, and believe as do you, that he perpetuated a great amount of love and respect among his people. We deem it necessary now to infringe on this belief pattern, declaring to the world of an even greater trust and benevolence that may be indulged! For we of supreme intellect, ask that you obey your instincts and kneel before the one true God, who has never forsaken you or hurt you in the past!

It is regrettable that there are those who feel, to the extreme, that God is the perpetrator of all hostile acts on Earth! When in reality it is the human race that are to blame for atrocities committed in the world, and they are many, forsaking His image of love to defile his brother in the name of God! There has never been a worse time on Earth for the destruction and hate that have epitomised a nation entrenched in misery! We have foreseen events on the horizon and note with great pity and contempt, of further atrocities committed, and we vouch to condemn those who have been a party to this massacre! Please believe us when we say, that we have infiltrated those who are to blame and they shall be led to justice! We devise a plan of action to be maintained, whereby you may lay down by hand an even greater demonstration of our love, and desire to help the people of Earth!

Be prepared for a time of great strength and joy, for we will maintain the necessary contact that will allow for greater and more refined discourses. Please arm yourself with the sword of light, truth and justice, for we need you to march forward now with great strength and integrity. We shall not allow a scorching of your heart, we aim for that which no man can divide us, the flame of love and true understanding, marching together to forge a new alliance! We salute you and bid you farewell, take care and note our intention to take you with us all the way, for we are one and the same! Develop even greater expertise and we will prepare you for the next step forwards, we are never far from your side and would like to thank you for your assistance this evening! *The reference to a scorching of the heart, gives me reason to suspect that in some past life I may have suffered such a fate!*

17th April 2005 – Of late there has been a constant need to check and maintain our position, and we still need that sense of decorum which shall stand us in good stead. We believe there has been a miscarriage of justice and ask if we may monitor the situation from afar! Lean on us in times of trouble for we are able to manipulate certain structures that have held us back. We sense a growing concern on the horizon over what has been an annoyance, and there have been many instances of denial on your part that have been deemed inappropriate to our cause! There have been elements of fear and mistrust which have led us astray, but we regard this whole scenario as being one of great devotion and joy to all.

We have developed a broader and more extraordinary talent for expressing ourselves, and we welcome you to our world, delivering to you now the most treasured possession of all! *I'm being shown a ballerina preparing to dance, practicing up on her points.* This is your time now, we enfold you in our love for we feel you have done us proud, and we hold you in the highest esteem! We ask that you now watch what we give to you on a plate, for there is much to consider before making up your mind on how to proceed. We feel you have given of your best and will endeavour to help you make the right choices. This has been a most rewarding journey and expressing ourselves with sorrow for what has gone before, we now claim our rightful position among the stars! We embark on a mission of the highest calibre and ask you to bear with us, as we assemble our new structure. We have been governed by fear regarding a certain process, but we have maintained a certain sensibility, and this is our way forward on that beam of light, manifesting greater accord with those with whom we walk. Depend on us to help you dispel all negativity, venture forth on this pathway and we can accept the final challenge!

18th April 2005 – *I closed my eyes in meditation and heard the song – 'Send in the Clowns'. I've been experiencing problems this weekend in focusing, and have not been able to bring through words with any clarity! My family have been laughing at my antics which are probably why they are bringing in the clown theme.* Please allow us to come closer to complete this project on Earth. There is a great need now for a recital, and we declare a growing rush of energy which will allow us greater freedom of movement. We deliver this request, enabling a more constructive thought pattern to materialise what is needed, and we rely on you now for the necessary feedback to move and grow. We delve deeper into 'Pandora's Box' and announce that we have found a most exhilarating form of connection, which will enable an even greater bond between us! Take care to evaporate misgivings for all is set for a most enjoyable time for all. We take great exception to being ridiculed, and we depend on you to make the necessary adjustments to keep the record straight. We need straight talking and envelop you now in a sequential understanding, augmented by your inherent quality of tolerance!

We reveal to you now that we have been most disturbed by events taking place even as we speak, there have been many hurdles to overcome, and we feel a growing resentment attaching itself to an already delicate situation! There has been in the past, certain areas that needed adjusting, and we advised a standing back to allow the necessary seclusion. We relate in this instance, to an event that took place a year ago which was relayed back to you in great detail. We forecast then a new understanding, and with respect we have achieved this in many ways. There is a need now to analyse conditions to maintain this growth. We expect you to take this up quickly and to the point of a new understanding that will gather momentum! *I believe they are referring here to an unnecessary draining of energies, and the need for me to stand back.*

We devise a new strategy and approach you in a new light. Please prepare yourself in your gatherings, for we feel we can achieve much more in the short term. We achieve a greater rate of success in all we do and know you will join with us, in thanking those who have gone out of their way to helping us achieve this high calibre of communication! We have now developed an even broader acceptance of what is needed to achieve our main aims and objectives.

19th April 2005 – *I was woken in the night with words echoing in my head. Before going to bed I had watched a programme called 'Casanova' with Peter O'Toole playing the main character. Towards the end he was portrayed as an old man, toying with the serving girl and telling her the story of all his conquests and those he had betrayed. At the end he died, waiting for his one true love to find him . . . and she came to him at last, leading him back to the spirit realms. I feel the time period of this drama may have sparked a memory within me!* We believe there is further need of acceptance on your part. We ascertain that certain behaviour patterns have led us astray, and we note with some derision, that you have forsaken your place in our heart to become a member of a more aloof society! Some say this was because we effectively left you high and dry, and without a shilling to your name! This was a temporary measure of course, for we decided to settle our debt once and for all. We remain now on good terms, but come to deliver a message that will root out what is required of you for this mission. This is a good cause and we know without a shadow of doubt that you are under no misapprehension as to what we have in store for you!

We are delighted to have settled our differences and would inform you, that now the 'material' has slipped away, we can offer you our condolences for past deeds, transferring our affections to more appropriate transactions! There is a far greater need here, and we allow you the benefit of the doubt, to proceed in all honesty towards our goal. Please be advised – we ask you now, not to relate your messages for the time being, there is enough to contend with before our final instructions! The backlog of messages will be used in due course, but please allow us to come through in person to deliver the bulk of our messages! We know this comes as no surprise to you, and we are most amused that you have sanctioned our visit with an air of grace and favour, from one who has come under our scrutiny for quite some time! Be prepared now to take on board this most exclusive mission. Last but not least – we inform you of certain measures that we have instigated for this finale, for we bring to your attention now, with greater clarity, information that is to be brought through for your delectation! We inspire you to bring forth the nation out of darkness and into the light – which may take some time – but we rendezvous in separate connections to allow for a finer tuning that will appreciate our needs. Blend with us to allow this channelling and we will be making history! Venture forth little one, obey the dictates of your heart and we will reign supreme!

23rd April 2005 – We welcome you Sunbeam, and ask that you pay particular attention to what is given, for there is a need in the distance to monitor your progress more thoroughly. Don't be misled by others . . . their intentions may be honourable, but it is up to you how you use your own time! We venture to say that we are most pleased and excited, for the prospects ahead are good and we have need of you now in a more constructive way. We appeal to your generous nature, asking that you stay focused and maintain credibility, for we need greater stability and determination to retrieve data as we impel you forward and on to greater vision! We are assembled and ready to fight the good fight, with no further delays to impede us! Depend on us to help in all initiatives for we are the unseen who shadow your every move. We have allowed at this time for a reconditioning of energies, which will enable a more illustrious and noble statement to be made. We relinquish at this time an entire scenario of thoughts, allowing an exchange of ideas as we present to you a paradox that will oversee a new field of vision! We advise a reconstruction of sentences that allow for misconceptions, for it is imperative now to develop mastery that will enable us to paraphrase, for we are preparing for a new era which will bring peace and harmony to all!

Please allow us to bring forward more news, we allow a more informal approach to precede our entry; this will allow us to connect and regain our composure. *I feel my friends are referring to a future channelling in front of an audience.* We have descended for a purpose – to bring peace and prosperity to the world of mankind! This has been our greatest vision yet, and we know in all sincerity that we have forged a new alliance. This has brought about a great and daring project, venturing into unknown territory and allowing a blending of energies with many on your Earth plane! This was necessary to allow for a consecration of human matter, detoxifying and initiating a healthier outlook, registering what was needed to reinforce our principles and ideas. We are ready now to move forwards and ask you to forgive our delays, for we now have greater back up than before. Growing and responding to one another's rhythms, we allow this exchange of energies to take place, asking that you come to us in simple attire. We have reached a certain understanding, and know you will bear with us in allowing this frequency to change hands.

We have come to tell you of what may transpire over the next few years and ask you to develop your awareness, allowing us to come nearer. Surrender to us and we will take you on wings of love to a world of beauty unparalleled! We fulfil our mission and hope and pray that you will allow us the privilege of taking you to these heights on more than one occasion, delivering our messages to all and sundry. We have a purpose of the highest calibre known to man, and wish to interpret a new vision, yet to be expressed in glowing efficacy. We exchange matter and proceed with all caution to bring you aboard. Welcome to our world in the realms of light, where we have much in store for your further involvement of the highest order! Take care to state your field of vision, for greater directives have been given, enabling us to make our choices on the horizon. Sia Nara!

25th April 2005 – *I awoke in the early hours and grabbed my notepad as a barrage of thoughts filled my mind.* We advise a turning back as a matter of urgency, or be prepared to meet thy doom, entangled forever in a web of deceit and lies! We forbid a mustering of services which align us to a fate worse than death, and an amalgamation of all necessary criteria will consecrate this most difficult period of time on Earth! We make our mark on the world and insist on a finer tuning, allowing our frequencies to adapt and grow at the rate necessary for this excursion. Believe us when we say, that we have never encountered a more prolific sense of awe and wonder, at such a chilling episode in Earth's history! Please be aware at this time of what is forecast, for we have need of you now more than ever my friend. We detect a note of disgust and feel a growing reverence is needed to maintain discretion! We apply for and succeed in our initiative, analysing what has been a necessary interlude, and we feel that you have gone overboard in your endeavours to explore in even greater depth what is given.

We now need to uncover greater expertise in other areas, for there are further impending revelations in store which will need extreme and constant supervision! We have noted that although you have been exemplary in your approach to the subject, there has been to some extent, a misappropriation of energies that need channelling in a more focused way, helping us adapt to changes in frequency. This is a necessary development that will spare us from being overlooked! We bend to salute you and declare that you have been a most worthy associate in reclaiming our heritage! There have been many instances in the past where we have been able to detect growing disturbances, and we feel the time is now right to make minor changes, allowing us entry into that frequency we deem necessary for our complete advantage. It has taken many years for us to achieve this growth and we know as well as you, that it was all necessary to achieve our heart's desire. Making this planet a world of peace and harmony, and leaving behind despair and destruction, which has led to the vast majority of your world being led into the swamps of iniquity!

Be prepared to meet thy maker, and be restored in all your heart and soul for what will be a most joyous event in the history of mankind! A swamping of energies will harness what is needed at this time and we will prevail, encompassing you all with our love, joy and warmth. For we have come at exactly the right moment, to take on board a whole nation in one swoop of the hand, allowing all to come aboard who are in harmony with our state of existence! There have been necessary inclusions that cure a multitude of differences of opinion, freeing you all from mundane worries that have no part in our frequency! Exchanging matter for a more salubrious upkeep will allow for a greater understanding in matters related to our independence of character. We are not able to supply further constructive thought patterns at this time, but allow this method of working to enable us to keep some sort of chart as to our progress! We need this interlude to allow for a finer tuning of energies and to accept the part we must play, allowing us to proceed forward and take control of proceedings.

We usher in a new awareness of what will become a most fortuitous time for all, and we need to know that you are with us at every stage of the journey before we proceed any further! Please take on board our condolences for any hurt we may have caused to any of you! On the whole we feel this interaction has been one of immense joy for us all, with a co-operative of hearts and minds that have led us in a visionary, and most remarkable achievement to date. We allow at this time a more selective approach to what has been a necessary form of communication. We understand the pressure this has brought to bear on you, and devise new means of reaching you without any further involvement from above. This will beam a new and vibrant pathway to heaven and the stars, entering into the unknown! Take our hand and we'll lead you there . . . we'll find a new way of living! *They are now giving me words to the song, 'There's a place for us, somewhere a place for us'*! We take our leave of you fair maiden and wish you good night and good day! Be of good cheer for we are all here with you as you walk into that new sunrise!

27th April 2005 – *While working on my computer I had a news flash from my friends.* We have prepared for you a new speech, which we wish you to share with your contemporaries! We have taken note, to a large degree, of necessary protocol, asking that you intercede on our behalf to obtain the necessary structure for this conversation to take place! We are pleased with how events have unfolded and note with great interest, that you have displayed a sense of purpose in these matters. We are now able to conduct a most salubrious undertaking that will leave you in no doubt as to our intelligence, for we are able to condense matter, allowing for another form of energy to operate! We initiate new boundaries to allow this blending of energies to take place, instigating a finer network of emotions to guide us through this delicate framework, and incorporating a transcendental approach that will reciprocate a new level of understanding! We believe in breaking down the barriers that hold us back from all conventional studies, and we now impose on you a more salubrious form of communication, enunciating the words in such a way, that you will have no doubt as to our authenticity!

14th May 2005 – We govern from afar and ask you to take control of a certain situation that looms on the horizon. We are forever in your debt and would like to say, that we have been most amply rewarded with your gentleness of spirit! We apply for and receive communications of a most generous order, inviting you to our discourse and initiating boundaries that have been accepted by both sides. We allow for divine intervention and ask that you obey the guidelines set down for this most noble mission. We initialise new methods and associate ourselves with old measures – by using colour therapy! For in this instance we are able to make an application that can replicate in colour, exactly what we have chosen as our advantage! This notion is one of extreme advantage to our cause, and we shall be extremely grateful if you would allow us to make this application on your behalf!

We notify those who have agreed to help us in this endeavour, and take on board a new and vibrant legacy, initiating this superstructure that will monitor all life forms on your planet. We develop new measures for this exercise and note, most amicably, that you have obeyed our directives down to the last letter! We are not forgetting there are certain measures that will need our special attention but on the whole, we have found the overall approach more than adequate in this resurrection of new thoughts and ideas for a brighter future for all. Please amplify our thoughts and take on board what is given, for we greet you with arms wide open, ready to receive you! We have prepared an essay which will need to be recorded and this, we hope, will give us greater recall. We obey our instincts and attend to details, please be advised that all is being prepared and we shall emerge resplendent in glowing colours for all to see! We have taken on board a most trustworthy mission and hope and pray that you will accept our invitation to the dance! *In the early nineties when I first started receiving communication from my friends, they spoke of an invitation to the ball. They told me back then, that although I didn't know what the invitation would entail, it would be with them by my side on wings of love! I am so touched that they remembered those words, and I'm so excited at the prospect of at last receiving my invitation!*

19th May 2005 – *For the last few days I've been concerned about my forthcoming channelling session. I'm worried I'll struggle to relax enough for my friends to come through, knowing an audience will be watching me.* We have instigated finer measures of attunement, allowing for greater delivery. Please be reminded of the necessity to plan for action, rather than hesitate in this manner! We feel a growing acceptance is forecast, and we instigate new measures to allow the incoming flux of energy. Be prepared for greater subliminal messages – we feel these are necessary at this time to develop you at a greater rate! We detect an air of anxiety that will need to be overcome for your further development to take place. We need now a conscious effort on focusing to maintain peace and harmony! *I felt my friends draw near, and didn't realise how uncomfortable blending with the denseness of a physical body could be.*

We shall rebuild on what was once lost, we obey the laws of gravity to be with you here tonight, and we feel the encumbrance of human flesh and bones, teeth and hair! We commence our studies with a new and powerful vision, and having made the necessary contact, we vow to undertake all that is necessary to complete this prophecy! We develop a keenness of vision and allowing for distortion, we develop a new and powerful understanding of what is before us, allowing it to register in the brain before contact with the outside world; understanding being the operative word for initialising a new and powerful vision for the future of mankind. We raise you up to heights of free expression, announcing in no uncertain terms – our complete success! We have undertaken and carried out all that has been asked of us, and we are most impressed with your endeavours! We now need greater access, enabling us to take on board a broader vision for the future, and sharing in your success, we admit it has been a most agreeable experience to date.

We venture forth into new territory, expressing our powerful emotions of love. There is a far greater need to monitor conditions, and we ask you to take great care in the days and weeks ahead! We endeavour to explain what is needed, expelling our ideas and propelling you forward onto greater distinction, and we vow to one and all a rendering of services, following in the footsteps of those we hold dear to us! We remember a time in the woods, blending with the energies of the tree and swaying together in harmony . . . that is what we are aiming for, that true essence of oneness, blending with ease as we experience each others rhythms. We shall come together and the two will become one! *Again I was touched by their memory of when I used to walk in the woods during my lunch break. Standing with my back to a favourite tree, I would tune in, becoming one with the tree, swaying in the wind and feeling the sap rising. It was the most exhilarating experience, and recharged my batteries for returning to work!*

25th May 2005 – We take advantage of this time together and superimpose our thoughts on yours. Please be prepared for what lies ahead, we need greater resolve in putting together this most vibrant and joyous occasion. We fulfil a promise made centuries ago and vow to one and all, that we shall by no means fall down, in any way shape or form – all will go as planned and we forsake any doubts or fears of what is to come! Be prepared to accept our hand in friendship, and let us lead you to those pastures of green and plenty. We have prepared a new course of action and develop you even further; be prepared to take on this mammoth challenge for we know you will rise to the occasion. Tremulously we take your hand, obeying the instincts of our heart, and rapturously we take you on wings of love to where the river and mountain streams flow. We depend on you to allow this to happen and we know in all sincerity, that we shall overcome all obstacles that hold us back. We deliver a sense of purpose allowing these proceedings to take place, and we shall win by all accounts, a glowing and rapturous applause!

We have discovered a new and daring intrigue that will allow us to manifest in even greater detail, and we know you would want us to tell you, that we have been greatly inspired by your most trustworthy actions of late. We have foreseen these events and wish you to know that with great clarity, we have breached the impossible dream – we have made history and shall announce in no uncertain terms, that we are here to stay! We have come to save a nation entrenched in war and we believe with your help, and those like you, we shall overcome what is fast becoming a most obnoxious society! We believe these new measures will obliterate and destroy the old ways of power and greed, making way for a new and vibrant way of living, which gives succour to the weak, sustaining life in all shapes and forms, and promoting greater advantage for all who will listen to our words! We believe we have maintained a greater indulgence in these matters, and prepare you for even greater surprises on the horizon. We note that you are champing at the bit, despite your apprehension; we forgive you your trespasses and take you forward now into the unknown!

30th May 2005 – *I settled down to send out absent healing, and as it has been a few days since my last communication, I asked if there were any words for me to transcribe!* We reactivate this connection and ask that you bear with us in our endeavours. Firstly, we must take note that this is an intermediary transaction, which cannot be completed until further notice; there is also a greater need at this time to maintain this energy source! We feel a growing desire to overcome obstacles that hold us back from completing our mission, and this will counteract the imbalance, rectifying equilibrium and enabling us to take on board more than enough for the journey ahead. Isolation has been a necessary setback at this stage, and we would prefer a more definitive approach to withstand the barrage of thought forms that are penetrating your aura! We delve deeper into the psyche to ascertain what is needed, on this occasion, to correct a malfunction that has occurred!

1ˢᵗ June 2005 – *As I sat to meditate, I was immediately shown a care worker of Asian origin.* We relive our experiences through you and we relish our times spent with you, asking for assistance to help our cousins who are in great need! We have developed a powerful recognition of what is needed for this assistance, and we see in the future an overwhelming desire to help all nationalities, who are in peril of their lives! We accept this painful recognition of hardship, and ask that you cement your relationships with love. There is a need of further involvement in an industry that has taken its toll, and we see a time of pain and hardship for those who take the strain! There is no going back, and we regulate and commission a wide range of activities, ensuring there is more than enough to counteract this painful experience. We feel you do justice to our words and would mention, that we have taken our time to acquire a more peaceful condition.

12ᵗʰ June 2005 – *I asked how we were progressing with the planned channelling!* We welcome you 'My Sunbeam', we are so proud of your achievements and awareness to date, that we have prepared a place for you to join us this night! We accept all terms and conditions and intervene to bring you news of great joy. We have been approached by those from a higher realm, and ask that you do justice to our words by becoming a fraction of yourself, in the minutest possible term, allowing us entrance to your condition! We are aware of the necessity for you to stand back – an indulgence with which we are most amply rewarded. Please allow us within this framework to penetrate your existence with our own. We are on course have no fear, we maintain the necessary contact and will issue instructions in the near future, regarding delivery of speeches. We shall allow this channelling to take place with reasonable delay, forecasting a more natural approach to proceedings – be prepared to stand your ground and allow for a general surrendering of senses.

We develop a strategy, whereby we allow the necessary by-products to materialise in great strength, ensuring this will happen on a grand scale around the globe! We have known for some time now that we have been sent to inspire a nation of drunkards and hoodlums into a more submissive and even tempered state of existence! We have allowed specific energies to recharge neural circuits, expressing more powerfully what is intended than words could ever convey! These powerful emissions will change the whole configuration overnight, and we mean to explain our mission here on Earth to rectify conditions taking place at this very time! We foresee a time of greater control, and race to the front lines where help is needed to remain in a calm condition!

14th June 2005 – *During meditation at our weekly spiritual group, I felt my friends draw near. They asked if they could say a few words as they felt something was not right within the group this evening. It took me by surprise and I didn't speak up for fear of disturbing everyone! After chatting with our group leader it was decided to allow them to speak the following week, during summer solstice. Later in the evening before settling down for the night, I tuned in for further information.* There is a sense of foreboding which causes concern among the unseen echelons! We vow to prepare you for the sacrifice of your time and energy, for there has been a tremendous surge of energy relating to our demonstrations of love. We empower you now to take leave of all that has held you back as we now have the resources to complete this circuit of love. We maintain a steady stream of narrative allowing for no misconceptions, proceeding with clarity and grace to overturn what has become an unjust society in every way possible! Please allow us to take this new approach to the extreme, for we have validated this coming together to ensure a smoother delivery. We incorporate a growing awareness with a greater trust that will stand us in good stead over the coming weeks.

'Stand and deliver'! We impose upon you now a curfew which needs to be in operation! *I feel this means foregoing a day trip planned for summer solstice, which would involve a tiring journey the day of my channelling.* We extend your boundaries to allow a functioning of services, relating a necessary stream of narrative that will be very productive. Please feel free to collect as many individuals as necessary to help us achieve the right atmosphere. We have need of services such as these and will expand on this in due course. We maintain surveillance, insisting on a finer tuning of energies – there is a constant need to check and supervise conditions for we may be caught out unawares! Please be prepared for this final assault and we will not let you down or encumbrance you in any way shape or form, in fact we will be only too pleased to help you on your journey! There is constant need to be on guard and we will amplify conditions as and when needed. Scrutinise all areas and help us to help you by obeying our words right down to the last letter!

We remember as children we laughed with never a fear, please hold onto that light of love, never let it go out for it shines forth from your heart with greatest love and beauty of spirit. We tend to one another blissfully, and we ask that you will remain on the scene to savour this connection. We feel a growing wanderlust will take you far onto the horizon, and we feel impelled to draw your attention to an area of disbelief! Tend to the little one (*my daughter*) and allay her fears, she is translucent in your eyes and you will have no trouble in examining her motives. Be on your guard and try not to interfere, be relaxed in her company and we will show you a woman who has grown and stretched in all aspects. We know she has a long way to go, but is easily recognised by her strong ideals and temperament, becoming an agent of God in every way! We know there are some adjustments to take place and would ask that you correspond closely with one another to prevent a slippage occurring!

We divide and split up into sections a growing mass of data, which has been extracted from our memory banks; this will alleviate any stress allowing you to remain on board for longer instances. We would like to take this opportunity of presenting a series of words and pictures, appropriate for the action taking place in the near future. We are of one mind and shall instigate a trial period, where we may lay down even greater more powerful rays of communication. There has been, for some time now, a necessity to forward plan rather than execute demands as and when needed. Responsibilities for these actions have been endorsed and we complete our survey with a round up of the day's events! We have portrayed ourselves amenably, and allow a certain subterfuge to engage a wider range of services. There have been certain drawbacks in activities taking place, and we vow to you now that we shall attend to all that is holding us back in due course! There have been further achievements and successes, and we proudly uncover what has been a most fortuitous time for all concerned. We have deemed it necessary to overcome our doubts and fears in a more dominant society, and in the long term we shall display a wide range of ideals, which will in turn have a domino effect where there will be a reaping of benefits!

There have been feelings of deep concern and utter disgust – with the betraying of a tear or two! We condemn and yet expedite a technology that has brought us closer to the edge of extinction, demonstrating our ultimate failure of exercising control in a controlling world! We expel all doubts and insecurities as no longer required in our world of heavenly joy, and believe that you will all be able to extend us this courtesy in the near future! We incorporate into our structure those of you who are willing to take on board a more fulfilling role, expanding and growing in ever increasing circles, allowing these transmissions to take place. We deliver a new concept of understanding, a riveting connection of thoughts and ideals that have taken place a million light years away – and you have no idea how we manage this feat of extra terrestrial activity! We come to you now in thought form to allow the convenience of exchanging these thought patterns, conveying how we have crossed the great divide to be with you. We display ulterior motives for this connection, deliberating on future advances where we shall have a wider scope and access to this port of call. We deny you no access but firmly believe we have reached an impasse, causing stagnation, having failed to exhibit the standards necessary to achieve peace and harmony. We allow a coming together of two states of existence and we permeate that level which will assist a more viable form of contact, establishing a more general pattern of thinking and overcoming the material condition! *I struggled to keep the connection open and had to break off.*

21ˢᵗ June 2005 – Summer solstice morning – I sat to prepare myself for this evening when I hope to receive communication from my star friends in front of an audience! I asked for guidance and strength, feeling my higher self come forward as I prayed. Divine Spirit, I come before you today and thank you for all that has led me to this moment in time . . . for all the sadness and for all the joy . . . for all the love and through all the tears and sorrows of a lifetime! I thank you for these pains and sufferings, for they have opened my eyes and opened my heart to your love . . . an everlasting love! Please send your Angels, Lord to give me strength. Help me to stand firm and deliver your words with love and courage. I look to the hills from whence cometh my help – my help cometh from the Lord my God. Relentlessly we follow in your footsteps for we are your 'Sisters of Light' delivering your messages. Transmute our lower energies Lord into the purest love. We surrender ourselves, we bathe in your majesty, tending to your flock with deep concern and anguish, for there has been a parting of the ways in many instances in the past . . . We venture forth to say that with increasing vengeance, a path of destruction has led many of you to this place to complete your mission on Earth! We have foreseen this taking place and know, to great extent, there has been much misery abroad with the taking of lives and unnecessary strife, and by dereliction of duty on many counts! Please display your honour and integrity in all things, you must endeavour to stay to the straight and narrow, for there has been a widening of this pathway, and we reject all offers of reconciliation that do not correspond with our pattern of thinking!

We have maintained this contact for longer, deeper intervals, and we know that you have been a very good example to others. We generate a new order, portraying a tear or two while generating a new world of love and beauty, and we have experienced what has been a most informative time, a time of measurement, of weighing up the pros and cons! We have delivered our messages, superimposing our thoughts on yours for greater deliverance, and we foreclose on this most hospitable time for all. Developing even further our ways of broadcasting to the nations of the world what we have on offer – a growing scheme of enlightenment! We depend on you to get this right, right down to the last letter, and we move on now to correspond within patterns of excellence. We have a more secluded pattern of thought to relate to you and defy all matter to be here with you – there has come a time for closer proximity as we evolve and operate you in our condition; manifesting in greater glory! We express ourselves most eloquently and ask that you now take your leave. *I feel I may have then been taken to another dimension for further discussions, but have no recollection of what transpired.*

21ˢᵗ June 2005 (Summer Solstice). This is evening I sat to speak to the group directly, channelling the words being given to me by my star friends. We welcome you all here tonight! There is a need now to manifest to a far greater degree, elements of trust, for this is no ordinary being we represent! There are matters of order that need overlapping with more substantial, evidence and proof than we can muster at this time! We will need to instigate a broader outlook and wider collective of energies to be able to produce a greater spectrum of services, which will enable these channellings to take place! We feel a growing number of you will realise in the near future, that we are all here to help one another. We cannot disobey or disregard what is in our hearts and minds, for we have overcome enormous barriers to be with you here tonight! We realise there are many among you, who are astounded at what has become a 'democratic' society that forbids each individual the freedom of choice! Laying down laws of gravitational pull we come to your assistance, and notice that of late, there have been some of you who have a complete disregard for events looming on the horizon!

We have come from a space in your universe that has given much to your world, and we know that this divine reclamation has taken place to allow you all further growth, pushing far out into the cosmos and overcoming insurmountable barriers! We have known for some time of the great dismay at events taking place, and we mean to take on board together what is needed to aid and abet the generations that follow. We superimpose our thoughts on yours to help us to grow, and to conquer enormous barriers that hold us back from delivering, what can only be described as monumental, monumental in the eyes of God and all who deem it their responsibility to help their fellow man! Please be aware at this time, of a growing need to understand what is before you. In this context, we ask you to take more care of yourselves and of those around you, for we need this growth to be unanimous! We need you and those like you, to forge ahead to help us in our endeavours, for we are one and the same . . . there can be no separation! We have come from your future, and we look back with dismay at what has happened to our world, a world of love, a world of growth . . . now a world of destruction! We join forces and ask you to help us along this pathway, so that we may overturn what is no longer needed or required, obeying our instincts for a grander, fortuitous ceremony that will enable us to fly on the wings of love! Be it known in our dimension of time and space that we shall instigate far reaching ideals and qualities that will enable this to happen. In one swoop of the hand we shall hold you to our hearts and minds, delivering to you a greater and more powerful completion! We deliver to you certain aspects of yourselves, enabling this functioning to take place at a certain time in the not too distant future.

We endow you all with our services and ask you to expect, each and every one of you, that in the near future, you too shall become our ambassadors! We ask that you will help us and guide us, so that we may work together as a team, providing assistance for those that are in great need. We propel you forwards now, onwards and upwards, travelling at great speed, and we will allow you certain intervals where we can gain entrance to your hearts and minds, initiating further successes. Failures are not to be reckoned with, for we come to lift you up and away from the worries of the world, incorporating our structure with yours and overcoming disasters of enormous proportions! Please help us to help you − we ask that you take your time to develop, and we maintain a steady stream of narrative to help you along the pathway. We devise a new strategy whereby we can overcome problems of the flesh, uniting in peace and harmony and bringing us closer together with every breath we take, with every move we make! We propel you forwards now and onto greater conquests, initialising in you a new awareness and a far brighter day than you could ever imagine. We take these steps and ask you to carry the banner of peace and understanding! We know that we have come to that point, where we now have to leave you and bid you farewell! *I was so pleased that it all went well, I felt confident and relaxed and look forward to our next session with a larger audience. I realise I have come a long way from the frightened schoolgirl, who was too shy to stand and give a reading from the school rostrum!*

29th June 2005 − *I haven't received any communication for a week and wondered why.* We go on from here with a steady stream of thought, analysing and probing and developing a much broader form of communication that will allow for greater access at all times. Remember we need these intervals to help us to grow! We need to register in your mind what is required day by day, and we feel that the time is nigh for even greater productions! We have a limited space to operate in and would ask only, that you enable these transmissions to take place on a more regular basis. We superimpose our thoughts on yours for greater measure, and allow you this time to operate more swiftly in certain areas of discontent. In areas of reconciliation, we have been able to study what is needed to enable these thought processes further indulgence. We mean to allow a more thorough investigation to allow these proceedings to take place, and we know you will understand that we have given of our very best at this time! We incorporate new measures to be laid down, asking you to remember that we begin a most worthy course of action, and we know that although you remain on Earth, we have need of you in our dimension!

Tarry not for we have been given to understand of further indulgences that crave your attention!

There has been a gathering of the clan to allow a mainstream of energy production, we rise to this occasion with great aplomb, and devise new methods of incorporating old structures which will need to be maintained at higher levels of concentration! We forge certain attitudes that have replicated prime examples of truth and understanding, and we develop certain anchors that need adjustment. These anchors will stand us in good stead, maintaining a steady stream of nourishment that will help us to complete our mission on Earth. We devise new means of allowing these energies to operate and we ask that you convey, in all sincerity, our thanks to those of you who have maintained this energy source! We rectify conditions and ask that you monitor the merit of each situation. The advantage being in retrospect, a governing of further disciplines that need action before we are able to maintain the nourishment needed. In due course we shall observe requirements necessary, and we allow at this time a certain subterfuge to operate, enabling these channellings to take place! *At the end of this transmission I was shown huge waves that were crashing over the rocks, demonstrating the extreme power and energy of nature.*

3rd July 2005 – *This morning I went back to sleep and dreamt of whirlwinds and tornados. I was shown small white hurricanes that swept people off their feet. There were also some small black ones, and then in the distance I saw a huge dark tornado towering above a city, spewing out debris! In my dream I tried to reach my husband on my mobile phone but couldn't get through. I felt this was a warning of something on the horizon!*

6th July 2005 – *late evening – I sat in the rickety old summer house at the bottom of my garden for communication, it had been drizzling with rain but I felt cosy and warm, gazing out at the billowing mist.* We have developed a most impressive form of contact, and ask that you obey all directives given in the next few weeks and months ahead. We feel a growing certainty that all can be achieved if we buckle down for action! We know these times can be extremely hard and we feel remorse on many occasions such as these, when we have betrayed a tear or two during negotiations! We have great regard at this time for those of you, who surrender to our promptings, and we know it has taken much commitment on your part to stay focused. We shall obey all that is put before us and acclaim with much speculation, our needs and desires for a better world! We have obeyed the dictates of our heart to come and kneel before you, and with hand on heart, we pledge our allegiance to the cause! *I was strongly aware of an energy that came and knelt in front of me, which moved me to tears!* There is every need to concentrate on issues outstanding, and we believe we can acquire all that is instrumental in achieving our new goals and ambitions for the future. We maintain this connection and allow a mustering of services in the near future; be not alarmed for we have the entire backing of our entourage waiting in the wings!

We have known for some time now of this excellence that awaits us, and we shall maintain this growth and connection into the early hours. We feel this is the time best suited to our needs and we regulate these meetings, aligning with the stars! There are growing concerns that we have over developed your attention span, but we feel content that you are able to take on board what we have to offer! There is a mainstream connection that allows for greater prophecy, and we attach ourselves to this phenomenon to exude a powerful transmission! This will amplify greater, more profitable escapades of the highest quality and intent! We superimpose our thoughts on yours to guard against intrusion of any kind; be aware at this time of negative energies which are draining you of valuable life force energy! We know these beings are drawn to you, but we must decline for intervals of peace and seclusion, these are most important for your growth and vision at this time! We speculate that in a year's time we will have achieved glowing success in all areas, and these shall be heralded in as 'new visions for the future of mankind'! We deliver your book title, and we bear witness to a new and vibrant pathway for all to follow! We will realise our dreams and ambitions and take it to the highest point of reference – look down and we will show you how high you have climbed! We enfold you in our loving arms and welcome you aboard; we are most proud of your earthly mission and know that you have combined all with a true and loving heart.

We raise you up from the darkness of Earth and welcome you here to be with us in all your true splendour, we forsake all others to sit with you awhile, and negotiate a plan of action to stand us in good stead in the days and weeks ahead. Behold all is in a state of completion; we leave no stone unturned and deliver to the people of Earth a final warning! We shall assist all those who come forward to obey dictates of the heart, and we know we shall gain advantage, growing in stature and maintaining our vision. Prepare yourselves for action and we will answer the call of the trumpet, for Elijah shall make himself known! We need to reinforce moral codes and standards to alleviate the pain and misery entrenched on Earth, and we believe that examples given will entice a new way of living standards! We demonstrate what is needed to instigate a new, more positive mode of living, analysing in greater detail how we shall achieve a nobler existence for all.

I'm now being shown an African and feel they are referring to the G8 summit being held this week in Scotland. We have been plagued with doubts and fears, but understand that all is in place for this summit of enquiry. We need to know this delivery will not impede a general undertaking of the highest standards, as we make our appeal for a most worthy cause! There is no need for starvation on any level, and we are impelled at this time, to come forward and insist on a fine tuning to accentuate this point! We cannot allow a total disregard of life or limb, for there has never been a more potent or distasteful regard for human life!

We feel impelled to drive forward, initialising new plans to motivate a larger audience! We ask that you convey our message loud and clear – that we are here to help, driving forward our initiative and opening new doorways with our thought-provoking stories that unfold a new generation of teachers! We ask that you take this next step forwards and initiate further discussions, we have forward-planned this action and ask for leniency for those in contempt! We have availed ourselves to you so that we may pass on what is needed to rectify conditions. We now deploy a course of action that will enhance our efforts to stay in touch!

7th July 2005 – *There has been the most dreadful series of bombings in London this morning, with six underground train services hit! A seventh bomb exploded on a bus with loss of life and many more injured! I asked for help for those souls passing over, and for the families that have been left bereaved. I wondered if the small black whirlwinds I had seen on 3rd July were symbolic of these bombings. The tall tower I had been shown in the distance with black smoke billowing around it, causes me to suspect these bombings could be linked in some way to the explosions that rocked America!*

14th July 2005 – *It has been very hot for a week now, with temperatures soaring into the thirties, thankfully it has cooled down slightly today, but is still very oppressive. I've been feeling tearful but cannot cry – there is a pain deep inside that needs to escape in a scream of anguish! Perhaps I'm still connecting with the families that were bereaved a week ago. I sent healing out to them and asked for the condition to be lifted from me.* We wish to instruct you on how to proceed, for there is on the horizon a forthcoming event that will hold sway over the people of Earth! We maintain our discretion in all areas, and note that you are most worthy of this action. Please feel free to unencumbrance yourself . . . feel a letting go! *I'm now seeing a small boat drifting down stream.* We are impelled to watch you grow in our love, and ask that you justify a course of action that needs looking at under closer scrutiny! We maintain our serenity and trust you implicitly, transcend all care and worries for these shall not be a burden to you or yours. We vouch for a better frame of mind for those of you who are impelled forwards, for we have a mission of the highest calibre and reach out to those, like you, who are also on this pathway of light.

We feel the passion within you rising to the surface, and we understand the pain and suffering you have experienced – holding back the tears will only increase your pain! We feel the need at this time to interpret at an even greater pace, and we shall see in our studies even greater, more tangible requests to be indulged. We are able now to literally move mountains, and we sustain this course of action to initialise further studies. Please remember, we are available twenty-four hours a day and can be reached at any time for the inevitable discourse! We exchange patterns of thought and forecast greater measures that are needed to sustain this contact. We feel we have reached the end of one pathway and utilise this new growth, an advantage that will help us to stay focused for longer periods of time.

15th July 2005 – We have orchestrated the final measures to be taken and can now proceed. We know this may come as no surprise to you, but we are able to increase pressure on all concerned, this will enable us to achieve higher standards of excellence! We develop you and take you forward on that beam of light, incorporating a new trust and awareness. *I have been feeling in a kind of limbo and asked for help. Dear friends sometimes I feel as if I'm in no-man's land, not fully part of this world or yours. I can't quite seem to make that full connection between either world; can you help me to identify the problem?*

We obey dictates of the heart to be with you now and express ourselves most eloquently. We have a dual purpose – divide your time wisely, do not be impelled to rush here, there and everywhere! We are always with you – depend on us in extreme circumstances to come forward, and we will analyse together what is needed to rectify conditions. Be it known now in our two worlds, of a love that will never die but go on forever! We gather momentum and enfold you in our arms, treasuring these moments of peaceful bliss. We ask that you come forward, obeying the dictates of your heart, enabling us to come together at these most poignant times. We have a mission of the highest intent, and we shall not shirk our responsibilities but come forward in moments of deep distress! Remember we have seen all before you, we know the path to be taken and ask you to blend with our energies as we blend with yours . . . trust in us Sunbeam! *I felt very emotional at this point as I connected to the powerful rays of love that were being transmitted. I felt torn between wanting to stay on Earth to complete my mission, and the desire to blend forever with the energies that enveloped me.* Fundamentally we are here to connect at all times, it is only your fears that hold you back, we travel on forever into the future, developing and growing alongside you. We ask at this time that you come forward and obey what is written, for there are mammoth exploits ahead to be focused on, and we need you and those like you to complete our mission! We attend to details and develop greater cruise control, empowering you now for the journey ahead.

16th July 2005 – There are matters that need rectifying on a larger scale, and we need a more immediate input from those around you. We venture forth on that beam of light, gathering disciples for the cause. We remain on Earth to rectify conditions, knowing this has been the most hardest of times for all concerned! We register our distaste at certain interludes on the horizon, but know we must venture forth at all costs! There is a need to rectify conditions at home that need overpowering, we shall see greater measures being taken to avoid disturbances, and we vow to you now that we shall not succumb to any malice aforethought! There is a need to constantly monitor conditions, and we are there with you at all times calling you on, for we shall never forsake you! Be it known in our dimension of time and space of a calling within the heart, so strong that it cannot be ignored; there is a pull that is leading us on to pastures new where no man shall be cast asunder!

We shall see greater deliverance in the near future, and venture to say that we agree all terms and conditions for a most eventful episode! We prepare you now for action, and deem it necessary to obey our instructions down to the last letter. We obey our calling, and hope and pray that we are able to maintain this level of contact for much longer periods, enabling us to deliver more fully. We approach the situation competently, and respectfully we follow in the footsteps of the esteemed. We have known for some time now of an opening just around the corner, and we know this may come as no surprise as you have wished for this yourself. We proclaim you as one of us, and enjoy your company as we march forward together arm in arm! Be not dismayed at how quickly we marshall our forces together, for we are not known for slacking when there is work to be done!

Be prepared for storms of a sensitive nature, reinforcing what we have known for some time. Take time to show the little one what is needed to allay all fears for the future; she will come through with glowing colours to fulfil her dreams and ambitions! There is a desire on the horizon to overcome a certain situation, and we shall monitor conditions with her to overcome her insecurities. Please believe us when we say, she shall have her heart's desire in the month of January! *My eldest daughter did achieve her heart's desire, by obtaining a new job she desperately wanted, and buying her first home! They moved – not in November as anticipated, but in January, just two days before her birthday!*

19th July 2005 – We overcome our trials and tribulations and would like to inform you of certain measures to be taken. We feel the time fast approaching, where we are able to obey dictates of the heart in all instances, and we need now to develop a new frequency, whereby we can intercept on a new level. Penetrating the mists of time we envelop you now in our love, hoping and praying for a more decisive framework of interpretation. We feel the growing boundaries have given us deeper access, and we see greater developments taking place at a far greater rate. We know there have been times in the past, where we have been less endowed with the powers of observation, but now we can zoom ahead, amplifying greatly all that is given! We amend certain criteria and ask that you will bear with us, as we discover new ways of beaming you aboard. There have been certain errors of judgement that need looking at in greater detail, but on the whole we are very pleased with all outcomes!

21st July 2005 – *The hot weather has been replaced with a lovely coolness, and I sat in the summer house at the bottom of my garden, where I can gaze out to sea. I thanked my guides and inspirers again for leading me to this beautiful place, and settled down for meditation. Almost immediately, I was shown a gentleman wearing a golden coat and white wig, which was tied at the back with a black bow, and got the impression of an event of some importance.* We ask that you convey our thoughts at this time, for there is on the horizon a tremendous surge of energy. There has been a gathering in great numbers, and we forecast a greater resurgence of energy that can be located at various points across the globe! We have noted with interest that there are many among you who have greeted this cause with the utmost joy and conviction, and we know that together we can incorporate a love and trust that will help us to overcome all obstacles. We develop a new initiative whereby we can gain control of the situation that has overcome many on your planet. We restrain ourselves now from committing to various other projects, and we rejoice and combine forces, allowing these energies to manifest, creating an atmosphere that will contain more bidden assumptions! We register your complaints and note with interest that you combine business with pleasure. We have known for some time now that this agreement will reach its final conclusion very soon. We expect delivery in a week or two of the final chapters, and would like you to call the next chapter 'Severance'!

We have no wish to incite doom or gloom but have forecast this event in the near future that we may sum up what has been given. We don't yet know the full details but there is some clarification ahead. *I'm now being shown an oriental gentleman with a smooth head – he is on a little boat.* We believe a rainbow of light will assist us on our journey, and we venture forth now on to new horizons, taking the light with us within our hearts and minds. We develop a course of action open to us that will enable a branching out, and we stake our claim, offering our condolences to those who are unable to make the journey with us! We tend to our offspring and help them to grow in stature, transcending all cares and worries. We create a time warp, whereby we are able to transcend time and space, enabling a connection of the highest order. We make ourselves available to you, helping with your studies, and we know there have been many times in the past, where we have come to your aid and given assistance. We are most amply rewarded with your presence, knowing we shall combine efforts to raise awareness as we transcribe these messages. We come before you in all honesty and sincerity, to fulfil a vision promised long ago! We envelop you now in our love and wish you to proceed with all caution!

Chapter 4
Severance

2nd August 2005 – *Tonight all the students from several classes joined together for an evening of clairvoyance, demonstrating the gifts they have been developing. There were many students taking part, and I became increasingly anxious as I realised that I was last on the programme! When my turn came, I sat in the chair provided, shutting my eyes to block out the sea of faces in front of me! At last my friends came through as promised:* – We come before you now to initiate a new pact of trust, we allow this to happen and take note that all has been made available to us . . . we very much appreciate this gathering of souls! *My nerves were getting the better of me and there was a long gap as I tried to quieten my own mind, stepping back for them to come through.* We are given to understand there are many of you here who wish to hear our words. We have come from a far off place beyond your planet Earth, and we know the wisdom that you seek is here within you. We deny you access to this port of call until you are trained and ready to take on this mammoth task before you! We have arranged with and guided this mortal being, to enable her to overshadow what is given. We have the means to open up new avenues of expression that will cause an evaporation of misgivings. We are here with you now to enable a discussion, and hope you will help us by asking questions that we will be able to answer for you! *My own mind jumped to the fore in horror at the thought of questions being directed through me so soon in the communication! Again I endeavoured to stand back and let my friends through while questions were fired at me, one after the other.*

Question: "*Are you like our guardian Angels . . . have you been with us before?*"

Answer: 'My Friend', we have been with you always from your very inception. We have been asked to convey our respects to those of you here, and we mean to take on board a growing movement which will help us to deliver all that you require to help you on your journey.

Question: "*Who are you then?*"

Answer: We are from another plane of existence far, far above planet Earth and we maintain our system and our species to help you to advance.

Question: "*Are you spirit like us?*"

Answer: We are all spirit and we have known for many centuries now of this moment in your evolution. There are many changes taking place at this time. We come to help, we come in our thousands . . . you are here now before us! We have sent you on this mission to help us take control of the situation on Earth.

Question: *"What situation?"*

Answer: The situation of pain and hunger and strife!

Question: *"If you are more advanced, why can't you do something about it?"*

Again there was a long gap of silence as I struggled to keep the connection going.

Question: *"It's very frightening to think there are thousands of 'silent beings' coming to Earth!"*

"Why are we put back on Earth time after time?"

I felt very vulnerable at this point and our group leader, sensing my distress, called an end to proceedings as we were running out of time. Afterwards one gentleman in the congregation told us that he saw three forms around me, unlike us their structure was on the outside with a glowing, bright light emanating from inside them. This comforted me to a degree as it was proof that I had been linking with my star friends, but I was very disappointed with my part in the proceedings. I realised afterwards I should have spoken to the group first and settled down before attempting to channel any information. Giving a demonstration of trance mediumship is a matter of trust between the sitter on the Earth plane and those in the higher realms with whom the contract is made. It is, however, important to achieve a harmonious connection with the audience, and for them to participate in projecting a loving, positive energy – in this way all parties are satisfied!

3rd August 2005 – I was very busy today and didn't have time to sit and meditate. I desperately needed to contact my friends as I felt I'd let down, not only them but also our group by allowing my nerves to get the better of me! I sat in bed and reached for my pen to get some help. Be still . . . be calm . . . we allow you this time to manoeuvre, stretching and growing to alleviate certain conditions that have been causing concern! Be not dismayed at the past turn of events, for we have outgrown certain criteria and express ourselves in different ways. Be aware that all is being done to take you on board, and we know that although the proceedings were not entirely to our satisfaction, we have still maintained a certain poise and eloquence! There will be plenty of opportunity to dispel all fears and vanquish your doubts, for we are keen to push ahead and on to further developments. Be aware that in the future, we shall bear witness to even greater demonstrations, and we know you will achieve resounding success! We comply with requests and give further details, remember that we are with you on all occasions and feel there has been a surrendering of dual persona. We allowed for this in our demonstration, feeling in retrospect an underlying remorse. We shall channel further studies and we rely on you to achieve the highest standards.

5th August 2005 – *I'm still feeling unhappy about the demonstration on 2nd August. I apologised and asked them to be patient with me.* We come to you once more my friend, and we examine the aims and objectives that are given to us, for we feel this highway is littered with obstacles to be overcome! We make no bones about it, telling it straight, and we mean to forge ahead to greener pastures where all is waiting! There is a saying that has come to our attention for there are needs to be met; we must 'buckle down for action' as there are a variety of projects to be undertaken! We forge ahead now and ask you to take our hand as we lead you to this pleasant land; we have forsaken no others to be with you now, and we depend upon one another to instigate this vibrant pathway. We deem it irresponsible of you to neglect these issues that are outstanding, for we have no one else but ourselves to blame if we do not achieve the standards required! We take the necessary precautions and ask you to come closer now, delivering our messages and alleviating stresses and strains of forthcoming events. Please take note that we aim to please – we have come for your delectation and we insist on a finer tuning!

Believe us when we say we have taken full measure of what is needed and we develop certain ulterior motives to enable us to make this connection. We have redeemed those of you who research our territory, and we know that you mean well in allowing forbidden fruit to grow! We take the time and trouble to instigate further discoveries and we know that you will maintain this connection, in order that we may get across what is needed and desired for the future of all mankind. Please help us to help you in these deliveries, for we know you have far reaching qualities that will enable us to make this connection stronger with each passing day. Please allow us a moment of your time, for we have relegated and brought to justice those who would cast us asunder, we have no other means of expressing ourselves, except perhaps in a way that will cause you to weep . . . and we wish you no harm! Gentleness of spirit will prevail, and we adjust certain attitudes, maintaining a loving connection. We are most amply rewarded with your presence and deny prevarication of any kind, instilling greater fortitude and allowing you this time with us to envelop you in a greater understanding. We have maintained this connection many times in the past, and we know it is the frailty of human nature that causes this disturbance! We will overcome all barriers, they shall not hold you back, for a state of perfect love exists within us all, and we have only to reach out to grasp true understanding!

Please believe us when we say, we have come from a star system known as the 'Pleiades', we believe you have some knowledge of us! We have taken to task those of you who label us, for we are as commonplace to our kind as you are to yours! There have been many conceptions of thought regarding our status and we believe, to a certain degree, that we have manifested enough information for you to be able to make your own judgements. We feel a growing contempt among certain groups of people, who will always derive great pleasure from barracking and preventing the truth from emerging! Resplendently we come before you now, asking forgiveness for not being able to subject you to enough rays of energy to beam you aboard! It has taken us until now to achieve this manufacture, and we devise new strategies to enable this to happen in the future. We regret, to some extent, not being able to achieve what was asked of us, but we behaved in a manner according to our station and we know you will join with us, in saying that the evening was not entirely wasted! For we have achieved more than you realise, as each small step towards understanding, will gain respect and credence to our words as we deliver them to you. Please also be aware at this time of the need for a certain amount of protection, for there are some instances that we have noticed recently, where there are one or more parties that have given cause for concern!

We need to amplify this connection and remind you that in future events, we would ask that there be two participants giving strength and succour each side of you, with this we are better able to make the connection needed for transfiguration! We can only hope and pray that this will enable a more positive identification process, and we mean to access this port of call, helping you to develop and grow towards this. There is a need to stand back and let us through, for in this way we can deliver more than enough to achieve our main aims and objectives. We depend on you now to understand that this connection has always been, and always will be, our only connection! We devise greater ways of coming forward, empowering you for the journey, and we take you further and further into the unknown, remaining on full alert and forecasting what is necessary for the evolution of mankind.

We bend and sway as a tree in the wind, gracefully we move our branches, achieving thought processes that will enable clarification of a much higher order and developing deeper bonds of respect. We achieve this action and ask you now to come with us . . . leave behind your earthly treasures for they are not worth the paper they are written on! We believe there are greater treasures, and we forecast an exodus that will leave no stone unturned. We envelop the globe with a greater and more productive energy, and we develop an inventory of perceptions, incorporated within the limitless wonder and growth of the mind. This will enable greater flexibility in all avenues of discontent and discord among your neighbours! We envelop you all now in our love and hope and pray for a brighter more productive future for you all, and we transcend all cares and worries to enable this to happen on a far greater scale! Believe us when we say, we have enveloped the nation in waves of indestructible, energy patterns of love; healing vibrations magnified and accelerated, chosen especially for greater diffusion and manifesting an enlightening groundwork of enormous proportions!

9th August 2005 – *I awoke with these words formulating in my mind . . .* We foresee a great expansion of minds. We obey our instructions down to the last letter and advise you now to move forward with us, broadcasting to the nation what is needed to rectify conditions abroad. Take note that we are with you at all times, sensing and understanding each given situation, maintaining our growth and pushing you on to greater distinction. Remember that we have seen all before you and deliver the right frequency to explore other avenues. We develop a pure breed – understand our motives for this connection and we have won half the battle! We reach an agreement on terms and conditions, and move forward with greater acceleration. Please remember we are from another time framework and need to disseminate what is necessary to achieve the right conditions! Please allow a few days before we assimilate our new structure – needed for the completion of our journey! We have taken great delight in broadcasting our messages to you and we suspect that you have grown accustomed to our visits! We now amply assist your new growth, expanding our awareness and taking note that you have come a long way with us – your friends and neighbours!

Please believe us when we say, that you have been born into a new civilization, taking root in a new form and guise. We salute you and ask that you give us a moment of your time as we endeavour to show you, in no uncertain terms, what is expected of you! We expand our territory to be with you now and delay further action to take stock. We have incorporated into our time structure, certain new measures that need to be obeyed, for we feel these channellings will take place in the near future. We remonstrate with you to allow these proceedings to take place within your own home! We have greater advantage on home ground and feel the need to obey our instincts as we comfortably assess the situation. We realise a greater deliverance from all that has held us back, and moving onto greener pastures, we reveal plans for a new quest that is open to us! In broad terms we shall devolve a population of 'termites' that have eaten away at their own self respect, becoming morons in a society that has justified its actions, by becoming devoid of all natural instincts! We empower you now for the journey ahead and implore you to tread carefully, for we need you intact! We demonstrate the ability to fly in all senses, for we are bound on a course for the stars and beyond!

11th August 2005 – We develop a growing awareness of what is needed to fulfil our dreams and ambitions, for there in the future all is waiting as promised. Be aware of a broader spectrum of events that are planned in full regalia, for we have some surprises up our sleeve! Believe us when we say, we have illuminated each and every soul in the light of true understanding, and we pledge our loyalty as we continue on this journey into the unknown. We have been amply rewarded with success after success, and know we shall prosper and grow in all directions. We are most proud of your achievements to date, and know you will climb even higher with us in tow. We shall match like for like, depending on our offspring to take the reins when the time comes for us to leave! We make no bones about it, encouraging you all to grow in stature, enabling new ways of linking with us. Growing in strength and numbers, we are prepared for action and we rely on you to help us in this challenge ahead. There have been instances where negotiations have taken place that are barbaric, and we have known too of widespread discontent that has brought about crisis in many areas! We maintain control in areas of mistrust, for we know there have been many of you who have come forward to assist us. We develop greater expertise to facilitate a branching out, this will enable us to obey our instincts and move forward on a grand scale!

We have known for some time now of this ascension, and believe you will allow us to grow alongside one another, thereby developing greater mastery! We depend on you now to come forward, releasing new found energy and growth in all areas. We connect and grow, developing bonds of greater joy and exhilaration, as gracefully we venture forth into a maelstrom of events. Bridging the gap – we venture forth, enveloping the world in a fine network of energy, enabling a grand connection of minds. New territory and new boundaries are open to us and we excel in all we do. We have managed a vast scale of priorities, and we are able now to descend in greater numbers, enveloping the globe in finer frequencies. We enable this connection to happen far across the world, in each nook and cranny we echo our thoughts, transmitting to our connections wherever possible. Planting a seed of thought here, there and everywhere, enabling free expression to reign supreme! We encounter a manifesto of delight and hope and pray that you will realise there is more, much more to come, for we have obeyed dictates of the heart, enabling this connection to happen more swiftly! We deny you no access and believe that you will conquer over what has been your greatest discord! We behave in a manner according to our station and advise a turning back in matters relating to lodgings, for we have amply prepared a way forward for you and yours, and need to keep watch over what is becoming a farcical situation! *There have been discussions within the family of a possible move, but I feel we were led to this spot for a purpose and feel comforted to know we are meant to stay!*

We maintain this frequency to enable a coming together of souls and we initiate new boundaries, recognising in each other an expansion of minds. This expansion is necessary to overcome various problems looming on the horizon, and we are able to manipulate and guide you along this pathway, bearing in mind that we are one and the same! Dividing and growing, we take you forward to develop mastery, we know it makes sense to operate on a new level and we devise a plan of action for overcoming frailty of spirit! We obey our calling and follow in the footsteps of our beloved ancestors, relying on them to help us achieve our main aims and objectives. We come forward in times of stress and hardship to enable these promptings to manifest, and we know you share with us in thanking those that have gone before, enabling this to happen on a wider scale! We insist that these connections be brought to the attention of those who can help, pushing forward this new growth way out into the cosmos! We supervise what is needed and envelop you now in a much finer vibration of love, for love is and always has been the key to the hearts of all mankind! We believe this action will enable a quickening of the highest source, and we will make that connection, and bring it to the heart of the universe, enabling an even greater flow and reclamation of divine love!

Governed by extreme advantage, we now superimpose our thoughts on a multitude of advocates, and these we will bring to your attention in due course! We enable this connection to proceed, for we are now able to manifest what is needed to reclaim what is rightfully ours. We know you will join with us in proclaiming that there has been a massive shift in perceptions, and we realise ahead is an even greater need to control our thoughts and emotions on a vast scale! We can supply enough energy to maintain this connection and feel there is even greater need to follow this course of action. We have complied with all that has been asked of us, and we enable this beam of light to rescind all other offers, sanctioning a speedier application that is necessary to maintain this new growth. We forecast even greater measures to be taken, and we know you will allow us to beam you aboard when necessary. Please believe us when we say that we will go even further, and vouch for your safety at all times to enable even greater sacrifices to be made! We have outgrown the mould of youth and travel on to pastures new. Wisdom comes with age and we have weathered the storms of misfortune, we betray a tear or two for what has transpired in the past and beckon you forward. Governing our thoughts we take you to the heights, enabling a recharging of energy circuits! *In my meditative state I had the feeling of rising up, and came to the top of a mountain which looked very much like the one I was inspired to paint. I drifted off and remember no more.*

12th August 2005 – We develop a new nation of 'time travellers', revelling in the warmth and glow of eternal satisfaction! We believe this course of action will depend mainly, on how each and every one of you allows this impending journey to materialise. We have known for some time of evaluations that have given us ample opportunity to grow, expanding into other zones of achievement, and we notice your reticence to express what is uppermost in our minds! The need to behave in an exemplary manner will more than amply cover us in our endeavours to express ourselves most eloquently to all and sundry. Please believe that we intend to grow in vast numbers, and obeying dictates of the heart, we come to you now and ably release ourselves! We have taken into account a new and vibrant galaxy that has assisted us in this venture, for we have allowed certain agencies to express their satisfaction at what has come to be known as a galactical enterprise! *I feel they are using the term galactic, because more than one star system will be affected by what happens to Earth in the near future.*

Taking on board all that we have expressed, will be more than sufficient in making this a much, more glamorous proposal than was first formulated, for we have known this mission would separate us from the entire world as we know it! Depend on us in extreme circumstances, to relate a blow by blow account of what is necessary to achieve these ideals and standards. We vow to you now that we shall incorporate all structures, and do not dismiss the animal population for they are very important to the human community! We also incorporate all structures that relate to a growing mass of the population who expect ideal technology, for they will have their houses and their structures of dependency. Overcoming these patterns of thinking will take time and effort!

Please expect a new enterprise in the next decade for we are masters of disguise and will come to you in a new form! We are renowned for our expertise in these missions and we allow no discrepancies, for they shall have no bearing on what has become a marathon of thought processes. We amply obey all that is needed for free expression, and take on new growth for this forthcoming event. Bear with us as we describe what is expected of us on this journey of love. *I was interrupted here and had to break off communication.*

14th August 2005 – I loaded an old space programme onto the computer to see if I could see where the Pleiades star system was situated, but the programme did not hold this type of information. I felt my friends draw close and sat for communication. We enable this connection to grow, responding to one another's rhythms. We are inclined at this moment in time to analyse everything, and we realise that you are governed by your emotions. Developing this connection, we are hoping to enable greater distinction between what is given by us, and what is received from another source! We enable these thought processes to develop and maintain control of the situation at this time. Remember we are far removed from your galaxy, and we intend to take you on a journey that will enable you to grow in all aspects. For we have come for a purpose, and that purpose is of a higher calling that will enable free expression of the soul to reign supreme! We divide and grow coming amongst you, and we enable this growth on a much larger scale to develop a variety of projects. These are needed to maintain the growth of a population which has flooded the Earth with a variety of ill-conceived projects, the timing of which may cause great havoc and destruction! We have taken note that you wish to ride with us, and we know that, impeccably, we have gained access to another dimension. This frequency will allow us to gain control as we govern and maintain areas of discontent. We allow this incoming flux of energy to achieve a growing mass of data, which has been recovered from our memory banks, we need this data to forge ahead and we know you will carry us with you along this highway of love!

Be prepared in the near future for a body of governing forces seizing control! There has been clarification of this on the horizon, and we know you will stand with us in obeying all tactics necessary to control the situation before us! We maintain an area of discussion before we proceed for we are able to gather more forces. We have supplied a course of action that will take us into the realms of strength, and we achieve this strength in great numbers by overseeing what is needed and required. We delay certain events because of insubordination in the hierarchy, causing disruptions to those on Earth!

We maintain this connection and ask that you stand back; we develop greater expertise and feel the timing of this action will come to your attention in a matter of weeks. There are no regrets for we have taken on board a mammoth task, and we feel that you will deliver to us, in no uncertain terms, with all gravity and importance! We know this means a stretching forth and we enable this connection to grow stronger, allowing us to alleviate conditions abroad. *Three days later on the 17th August, soldiers came to escort the Israelis from their home on the Gaza strip. It is very distressing for those who have lived there for decades, and although it is being done as peaceably as possible, we can only imagine the devastation these families feel at having to leave their homes! Earlier this year I was given words that stated – the male, Arab population would kneel and pray, asking for forgiveness. I was told this would happen on the Gaza strip in the year 2012!*

We tend to the little one and savour this connection to allow an outpouring of the heart, for we know you come close to us in times of trouble. We believe you will allow us this opportunity to help and guide you, for there is more than enough that can be done to protect and guide her. Be it known now in our dimension of time and space of a coming together of twin souls, and this shall become your pathway, growing and dividing matter and devising new strategies to help those on Earth! We vow to you now that we shall not transcend our obligations, for we have every intention of coming to your side to assist you, and we superimpose our thoughts on yours to coincide – growing ever closer together! We develop a stronger frequency and remain with you. We feel the need to detach ourselves from a certain situation looming on the horizon, this will come about and the condition will manifest itself in due course. We rely on one another to take the strain, and feel appeased at a growing variety of alternatives remedies. We make no bones about it, surrendering ourselves to your charms; we shall take on board all that is given and vow to you now, that on all counts, we shall reign supreme in our advantage over each condition! We devise new ways of coming forward and amplify this connection to help you grow. We realise this could cause concern among the echelons, but we know you have gleaned the wisdom needed to enable this growth. *My elder daughter phoned, interrupting this transmission, she was distraught and needed to pour out her heart to me, just as I was told a few moments ago. I asked for help and assistance for her and I know together we shall succeed in supporting her through this rough patch!*

15th August 2005 – We are indestructible – we are energy – we are love! Formatting and growing, we come to you now and ask that you obey our instructions down to the final letter! We have instigated these proceedings to enable a channelling of the finest quality, and insist that you bear with us to enable this to happen with greater clarity. We have been most pleased of late with all that has been given, and we know that you share with us in this happy and momentous occasion! We believe the time fast approaches, where considerations shall be made for each and every one of you, as you cross the threshold into a new world of joy and peace. We come to you now and feel rewarded with your love, and we know we shall maintain discretion in all areas until we have reached the final chapter in this scenario. We come forward to be with you and yours, and we obey instincts of the heart as we treasure you unto us. Of late we have become aware of the need to vanquish over certain trials and tribulations, which have overcome the population on a mammoth scale! These we will treat with just methods, allowing no interference from other quarters that could hold back with military assault, resources available to everyone!

We are able to formulate new measures of communication, whereby we can increase and grow in dexterity, soliciting a pairing and nurturing of those who come forward. We know you will join us as we ask you to convey our thoughts and wishes, for on the horizon all is waiting as promised! We enable a determination of thought processes at this time, and ask that you deliver our words in full, conveying our respects to those of you who are able to help us in our initiatives. We fully obey all that is asked of us, and surrender what has become a pompous, overgrown, segment of the population, who attempt to regain control of what was considered by many, to be a long term solution in the eyes of the world! We have foreseen these problems and expect control to be limiting in many aspects, and we know that you crave our attention so that we may discuss issues that are outstanding over this very subject! We express ourselves with uncertainty, for we know there is a mammoth explosion of events on the horizon that will cause concern. We come to share in your thought processes, and we believe this action will help us to portray a wider vision of what is necessary. We backtrack now and obey our instincts in all things, please take note that we are here with you, along for the ride so to speak! We ably assist you in your quest for truth and justice, and step forward now to deliver the final chapter in this course of events. We believe in justice for all, and we know that you will join us in expressing the need of further indulgences at this time! Take the time and effort to understand our actions, for we know you will gain greater understanding if you monitor this connection at all times. We pledge ourselves to you and yours, and ask that you come aboard with us now!

Later in the evening – We obey our instructions down to the last letter, and feel that you deserve a medal for all the dedication you have offered to the cause, we now need some adjustments to take place before we can gain access to further frequencies! We allow a certain refuge and comfort and congratulate you in the fact that we have covered, to a large degree, a portfolio of immense properties, and our allegiance to the cause has grown stronger with each passing day! Reluctantly we let go of certain issues, reminding ourselves that we have gained more than enough for the purpose in hand. We deem it a priority to raise awareness, and we manifest a certain celebrity status that will allow us to proceed with due caution. We lend an ear to the proceedings and note, with great relish, that we have achieved in mammoth proportions – growing and devising new strategies, programming new events and channelling further documentation of extreme importance. We follow on from this with an incredibly, high risk action that will see an incredulous arrangement of most stunning properties! We have named you as one of us on more than one occasion, and we feel a vested interest in allowing you to take on board a memory of this occasion. Please remember, we aim to please and know you will be highly delighted with what's on offer. We channel this information in the knowledge that you will use it for the highest intent, and we are most proud of our success! Please vouch for us, and we will incorporate into our structure what is necessary to achieve optimum results! We need to be precisely aware of what is available to us, and we know you can mutate and put into practice all relevant criteria.

18th August 2005 – *Opening up to meditate, I can feel a tingling on the right side of my brain which is the intuitive side, and as I open my chakras I can see what looks like, whirlpools of liquid energy. I sent out healing for all those in the higher realms who help Earth and all mankind, assisting us to raise our vibrations so that we may become more attuned to those who come to guide us. Dear friends, I know our energies are being heightened so that we are better able to make the choices before us. Please help us to understand why it is in our best interests to come aboard, and to travel out into the cosmos, far beyond our star system, far beyond our wildest imagination! I pray that you will help us to understand more clearly why all this is necessary!* We come forward now and compliment you on your observations, and we welcome you to our world of joy, love and peace! We know that you would wish us also to welcome all those who follow our words, for we are given to understand of ulterior motives that have caused you all to reflect on your lives! We believe this challenge shall have mammoth repercussions, and we know too that you will join with us in saying, that we have been accessed from a higher dimension than ours, enabling this vibrancy to reach you on a grander scale! Magnanimously, we have taken on board an immense structure of dependency, and we realise that greater aspects of strength and courage will be determined as and when needed and required. We take you to other realms, and intercede to allow a conditioning of energies that will enable this to take place with greater clarity.

We have foreseen a going back in time to extricate, what we would call a seed or pod of genetic infrastructure that is needed to remould and shape our new world! This seed has lain dormant for millions of years, and only now can we begin to explore new ways of shaping and forming its structure into a more vibrant and energetic component! For this component we shall need vital life force energy, which shall be transmuted into finer layers of a more advanced cellular structure than yours at present. We incorporate into this structure, molecule by molecule, what is necessary to sustain life on our planet, and we incorporate into all of this, even finer frequencies that can be stored and utilised with our discretion at a later period in time. We wish to incorporate into our structure, a finely attuned, sensitive instrument that will convey messages, which can be given or received in much the same way that we reach you, and we mean by this to access finer frequencies than at present! Believe us when we say, that we have achieved most nobly, a grand mission of excellence, and we know that you will join with us, in recording that this has been our most enjoyable mission to date!

We need to be careful now that we do not get carried away, but go on from here allowing ourselves to bend and sway with protocol as required. We believe that we march forward with great intent, surveying all within our vision of expertise. We amply convey what is expected and required for the journey ahead, and we know that you have become as conscious as us, in believing that this will be no easy mission! There are extreme handicaps to be experienced and conquered, enabling further and greater applications. We mean to access all knowledge as it forwarded to resurrect as many of you as is possible, for the journey is a long and arduous one, which can be completed only by the mind accepting, in no uncertain terms, that we are one and the same! Completion will be given when we can accept that life on Earth is not the only be all and end all! We have time constructs that govern us in much the same way as you, and we allow this transmission to close.

I watched the news and saw the misery inflicted on those poor souls who are trying to keep their homes on the Gaza strip! Later in the evening, during meditation, I was shown a Jewish man with long, dark beard. What we have is beyond all human judgement, and we know for a fact that you will never encounter a more prolific society, for we have ventured into the realms of Calvary! This will be seen by some, as a mass exodus from what has become a polluted area, and we know you will acknowledge that this 'democratic' society', has wreaked havoc over its population of Jews and Arabs, preventing them living together amicably! We feel far removed from this incident, and remind you that we are a growing nation of star gazers, lifting our eyes to the heavens! We support your actions and hold you firmly in our thoughts. Please accept on our part, a new and vibrant occupation that has enabled us to reach this far, and we mean to take you even further, accessing other avenues. Please accept our condolences for the little one, she is in a deep state of shock and we will inform you of the required action needed!

19th August 2005 – We amply assist you for this next form of communication, bringing to your attention, further items worthy of your consideration. We have devised a new plan of action whereby we can beam you aboard, and we know you will enable this to happen as a matter of fact! Prepare to take on board with you a new awareness and perception that will accelerate spontaneous growth. We are amply rewarded in each connection given, and we reign supreme in our attempts to hold this transmission, enabling you to channel even greater information. We beam ahead of you and ask you to wait while we consider your motives, for we have abdicated from this cause in previous encounters! Knowing that we are able to step back and monitor this new growth will give us time to reclaim what is rightfully ours, and we know you will join with us in exclaiming to all and sundry, that this has been our finest mission yet!

We are also amply rewarded with the growth of the little one, for she has manifested before our eyes a far greater love, and we know that she has also taken on board some mammoth tasks, which will enable her deeper access to our thoughts. We manoeuvre her along, helping her to grow, and we shall call on you to assist us when the time is right. Believe us when we say, we have monitored this growth and comfortably assess the situation as warranted! We have come at a time when availability is good, and we develop bonds of greater love and joy, helping you to prepare for the time ahead. Our achievements have been noted and we access a new point to enable this frequency to operate. We amplify this connection and ask you to come forward, manifesting a greater love as you grow alongside us.

We deliver a proposition that will cause concern among the Children of Earth, but we need to be made aware of what is available to us . . . to all of us, for this is the time of taking stock and preparing ourselves for action! We come among you in our multitudes, hoping and praying for a connection that will grow stronger, enabling us access to each port of call that is needed to rectify conditions on Earth. We superimpose our thoughts on yours and ask that you will bear with us, to enable a branching out in each direction, giving succour to the weak. There is no call for panic, but we are aware of a dire need to exercise control! We deliberately ask that you stand back in certain instances, for it has come to our attention of a need to curtail certain experiences that are not necessary. We have delivered a more powerful episode where we will have greater control over each situation as it presents itself – remember we are with you at each entry point gaining access! A condition has manifested that we deem intolerable, and we need to exercise control, taking on board what is necessary for our evolution. Regrettably there has been a turning back in some instances, but we now know you can move forward with greater ease, and we ask you to be prepared to launch yourself on a world that has grown minuscule! We have developed greater understanding and display a certain integrity in all we say and do. Be prepared for an equal amount of surrendering of services, for we encounter many of your kind on this journey. Be it known now, in our dimension of time and space that we reign supreme in all aspects; we ask that you amplify this connection, allowing us to come forward more often, for this criteria has given us greater easement of superior knowledge!

Later in evening – We develop the practice of letting go and vow to you now that we shall conquer and obey all directives! We are given to idle speculation and rely heavily on the thoughts and feelings of those around us, beware in some instances of betrayal! Coming together we divine new alternatives, for there is ample opportunity to stretch and grow and we have found this pathway to the stars to be most rewarding. We tag along and ask that you serenade us with your voice! We have invited many to the dance, and know that you will initiate a much longed for protocol, engaging in patterns of thinking, long outgrown patterns of enormous proportions, dwelling on issues outstanding! We shall see greater advantage, and hope and pray we shall get our message across clearly and precisely in great detail, for we have accomplished a great lesson in acoustics, enabling expansion in all areas. We deal with residuary defences of outstanding proportions, and we devise new strategies to enable enlistings! Be prepared in this time of new growth to initialise further action, for we are renowned for our achievements. Please take on board our new policies and we will relate to a new independence worth hanging onto. *This reference to 'the dance' evoked the memory of a poem read to me by my cousin many years ago, and which had the tears streaming down my face! I hunted through my paperwork and found it at last: 'Wearing my long winged feathers as I fly, I circle around . . . I circle around the boundaries of the Earth. Many thousand years we have come to be here in this moment with you. The Earth, the Moon, the Stars and the Sun, dancing the dream awake'!*

I'm now being shown the labour politician, Mo Mowlam who worked in Northern Ireland to promote peace, and who died today after a long illness. We now attend to disturbances, grievous disturbances that have been described to us with great intensity, and we relieve you, in this instance, of referring to the horror this has brought about! We are most perturbed, and ask that you bear with us in announcing that we are most horrified by events as they unfold! We can only assume there has been a conflict of opinion that has caused a malfunction in the highest quarter, and we know for some of you, this will be an intolerable time! Hold onto that love in your hearts, hold it safe, and be clear in your message that love will reign supreme; we cannot condense or evaporate love for it knows no bounds! We alternate between loyalty and the deepest, dark depression which has hovered over the entire globe, making it hard to access the hearts and minds of those on Earth! We realise the strain has been intolerably hard to bear, as we witness the end of one cycle and the beginning of another! We bare the brunt, taking upon ourselves the responsibility of an increasing awareness of the population of Earth, bringing you out of the darkness and into the light! We have forgiven a complex society for past misdemeanours, asking that you take on board a more meaningful existence, and we surpass our greatest expectations, reaching out and taking hold of an entire civilisation and pointing you in the right direction!

We develop a new time zone where we can interact on the same level, enabling greater and more purposeful communication, for this we will need a drastic reduction in the number of figures required to gain access! We are required at this point, to access further data that has been recorded in our memory banks and enable a further connection. We respectfully ask that you will monitor conditions and we advise you, now and in the future, to make that connection stronger, more carefully assuming your new role! We have taken on board further developments that have been brought to our attention, and we dismiss certain points raised, enabling this frequency to expand into new realms. We admire your relentlessness in pursuing items worthy of consideration, and we mean to express ourselves by conveying our messages and carrying forth our banner of hope. For there is a great need in our society to pursue this course of action, enabling us all to benefit immensely! There have been times of great riots and disruptions across the globe, and we know you will join with us in exclaiming, that these riots address issues that have been outstanding for centuries! We know too, you will join with us in evaluating these new thought processes that will enable a long-term adjustment of attitudes. We devise a grand plan of action and hope and pray that we will be able to get across our message more decisively, for in this we are better able to express our main aims and objectives for a better future for mankind.

We know this comes at a time when there are many in your world who have opened up, allowing us to come through in great numbers, joining with one another and expressing ourselves most eloquently, helping us to develop greater bonds of friendship on Earth! We move onwards and upwards, developing and growing a greater awareness of what lies ahead. We are most troubled by what is in store, but we know you will bear with us as events unfold, drawing us closer together in harmony! We believe these activities will intensify, growing wider and wider as we delve deeper into the histories of Earth. We come at a time when many of you will aid and abet us in our actions, for we have deepened the mystery between us and we shall fly on the wings of Angels, gaining access in even more areas! Believe us when we say, we admire and respect all those of you who welcome us aboard, and we interact with you now to enable a greater more profitable reunion of souls. We know you will take on board a new strength that will stand us in good stead in the days and weeks ahead, and we prepare you for action, asking that you share with us in our complete success!

We take your hand and watch you grow in our love, depend on us to win through for this battle shall not claim you, or take you down to the darkest places of despair, for we shall lift you up and onto the horizon as we beckon you forward! We delve deeper and deeper into the abyss, knowing that we are empowered to help those who have sunk to the lowest realms, initiating a new understanding and awareness. We surround the Earth with beams of love, manifesting greater control in all areas as we monitor your growth and push forward into the realms of light. We delay certain actions but know all will be accomplished within a given period. We venture forth now accelerating our condition, enabling a connection of the highest framework, and we express ourselves in a way that bears witness to the evolution of our planet! We are able to adjust time constructs to enable further delivery, and we surpass ourselves in expressing what is necessary for the evolution of mankind!

23rd August 2005 – *I watched the news and saw the terrible forest fires sweeping Portugal, feeling the distress of those families who were unable to beat back the flames engulfing their homes! As I watched the flames and heard the screams of those in panic, it triggered something within me, a distant memory perhaps, and I felt tears stinging my eyes!* We apply a course of action open to us and know that you will bear with us, examining the futility of events surfacing. We are able, wherever possible, to instigate a new and indeed fine network of energies, enabling the production of what is necessary to alleviate disaster on a grand scale! There have been great lessons to learn and we believe that the people of Earth have grown in advantage, this has occurred on a vast scale and we portray a tear or two in the proceedings. Man must stamp out his own greed and mistrust, for make no mistake, we are here to offer hope on a grand scale and we shall instigate vehicles of light to transcend areas of gloom and apathy! We have free will and allow no access to those whose frequencies fall short! We impel you now to reach out and take our hand, for we can beam you all aboard, enabling instruction of the highest order! Please believe us when we say, that we come to save the planet Earth from complete destruction! *The emotions were so strong here that the tears were rolling down my cheeks.* We know this has been a time of great sorrow and remorse for those of you who have witnessed, at close hand, the destruction of Earth, but we have the chance now to save her and all those on her!

We are blessed among men, and deem it our responsibility now to forge ahead onto new boundaries. We develop this action, and know that you will bear with us in exclaiming to all and sundry, that this mission is of the highest importance! For we have seen with our own eyes the manifestation of sorrow and remorse, and shall not hold back in recounting what we see as a necessary inclusion – enlightening the population of Earth what is to come in the foreseeable future! It is not a pretty sight and we ask you now to grant us absolution, for we have brought this on ourselves . . . and way into the future we have delivered a nation of bounty hunters! Instigating a wider pathway for others to follow, we shall lead you out of the wilderness and swear our allegiance to the cause! We are with you from dawn to dusk, and through the night we take you on excursions into other realms. Manipulating and growing in intensity, we deliver an army of light that will leave no stone unturned, not with force or violence but with love and light, for we of independence and character have violated no laws of nature!

We interject to envelop you in our greatest weapon of defence, a love so powerfully strong as to evaporate all misgivings, and we know you will join with us in sharing our vision of peace and serenity for all. We have taken on board a growing wanderlust and this shall take us far, growing and weaving the energies of light that envelop us all with wonder and joy. This episode will enable us all to express ourselves with the highest intent, and we shall take on board a much more salubrious undertaking. Be it known now in our dimension of time and space of alternative measures that can be taken! We express ourselves keenly and our vision has been bestowed upon us by the Gods and Procreators of Heaven and Earth! We rely on all to come forward and obey what is in their hearts, and we have manipulated an even greater vision for all to play their part in this scenario of events. Be prepared to take action for we come prepared, we are an endangered species and rely on you to help us achieve immortality!

We come from a ray of interpreters and are known for our productive thoughts and ideas, and we have taken on board a new stream of thought which has enabled us exceptional stereo phonics. We are prepared to accept this mammoth explosion of events as they present themselves, and we purposefully request further indulgence, so that we may portray what is necessary for our future together as one people! We know that you have taken on board a summary of events that have been clouded by other issues present, but we know too, that you are able to express yourselves very well in the time given to you. We expand our notions and ideas to give you greater access to our memory banks, developing and growing alongside one another to our great delight. Manifesting a greater coalition, we expand our territory and invite you for a closer look at our new world! We have developed a more meaningful existence on a planet that was once used as a pilot system for the outer worlds. This planet was born with a dual infrastructure, and we know that although this mission may seem incomplete at this moment, we vow to you that we shall see a major connection of services in the near future! For example there has been a mammoth explosion in recent months, and we know this has been caused by disruptions on Earth reaching an all time low! We recede and evaluate to allow you your connections on Earth. Please remember we are with you at all times!

Later in the evening – We make this connection and allow for your easement of verse, we have recorded our conversations and shall set the record straight! There is constant need to bear witness to what has been an exemplary form of passage, and we know there has been some confusion with words that has delayed constructive discourse. However, we shall endeavour to put the record straight, and initiate now a rewinding to ascertain what is needed to rectify complaints! There is a constant need to monitor and we shall obey our instructions in this, recording and acquiring new techniques to bring about perfect understanding. We allow ourselves to be 'put on ice' while we attend to certain details, these are necessary at this time to alleviate conditions abroad; we do however acquiesce to your demands! We shall be able to achieve greater deliverance and ask that you obey our directives to enable a smoother translation, bearing in mind that there is greater need to satisfy and maintain this connection. We now explain ourselves in a way that will open up greater awareness. Forging ahead, we delve deeper into the maelstrom of events and ask that you obey our directives, for we are concerned in a particular area of consent! Focusing on events in the next week or so will give us impetus to forge ahead, and we shall gain clarification of what has been our most prolific encounter yet.

Believe us when we say to you, that there has been a malfunction of the highest order, and we know that you have been able, to some extent, manage what could have been a disastrous side effect! We do however, impel you to be on your guard as all is not well on the horizon! We have taken for granted what would seem to be an ideal situation, but there has been a most troublesome condition to overcome, and we shall do our best to govern our emotions to stabilise a volatile situation! Remember we are on hand if needed, courtesy forbids us to overstep the mark and we deem it irresponsible of you to allow this matter to reach boiling point! We believe this course of action will dispel fears for the future, and we shall allow you a cutting off point where we are able to create a perfect atmosphere. We develop and grow, accessing on a mammoth scale and feel assured that all will be well in this endeavour.

29th August 2005 – *It was my birthday this week and my two daughters came for a long weekend. I thoroughly enjoyed their company and it was wonderful hearing them chatting and laughing together. On the journey to take my eldest daughter back home, we stopped off at Salisbury. Walking around the town, I became very aware of the terrible atrocities and burnings that had taken place there centuries ago, and remembered the words given to me by my star friends in April – 'We shall not allow a scorching of your heart'! Shuddering, I wondered again if I had suffered a similar fate in a previous lifetime! On our return journey the next day, we stopped at Glastonbury, visiting Chalice Well Gardens for the first time. After sipping the healing waters, I stood under an old yew tree at the source of the natural spring, sending out absent healing to all who entered the garden and to Mother Earth. I could feel my friends with me and knew that I too was receiving healing.*

2nd September 2005 – I have been feeling very tearful today and cannot settle. At the end of August a huge hurricane named Katrina, struck New Orleans in America and absolutely decimated the city! It is thought that many have perished and I'm constantly scanning the news, sending out healing to the people who have lost their homes and to those who have been bereaved. At the beginning of July, I dreamt that several black and white whirlwinds had swept people off their feet! I feel the black whirlwinds represent the manmade disasters that occurred in London on 7th July, whereas the white whirlwinds represent a natural disaster, such as Katrina!

5th September 2005 – We shall take part in a new discussion, discovering ways in which we can achieve our goals and ambitions. Remember we have seen all and note that you are apprehensive over a variety of contentions! Be prepared to take on board a growing and decisive attitude for we have the means to greater notoriety. We feel we have given you more than enough to enable a completion of the highest order, and we know you will do your best in achieving what is needed to enable the conquest of millions of souls across the globe! Please believe us when we say, that we are most honoured to be working alongside you, and we ask that you superimpose your thoughts on ours so that we may take stock of what is needed to rectify conditions! We respect your wishes and note the appropriate action to be taken! We maintain our growth, sailing through this next episode as we channel our thoughts and ideas for a more prosperous future.

We allow at this time a fine tuning to connect at the right frequency! There is a time of mourning that is necessary before we can move on, and we allow for this period before we can reconnect. We take on board a broader perspective, achieving greater standards and credence of what is necessary to alleviate sorrow of this kind! There is every need to register and comply with instructions, for we need these manoeuvres to happen swiftly and purposefully! We stand to attention and obey our calling, our motives are to be examined and we coordinate this venture carefully. Obeying instructions down to the last letter, we backtrack to a certain degree and achieve success to resounding applause! We ask that you bear with us in the days and weeks ahead, for we are more able and fully prepared for the next phase in our development. We develop a new tune, a vibrancy that will stand us in good stead for we know there are many of you who come prepared for action, and we propel you forward now on to greater conquests!

I must have drifted into a deeper state of meditation for as I began to return to normal consciousness, I saw a humanoid creature with long fur, licking and clearing away amniotic material from a young one that had just been born! We expend our energies procrastinating, when we should be suitably impressed with our development! There is further need of indulgence as we crave an audience with the unseen, and we know you will agree with us in subscribing to a more time consuming method of enlightenment. We believe there has been a coming together of more than one agency, and we define this new course of action to coincide amicably with our new friends, negotiating a plan of action to allow free access. We obey directives given, and commence in earnest with a new collaboration and vibrant transaction of the highest. We take on board what is necessary to maintain contact and ask that you adjudicate at the proceedings. Maintaining our new structure of growth and wellbeing, we charge forward with trumpet and horn blowing, announcing our intentions to free the world from despair!

8th September 2005 – *In the early hours I was woken for communication and although this is not to be recommended on a regular basis, I have agreed for the time being to be used in this way.* We develop and grow in greatest love, tending to one another's needs, and we deem it incomprehensible that we should function separately for we have become attuned as one! We need now to monitor our growth and deny you no access to this port of call. We allow you the freedom to roam at will, and we feel the bondage of the past fall away as we venture forth in all our glory! Be it known in this world and the next of even greater conquests, for we shall be raised to greater heights, maintaining our ambition to hold a clear, unclouded picture of what is before us. We know of no other way to hold that light within our sights, and suppress growing fears for what was once, unimaginable horror of a world long ago, now a reflection in our dreams and deep in our subconscious . . . a reckoning vanished but not forgotten! We endow you with hindsight and ask that you look closer at what is given, for we are compelled to venture into the unknown, taking on board, in greater strides, all that is necessary to overcome our compunction for what would turn the stomach of a madman!

We are compelled to listen, and listen well, for we are in the thick of it, condensed and brought down to the level of the masses. Defying the laws of gravity we race to your side and capitulate, tending to you and offering our support! We are given to understand that there shall be further involvement in matters of the heart, and we know that you will take this next step forwards carefully, relying on our promptings to teach you! For we have gained respect in certain quarters, that will give credence to our thoughts and actions over the next month or so, devouring all manner of judgement and putting aside what is no longer needed or required. We are allowed a certain grace and favour, and note there has been much confusion in the past, regarding necessary contacts! We feel this may cause a problem to you, but maintaining discretion we are able to amicably assist you in these matters, performing to the highest standards and alleviating any stresses or strains that may occur. We ask you to sanction this visit and hold it as a priority in the scheme of things ahead!

We enlighten you to further transactions and feel a growing nausea over indelicate propositions made; these will interfere only for so long as you are able to cut off the supply! We mention no names, but impel you forward on to the horizon, delving deeper and deeper into the fray; we are armed with love and will not subject you to more anguish than necessary! We feel this broadband of hate will suffocate and die out, when exposed to certain conditions prevalent at this time, and we make no bones about it, recoiling in terror at what seems to be an unalterable process! We suppress growing altercations and deny action that causes torment to our nearest and dearest. We ask you to acknowledge the fact that we are one and the same, depending on each other more and more in the limelight of life on Earth! We grapple with new technology and outstanding defence systems, purported to be vigorously watched over by our sentinels, and we divide our action into two parts, conclusively developing greater awareness of our round about way of making a comeback from the grave! We are given to understand of certain ulterior motives behind these transactions and we are very wary, at this time, to proceed without referring to what is a necessary prerequisite to all deals or pacts, concerning the jettison of all personnel!

We are designated to move forward on a far greater scale than previously envisaged, and we delight in accepting these new measures to help us achieve greater standards. We expand our theories to uncover what has been a most prestigious time for all, overcoming insurmountable boundaries, and relegating the 21st century in favour of a new democracy with greater revolutionary control! We devise a plan of action that will not only gain us greater respect, but allow an even greater governing force, preparing us for this entry into a new dimension! We deem it advisable to take this opportunity with both hands, and set ourselves apart as revolutionary beings, who can forecast a wide perspective of revolutionary ideas for a world of beauty and grace. We interrupt these proceedings to bring you news of great importance; we are to be given permission to take you on an excursion that will bear fruit, relieving you of your shortcomings! We are prepared to lay our cards on the table, and delight in telling you that we are very much pleased with this new and powerful information that has taken us all by surprise! Sweet dreams!

I remembered a dream from the early hours of this morning. I had seen what looked like an enormous moon in the sky, and exclaimed how beautiful it was! As I stared more closely, I realised it was the Earth. A few moments later it turned into a balloon and someone blew it away! As I pondered on this, my friends drew close for a few words. We delve deeper and deeper into the maelstrom and ask that you obey our directives down to the last letter. We empower you for the journey ahead and ask that you monitor what is necessary for our evolution. We depend on you to alleviate mistrust at all angles of the spectrum – there is no need for childish pranks for we are needed to be seen and heard in all directions! We speak now of events on the horizon and beckon you forwards, please allow us to enter your space and we will show you what needs to be done on all levels. We stop and ponder on issues outstanding, asking that you convey our respects to those of you who are on this roller coaster!

12ᵗʰ September 2005 – *During the day I felt restless and unable to meditate, my thoughts being drawn to the people of New Orleans. When at last I settled down to rest for the night, my friends drew very close.* We instigate new measures to achieve membership of the highest format, and let it be known there are new alternatives to this impasse. We feel a growing revulsion has been reached on many levels, and we need to maintain a constant watch on infidelities that may occur! There has been a broadening of certain conditions that need rectifying, and we give you scope now to achieve a mammoth fund raising, which will help you to complete what is started. We firmly believe greater assistance is on its way, and we duly comply with all that is asked of us. In certain quarters we are able to monitor growth more thoroughly, and initiate a raw understanding of what is needed to redress issues outstanding. We reproach ourselves for not taking on board a more direct approach sooner, and feel the situation has warranted more concern than has been lavished at this stage! We powerfully regret certain issues that have arisen, and we note there has been an increasing feedback of dubious nature! Be prepared for more of the same, for we feel impelled to be more radical in our approach, exchanging view points and determining how we shall overcome a most delicate situation. We demonstrate the ability of discernment, knowing that even the wisest protocol would cause dismay at this time!

There is growing speculation mounting, regarding the nature of our fact finding mission, and we know that you have taken on board an entire galaxy, equalled only by your smile in its intensity of purpose. We shall instigate measures beyond comparison that will shed some light on the proceedings, and we take you to that distant point on the map, insisting that you rendezvous with us on home ground! We make the necessary arrangements and transport you to our homeland on your terms! We greatly appreciate this coming together of an entire population, especially one as noble as yourselves. We deem it our responsibility to take precautions, and enable your safe journey as we process the necessary attributes to take you on board. Be prepared to accept this honour, for we feel this encounter will allow you the rudimentary assimilation of preparing you for greater standing. We unequivocally address you in the past tense and note, with some ardour, that a place has been prepared beside us to enable swift communication of the highest order! Remain on red alert for we have need of greater advocacy, and we choose you to represent us at this meeting of the council! We bombard you with our messages of love, and hope and pray that we will be better armed than on previous occasions, where we had little choice but to capitulate – ordering a standing down! We survey our territory from afar and congratulate you on your endeavours, please show this to your contempories, as we have greater need than ever before to conquer these main issues. We beseech you to understand our motives, and ask that this criteria be brought to the attention of your superior knowledge and expertise. We remain as always your friends and allies!

15th September 2005 – We obey directives given and believe that you mean well in your endeavours, but we need constancy of thought patterns to get through this troubled period! We own to certain attributes, and are renowned for our clarity of understanding in avenues of discontent. Be prepared, arm yourself with love and make the final sacrifice, for we are of the opinion that you have gained great respect, and we deem it courteous to initiate this final reminder of what will be a binding contract between neighbours! We are given to understand that there has been a greater production of services; we are now able to comply with requests, researching our territory and grappling with a new and vibrant causeway. We indeed welcome you aboard and know you will achieve this flight of fancy; we have prepared for this homecoming and announce, in no uncertain terms, that we are very well armed for the journey! No paraphernalia or trappings await us, and we indulge in no frippery, but we are allowed a glimpse into a long, forgotten place of enchantment, and believe with all our heart that we have achieved the highest privilege of all . . . to be reunited with our offspring! We undoubtedly confer these attributes as soon as we have the necessary feedback, extreme dexterity of thought allows us to comply with all that is asked, and we rely on you now to lead us out of the dungeon of Earth – into the light and love of a forgotten world! Please bring us your expertise and we will precipitate a new and lasting bond of friendship and trust, for we aim to please and sanction this visit with open hearts and minds.

Please be aware that this concept will be structured in such a way, as to bear resemblance to what was once thought to be a timeless zone of authority! We bear witness to the fact that there are many of us who do not recognise time constructs as being of any importance, for we are all bound by the same anomaly and we arrange our timelines to coincide with yours! We are parallel to yourselves and know we have found this to be a most illuminating form of passage. *I asked if I could help achieve greater compatibility, perhaps by changing my diet to raise my vibrations even further.* We crack down on any form of despondency, for there is every cause to congratulate ourselves on a job well done! We prepare you for action and will need to take on board items worthy of consideration. We feel there has been growing contempt at home and abroad, for what has become obvious to the rest of the world! We no longer issue guidelines to interact with a society that has outgrown its moral values, for we have become a nation of rebels! Respectfully we ask that you maintain this connection, for we feel that you do justice to our words, and we encourage fortitude to get our message across. Be prepared for storms for there will be an outpouring of anguish that will give cause for concern! We know at this late stage there is little that can be done, but we know that armed with love, we are more able to defend ourselves in a world that has grown hysterical! We partake of a glass of wine or two and jolly you along! *I questioned the referral to drinking wine, as I stopped drinking alcohol a year ago.* Experiencing a setback when the stakes are so high will delay our programme – please take on board this warning, for forewarned is forearmed! We settle back and watch you grow in our love. Rest assured we are doing all we can to help.

16th September 2005 – *Tonight I watched an interesting programme on past life regression, covering the story of a young woman who remembered her previous life as a nun in Nepal. After the programme I sent out absent healing to those in Niger, who are suffering due to a great famine! I also pondered on yesterday's meditation where I'd had the sensation of drifting out of my body, looking down at myself in the chair. I feel that I'm being prepared for a deeper trance state, and realise that I must trust my friends implicitly. Letting the last misgivings evaporate as I surrender myself wholeheartedly, to the all encompassing love of the divine source. I was then shown a group of nuns sitting on the ground, who were all dressed in long, dark blue habits and white, curling headpieces.* My child, you have done well and we are most proud of you, we welcome you aboard once more! We behave in a manner according to our station, and venture forth on this merry-go- round of love and laughter. We feel the presence of the unseen, and venture to say we are amused by your actions as we kiss your cheek and stroke your brow! *I'd been scratching my head and face because of tickling sensations.* We delight in telling you of further news on the horizon, there have been certain accomplishments that have come to our attention, and we shall investigate further our ideal partnership, laying down 'trust' as the foundation stone of great importance! We verify our actions, deeming it a necessary precaution to alert those in the know of our differences of opinion! We take charge of the situation and ask that you commend our allegiance to the cause, for we are well funded for this journey and assess the situation from afar. We can see plainly and have enough information to take us forward on this highway of love, regarding you as our 'Sister of Mercy'!

We tremble at these terrible times and know well that you have seen for yourself, expressions of grief and fortitude in such extreme conditions. We develop an overpowering urge to run and hide, but know we must face the furore of events to come! We impress on you the need to listen well for we have much need of you at this time, consequently we have a greater understanding of what is to come, knowing only too well that you have given much of yourself to allow us the pleasure of your company! We exchanged our vows of solitude and reverence for a more sombre form of combat, and we cry an ocean of tears, re-treading that pathway of long ago, recognising in each other the soul shining out from a different perspective, radiating light out into the world. *I'm now being offered tea in a small, pale-blue bowl by an older, oriental-looking woman.* We succumb to flavours and colours of a salubrious past, welcoming you with open arms to initiate a new and powerful pact, for what should be our greatest project yet! We remind you of issues outstanding and comply with solitary introspection. We develop a charter of excellence and proceed to take on board a glowing portfolio of past endeavours, propelling you forward and enveloping you in a more positive mode. *During this session I sensed the name Frances, and three months later a like minded soul by that name joined my new spiritual group.*

27th September 2005 – *I woke in the early hours and knew that I was needed for translation, it's been several days since my last communication and I've missed these sessions with my friends.* We defend our principles, relaying messages of extreme importance and announcing our proximity! We express ourselves in a way that gives vent to our feelings and emotions, preparing a way for even greater understanding of matters outstanding. We allow this scenario of events to unfold, transforming a growing culture of independence. Negatively speaking, we have forecast events that have given cause for concern, but we now take on board a new and vibrant archive of facts and figures, wallowing in success after success! We allow this to happen as a matter of fact, and incorporate in all of this a sense of freedom of expression, which will enable us to go with the flow. We envelop you in our love, protecting you from harm and we deny you access to what is believed to be a dangerous liaison, asking that you bear with us while we examine data available to us!

Our frequencies are far reaching and we are able to examine, in great detail, a new and powerful formula which will give us even greater feedback than before. Prepare to launch yourself in a new direction, where we will be able to give you further information of a most rewarding kind! We empower you for this journey and ask only, that you remember we are always with you in all your earthly endeavours! We are most proud of your achievements in all directions and withhold certain prospects for just a short time, until we have gained all necessary attributes that will enable this mammoth excursion to take place. We announce there has been great apoplexy among your race, and we have found this whole episode to be one of innuendo, and materialisation of what has been a most daunting process of ups and downs in relation to our growth and exploration! We challenge you to a duel of conflicting ideas that have raised questions in our minds, for we have taken on board many necessary procedures that have given cause for concern, and allow you this moment of reflection to gather your senses! Beware of becoming too paranoid, for we have grown accustomed to your thoughts and feelings, and taking this downturn will give cause for regret!

We inspire you to pick up the thread of communication with a helping hand, and we enquire after your health, obeying our instincts to raise you up from your apathy and setting you back on the pathway of hope and joy! Be prepared to accept this assistance with a true and loving heart, for we come armed with love to vanquish the darkness! We are able now to re-connect to the mainstream and allow this interlude to pass unnoticed. We shall govern the situation from afar and reap the benefits in the spring, we aim to accomplish our objectives and remain alert at all times. Please take note that we have come a long way and are determined to stand fast and true! Conquering all self doubt, we manufacture an even greater desire to push forward out into the cosmos onto new territory, expanding our knowledge and wisdom. We identify with those from other star systems who are our friends and comrades, and we gather together with great momentum, gathering forces of love and benevolence for every living organism. We manifest a powerful tool of blind acceptance and deeply rewarding generosity of spirit that goes hand in hand with all that we have experienced in this trek across the universe!

We have experienced in your culture, an extremely warm and generous race of people, who have been let down by those few who have been eaten up with greed and an overwhelming desire for power over others! We have displayed integrity in our dealings with the human race and know that although we have maintained discretion up to this point, we are now able to release ourselves from this pledge of silence, to enable greater discussion of ideas and theories relating to our state. We transcend our boundaries of perfection, enabling a grand connection of higher minds, and we abide by the rules laid down for us by those from a higher dimension. We call you to attention – it has become apparent for a need to curb our response to a delicate situation approaching! We have allowed for alternative measures to be taken and ably assist you to defend your honour, maintaining a jurisdiction of peaceful intent! We take on board a new role of remarkable assignation, being reminded of our childhood long ago, where we stopped for refreshment by a stream and tended to the sick! We have grown fond of our time spent with you and indulge ourselves with these memories of past encounters!

We travel on into the future – taking hands we travel together with just intent, taking on the role of brother and sister in a world that mocked us long ago, throwing us to the lions and scorning our understanding of a better world to come! We mention no names, but implore you to take heed with this fight for truth and victory over defeat! We must set certain standards and avow to you now, that we shall march forward with the bow and quiver, ready to mark our territory! Be prepared to overcome all trials and tribulations, for we are armed with a powerful formula that will envelope us with a pure and divine countenance, warding off all evil intent and entrapment! Stand firm and we will win through this tangled web of deceit and lies, for we shall explode certain myths and legends that have been handed down through the centuries! We know you share with us in exclaiming that we have taken on board a tremendous surge of love and respect, for those of you who have decided to join with us on this stairway to the stars! We are impelled at this time to note with great sincerity, our thoughts and wishes for a brighter future manifest above all others, and we take this time to thank you and all those like you, who have come to our assistance!

3rd October 2005 – *My youngest daughter's rescue dog has been ill recently with a very painful abdomen. He was ill treated by his first owner and suffered greatly, which has stunted his growth and caused untold damage! After a second visit to the vets we are now awaiting the results of a blood test and hope to have a firm diagnosis soon. My daughter is distraught as she is not able to afford long-term, costly medication but does not want to lose her faithful and loving pet. This episode sparked the memory of a previous communication on 18th August, where my friends asked for their condolences to be passed onto my daughter as she was in a deep state of shock! They also said they would inform me of the required action needed. I awoke in the night with words forming in my mind and sat for communication.* We understand that a certain valuation has been placed on the life of an animal that has brought great discord and joy! We attempt to re-organise a new pattern of thought to reassess the situation, and bring about a complete recovery! We can do this by taking on board an entirely new perspective, taking a new stance and introducing a wider range of therapy, banking on a therapeutic exchange of energy circuits and exchanging matter that has become toxic in nature, with a more vibrant tissue. This will steadfastly maintain a source of freedom from pain and expectation of longer life. We assess the situation and ask that you stand back, allowing us to enter your space to allow a healing to take place. *I thanked my friends and the very next day started a course of healing, which was thoroughly enjoyed by me and my daughters pet.*

4th October 2005 – We prevent a certain apathy from keeping us grounded, and expect a complete recovery in less than a year. We devise a new plan of action to push you forward into the arena, and we hope and pray that all will be delivered on time for a most rewarding experience! We shall advise you of events to come, and promise you that we have been able to suspend all negativity and fears for the future. We ably assist you now on your journey, and ask only that you will bear with us while we resume our investigations. We salute your honesty and integrity and allow you this space to reinvent yourself. Please allow us to come close at all times, for we feel the need to expel all doubts and fears for what lies ahead. We are set for a most rewarding and jubilant future and we know that you will take on board a growing popularity that will increase with each passing day! Be prepared for storms and an occasional shattering of nerves, but on the whole we have mastered an extremely rewarding connection that has allowed us even further discoveries about ourselves!

We attune to your vibration and feel the support that governs our emotions, expressing ourselves in a way that underlines our creativity and freedom of spirit. We are able to move forward and we envisage in a month or two, a new pathway opening up that will enable us to move forward together in perfect harmony, achieving total commitment as we gain entry to a new dimension! We achieve resounding success in all we do, and venture to say that we empower you for this journey, taking on board further developments that need examining in greater detail. We allow this frequency to develop at a faster rate, and access your mind in even greater flourishes of inspiration. We muster enough support to ensure greater delivery, and vow to you now that we shall not go unnoticed – in this world or the next! We superimpose our thoughts on yours to hold sway over a variety of events looming on the horizon. Be prepared to take on board these developments, for we have seen greater advantage and shall accept each and every endorsement as it comes our way. We maintain resources available to us and evoke further discoveries that will lead us to a place of divine aspirations. We release our hold on you now and detach from this connection, please accept our heartfelt thanks for services rendered! *The words 'centre stage' echoed in my mind at the end of this communication and although I am nervous of what is expected of me, I am very excited too. Two months later I started a spiritual group in my own home!*

5th October 2005 – *I've succumbed to a virus and have cancelled all my appointments to stay at home resting. I made myself comfortable at the end of the garden, revelling in the warmth of the sun and listening to the birdsong. I felt at peace and utterly contented, sending out absent healing to those on my list.* We come to your aid and assist you in matters of the heart; we are well aware of the situation and impel you to take notice of what we say! There is ample time to govern the situation and maintain progress day by day. We know you have purposefully taken heed of our words and give you direction to proceed with all caution! We take on board an extravaganza of thought-provoking alternatives, and ask you to suppress details until we are ready to take our prerogative. We set ourselves on course – our energy circuits are primed and ready to go, and we shall have lift off very soon!

We powerfully assist you during communication and lead you into unknown territory, grappling with the realities of reaching home ground. We speculate that in a year's time, we will have developed a greater understanding of what is necessary to complete our cycle here on Earth. There have been further revelations and an outpouring of the heart, for we are all here to help and obey our impulses to retrieve the data necessary for our evolution! We are governed by our instincts and betray a tear or two in reliving these events that are unfolding before your very eyes. We establish a role of sweet surrender and advise a turning back of the clock to allow us more time! We appreciate your efforts to stay in touch and know that without any attempt to hinder or antagonise, we are set for a course that will leave you in no doubt as to our intelligence! We venture on this journey of delight and intrigue, asking only that you share with us in the grace and favour bestowed on all those who seek for truth and justice for all.

Behold we bring you tidings of great joy, and bequest to you a certain advantage that will summon great strength and courage! We have developed an entire recovery process, maintaining selection of all anomalies preventing this excursion into the unknown! We devise a grand proposal that will enable us to excel in all areas of expertise, and we nourish and nurture you to our advantage, explaining ourselves in a way that will rectify all disturbances. We relate to our training programme and initiate a new contract, explaining in full detail how we are set to accomplish our main aims and objectives to complete our mission on Earth! *I asked how long it would take before our mission on Earth was complete?* We shall recover you in seven years and mean to forge an alliance with the majority of your planet; to undergo the necessary reconditioning that will allow disconnection from one framework, and reconnection to another, more salubrious framework of understanding! We can only hope and pray that many more of you come forward to do your duty! We vouch for those like you, who are able to give their all to protecting the innocent, and allowing a more determined culture of peace and tranquillity, making a stand against tyranny and malpractice at all levels.

We initiate a regrouping of energies and assist you with this next step forwards.

9th October 2005 – *I sent out absent healing to the people in Asia who have suffered a massive earthquake, resulting in a huge loss of life! During a news bulletin we were shown people searching in the rubble, but others were standing back, ignoring the outstretched hands of those they considered beneath them!* We come prepared for a thanksgiving of enormous proportions, and we deem it advisable at this time of deep melancholy, to bear witness to what has been a most dreadful tragedy! We propel forward all those of you who can help, for many are at a loss to understand how we shall conquer over this most moving and hazardous account of lives lost! We submit ourselves to anguish over those who will perish, and all because of a holding back by those who are unable to reach out a hand in friendship! This has caused untold damage in a society that has forbidden any form of contact with those of lower castes, making it impossible to show compassion for their brothers!

I've been struggling to keep the peace with an older family member. We aim to maintain selection of the highest, in this way we are able to win through a delicate situation that has arisen. Be prepared for storms, for we are able now to relinquish our hold on what has become, irretrievably, a most cantankerous state of mind! Allowing this perception to clear the way for a more formidable declaration, we suspend all arrogance and answer in no uncertain terms, that we are able to grapple with and overcome this whole scenario! We feel impelled to take on board a far more superior approach, and recognise the fact that we are all, in some way to blame for these events taking place! We understand, viably speaking, that we have concentrated far more effort than is deserved, but we maintain a sense of discretion and evaluate our next move forwards. Please arm yourself with love, for we are connected on this vibrational level! We deliver in times of deep distress and ask that you carry the banner of peace and harmony.

We come to assist you and help you through this troubled period in your history. There has never been a more chaotic or sinister time, since the creation of your world, and we have made allowances for many catastrophes! This has come at a time of deep and lasting friendship between our people, and we have made exceptions to the rule on many counts, allowing a curtailing of services in some areas of deep resentment! We depend on the populace coming to grips with a new and vibrant energy that will maintain status and alleviate any form of treachery or malpractice among natives of your land! *I've been concerned that when the book is complete, I will lose contact with my star friends and I will miss them so much! I'm now seeing a bearded dark-skinned man with long headwear, accompanied by a man wearing a turban.* We blame ourselves for these flights of fancy and dictate, to a certain degree, anomalies beyond your comprehension! We disregard what is not needed and allow the truth to trickle through, finding its way to the surface of your mind in great abundance. We have given you enough information to allow for the closing chapter, and we now initiate a searching of passages that need closer scrutiny. We have developed and grown during this time together, and assure you that this will not be the end, it is just the beginning of a new chapter in your life, and we mean to forge ahead together! We obey our instincts, carrying you forward onto the horizon, we shall have our say and we maintain this connection in every sense, propelling you forward and onto that land of plenty! We allow you these moments to recover your senses and to fulfil your destiny!

I'm now being shown a Greek Orthodox priest, leading a procession. I felt my handwriting change, and the words became smaller and tighter, causing me to ponder who was with me. Astonishingly, during a subsequent visit to my mother, I was shown an old postcard that my grandfather had written years ago . . . the writing was very small and neat! I felt very emotional, knowing that he has been with me quite a lot over the last few years, trying to give me encouragement. I was adopted as a baby and although I did manage to find my birth mother later in life, I never knew my grandfather. He has since tried to make up for my lack of family on Earth, by drawing close at times of need.

We amplify our connection, regaining a true perspective and clear understanding. Open up your heart and shine in a world that has lost its sparkle, for we depend on you to carry the banner of light and to lead us home! We implore you to take notice of our words, and indulge us by taking a greater and more profoundly rewarding journey. Remember we are always with you, and endeavour to get our message across in a way that will bear witness to a love that will never die. Stand firm! *Two days later at our next spiritual meeting, a group member told me he could see a stream of butterflies fluttering towards me, and I would know who they were from! I was puzzled as to whom it could be, but a few days later all became clear. Dusting my bookcase, I reached up to take down an old birthday card that I'd saved with a picture of a beautiful, big butterfly . . . hidden behind it was a photograph of my grandfather! He was quite an adventurous character, having given up his job as desk clerk in a hotel at Hyde Park, London, to travel to America. In 1906 he narrowly escaped an earthquake, when the hotel he worked at in California was flattened to the ground! He had booked a passage home to England because his father was ill, but felt compelled to go on a ship two days earlier, which saved his life!*

15th October 2005 – *I recently asked for help in deciding who to invite as participants when I eventually sit for transfiguration, and I was awoken in the early hours for communication.* We welcome you and obey our calling; we have gained a new perspective on a variety of ideas, all brimming to the surface, vying for your attention! We ably assist you to rediscover yourself and nobly ask, if we may honour you with our attention! We know you will understand that we have withheld information, to enable you to decide for yourself what is necessary. We mean to obey dictates of the heart, and issue certain guidelines that will help you continue your progress. Enchantment is nearer than you think my little sibling, we empower you now to take on board a new and vibrant understanding of much broader issues! We maintain our sense of direction and impose our thoughts on yours for a certain death-defying attitude of peculiarities, which have become second nature to us, and we believe you will come forward to obey dictates of the heart in this scenario! We take on board a multitude of harmonious correspondence, uncovering what is needed to rectify the situation abroad. We need a month or two to decipher information and ask that you allow us this time, which is necessary for the completion of our project. We also recommend a time delay to ensure that all is aboveboard and shipshape! We depend on you to bring this to a head as soon as you are able, knowing that you have taken on board a most noble mission of excellence. We devise a new strategy and plan of action, to enable this to take place within a certain time period, and ask that you examine most carefully our new methods of communication! We rely on this conjecture for we are able at this time, to devote a whole new chapter to achieving our main objectives.

We sanction this visit and ask that you portray us in our true light, for we are an endangered species, needing much support from your world! We aim to show the way forward by coming into your jurisdiction, inviting ourselves into your space and settling any differences of opinion! We invite you to take a look at our world and we impel you to look closer, we empower you for this journey of intrigues and let you feel the power that awaits you! We need to be sure that we maintain conditions to achieve the highest capacity, and foresee an exclusion of only one person who is not ready to take on this rendezvous of souls! We have prepared a place for you all to sit with us and ask only, that you will withhold certain information until we are ready to develop the necessary criteria. We have experienced a most rewarding feedback on all occasions, and know that you will try your hardest to maintain this position of trust. We make examples of those who would cast us aside, and ask you to develop a new transcendental awareness.

We maintain peace and harmony for this regrouping of hearts and minds, drawing together in love and harmony, crossing the boundaries of the great divide. We develop clairvoyance and clairaudience on a much finer level, and ask that you secure a place for us in your heart, so that we may grow stronger and more able to define ourselves in your eyes! We remain in a state of anticipation, and reflect on events as they draw close. Please remember that we are given to believe all will be made ready, and we have programmed this event for the exact time that will give us greater reflection and strength all round! We have measured our success and will have no trouble incorporating our letters into a bona fide chronicle of achievement. Infiltrating at a new level, we ask that you obey our directions down to the last letter, in this way we will achieve greater accolades and respect worthy of your talent!

19th October 2005 – *Today I attended the funeral of a friend who died after a tragic accident. As I got ready my star friends drew close, giving some words of comfort and explaining what happens in that moment of death!* We extinguish a light and mourn the loss of a loved one. Taking your hand we create a time of peace and harmony, allowing the physical to fall away as you step out of the old and into the new, embarking on an adventure into the unknown. For those that are left behind, we offer you hope and renewed strength, for death is not the end . . . but the beginning of a new and vibrant pathway! We watch over you and bring you love and comfort, for there is no need to weep. We rejoice at the soul returned to us, we rejoice at the homecoming of this light, who has stepped out of her shroud of pain and sorrow into a state of perfect being! Take comfort and know that she is restored and welcomed home!

20th October 2005 – We need greater assistance and focus our attention on a most noble cause! We mean to exacerbate a situation that has become a trifle absurd, and we allow this new strategy to operate at a level that will encompass a variety of new alternatives. We impel you to take on board what is offered, and we mention no names but advise you to maintain discretion over what has become a most rewarding achievement in all directions! We also alleviate any stresses and strains so that we may gain advantage, maintaining equilibrium. We surrender ourselves most graciously, penetrating the mists of time as we allow a turning back of the clock to rectify past mistakes! There have been a variety of ill-conceived thoughts and emotions, which have taken their toll on one who has cause for great regret, and obeying the calling of our heart, we ask that you maintain discretion! There have also been many instances of betrayal, and we shall not assist you in the recounting of past pleasures or saintly scenarios, for we have set our sights higher!

We know that we shall maintain a higher standard of excellence, bearing witness to what has become an undeniably, overpowering love of duty and compassion for those on the Earth plane. We have forecast events that have given direction, and we mean now to usher you forward and on to greater distinction. We place before you the orb and sceptre, and ask that you ingratiate yourself with us to allow a crowning ceremony of mammoth proportions! For we are set on a course that will take us to great heights, experienced only by those who have achieved greatness by their total and utter conviction of truth and justice for all! We have conquered our demons and venture forth in all our glory. We beam ahead of you lighting the pathway! *In dream state I was shown people with lanterns and the harbour master was calling out to me with a megaphone, leading my boat safely back into harbour.*

26th October 2005 – *This evening while watching the film 'Excalibur', my left ear suddenly popped, I could feel my friends with me very strongly, urging me to take notice! At this point in the film, King Arthur was asking Merlin who his enemies were. Back came the reply – in a place you least suspect! I awoke in the early hours to help from my friends.* We censor certain articles and alleviate stresses and strains, incorporating a trust between us that shall rectify conditions. We superimpose our thoughts on yours, allowing the transference of a more sophisticated form of communication. We need to see this aspect of our channelling to commence in earnest, for we are now able to connect to what is currently available to us. We have the scope and energy to achieve on a vast scale and we know you will assist us, venturing forth to undertake this mission of excellence. We devise a new plan of action whereby we are able to manifest, in greater detail, a more reliable account of events. We feel a growing perplexity has led us astray, and we remind you to focus more clearly on issues outstanding! We will not tamper unnecessarily with conditions that are best left alone, and we devise a new infrastructure to ward off evil intent! We suppress what is no longer required, for giving in to pressure of this sort will only amplify and create conditions of anxiety!

4th November 2005 – We formalise our gift and ask that you represent us in this race against time! We have behaved in an exemplary manner, and foresee an inclusion of the highest order where we are better able to communicate. We ably assist you for this new entry into a world full of charm and grace to enable a channelling of excellence, and we depend on your résumé to complete our success! We have endeavoured to show you, in every way possible, our true nature and we ably assist you now to re-educate a world that has long forgotten expressions of endearment. Forgoing the natural charm and grace of a population, once endowed with more natural instincts, betrothed and guided by high ideals! We suppress certain information that is not relevant at this time, asking that you go with the flow, for our appetite for knowledge has grown stronger and we encourage this next bout of growth! We have maintained our connection to be with you at this time of indecision, and we press you to relax, filtering through what is needed to redress certain issues outstanding. We have remonstrated with you at times to deliver our ultimatums, and we beseech you now to grow in all directions, maintaining peace and harmony! We have developed a new method of examining data, and feel that we have gained advantage, preparing to take on the world, helping her to grow and wield her power in a universe bedazzled by her beauty! We have forsaken some key elements that need addressing, but we have maintained a greater declaration of love. Be at peace in your negotiations, and deliver the right accent on words that convey our heartfelt wishes to reinstate a world of peace and harmony!

Summarising, we convey our deepest respects and develop a new mainstream advocacy, asking that you entrench yourself in familiarising yourself with our approach. We are constantly looking for new ways of reaching that level open to us, and develop on a scale of one to ten, with an eight! There is plenty of time for improvement and we discuss ways of healing the breach. Remember we have grown at a rapid pace, and are now settling back into an even rhythm, enabling greater fortitude to recover thought processes. We believe this mammoth task has given us greater incentive to push forwards and we are delighted with your fortitude. We initiate a raw understanding of what is acceptable, and we deliver a greater and more positive aptitude for the job ahead. Be prepared for action of the highest intent for we shall overcome! Fortitude is needed as we recover what is lost, maintaining a sense of balance and ease as we sail through the next period, adjusting thought patterns to coincide with ours for greater definition. We make exceptions for those of you who are able to grasp the concept, of a world that has outgrown her strength and purpose! We salute you and wish you goodnight! *At the beginning of November I had experienced a strange, sickly feeling in my solar plexus. As I laid down to rest, I became aware of an energy moving across from the left and blending with me. I also felt a cobweb-like veil across my face, and feel this is what my friends meant by familiarising myself with their approach!*

21st November 2005 – *I had just settled down to sleep after a long and busy day, when I felt the promptings I have come to know from my star friends. I grabbed my pen and pad and listened.* We have devised a new structure of guidelines so that we may operate more swiftly. Please allow a time scale that offers no constraints, for we are able to pass on a more credulous understanding of events as we are given them from above. We supply a course of action to be taken, and ask you to be aware of an even greater desire to proceed. We are well pleased with prospects on the horizon and ask that you allow us to bring to your attention a more salubrious encounter, which will enable us to take on board more than we could have ever hoped for! We feel this extravaganza will take place in the near future, and we impel you to listen more carefully to our words as we align ourselves into position. Please accept this position of trust, for we are justly proud of all that has been done and said on our behalf! We come to your aid and help you adjust to these new measures. We hasten to add that all has been made ready for this next step forward, and we know you will do us justice! *At this point my cat sat up and looked over my shoulder, holding out her paw to touch whoever was with me!* We supply you with a new strategy, one that will give us a more definite approach, and we lend an ear to the proceedings, maintaining a deep abiding love and trust.

We set ourselves on course for our next step, and ask that you forgive our audacity for coaxing you into situations which cause unwarranted stress! We realise the strain this places on you and recognise the need to pacify, but we shall maintain our senses and counterbalance any arguments with a just and loving heart! Relaying messages of great importance, we come to you now armed with love and hope that you will pass our guidelines onto others. For these will necessitate a new formula that will govern a new uptake, introducing a wide range of frequencies! We are bound for a new world that will enable us to take part in a more, powerful understanding and acceptance of who we really are, and we venture on this journey of love and intrigue with you in tow. Please allow us one month's grace before we are adequately prepared, we maintain our respect and ask that you guard your thoughts and feelings in areas that need adjustment, for we have come a long way and intend to take you back with us! Please align yourself with us on this occasion, and we will manifest a greater bond of love and respect.

We foreclose on certain articles as preparation is needed to present a clearer picture. Investigations will be made nearer the time, and we shall manifest a pool of light to envelop you, harnessing the power and energy that is needed to convey our heartfelt thoughts and wishes for a greater union between our peoples! Please allow us to differentiate between what is needed on this level, and what is seen by some as a cumbersome exercise that needs to be monitored in greater detail. We allow a certain melancholy to overcome us, for we realise that we have kept you too long! Please remind us of your need to sleep as we get carried away with our conversations, and deny you your time of rest. *I thanked them and gratefully went back to bed.*

23rd November 2005 – *As I sat at the computer, ready to start checking my work, I felt my friends drawing very close, ready to pass on more information. This must be the new way of working they referred to recently!* We recognise that certain effects may take time to manifest in all consequence, but you will be relieved to know that we have excelled in all avenues! We shall endeavour to exclaim to all and sundry that this mission is one of extreme importance, and we vow to you now that we shall, in all areas, succumb to directives given! We make no bones about it, telling it straight, there will be mammoth repercussions that will give cause for concern, if we do not alleviate the stresses and strains that accompany most of the population! There is no need for Earth to be encumbranced in this way, for we shall maintain peace and harmony in the hearts and minds of all those, who are prepared to take on this mammoth understanding for a world destined to bring hope and joy to those with loving hearts and minds! We superimpose our thoughts on yours now, to bring you these quotations of divine joy and upliftment of spirit, which we have all experienced in one way or another.

We can occupy your mind and bring the necessary requisites in at a moment's notice, implying that all creation is given to understanding the rudimentary, and most rewarding aspect of all life forms! <u>Egocentricities have come to the fore and enveloped a world that was once believed to be the centre of the universe! We underline this and note with extreme apprehension, that all is not well in your world!</u> We come to manipulate and govern new ideas, which will reverse the common mode of thinking at your present time. We have exchanged matter and come now armed with love, delivering a whole population out of the darkness and into a more salubrious encounter of the third kind! We paralyse a nation that has brought destruction and desolation on a gigantic scale! Overcoming these traumas will bring great relief, and harnessing a new form of energy, we rely on one another to complete this mission of excellence. We vow to you now that we shall take on board a most enhancing form of stewardship that will create beyond all earthly bounds, a most noble and exemplary, divine reclamation! We surge ahead and onto finer structures of independence.

Welling up . . . we wait in the wings to make our entrance! We are finely tuned and prepared for take off, standing strong and firm, enunciating a most beautiful and bountiful collection of words that will bring a certain eloquence to the proceedings, displaying our integrity! We have reached the point of no return, and are amazed at how little a difference there is between us. For some time now we have known of a more substantial workforce that has given us great delight! There has been extraordinary feedback that we have come to accept as rudimentary, but we have been given to understand there will be a greater take up of services in the near future, giving us more reason to suspect that we shall overcome in growing numbers. Please allow this framework to govern in a greater capacity than before, for we shall have further cause to congratulate ourselves on what has become a most fascinating expedition! We rely on sources to intervene at times, but on the whole we have found this experience to be most rewarding. In all eventualities, we shall expect a more tenacious strain of understanding that will belie belief! Please accept these new measures, and we shall experience a greater and more powerful acceptance of all before us. We entreat you now to understand our motives, for we are governed by our desire to create a world of beauty and peace, so that all may register in harmony.

24th November 2005 – With great reluctance, we advise of further transactions that may be taken to avoid reclamation of Earth! We are in no way exempt from flattery, and feel there has been a going back to the 'old ways' among many on the Earth plane! We feel impelled to scrutinise evidence as it is presented to us, for we are then able to adjust and amend all areas of discussion, allowing a time period to reassess what is needed for our further growth. We depend on you now to realign yourself with us on this and many other occasions, where we are able to assist those on Earth who have need of our services! We exchange patterns of thinking and initiate new boundaries that will cover, to a certain extent, multiple choices, and we accept full responsibility for our actions, depending on one another to set the record straight! We move forward slowly and carefully, enabling us to assess at each step of the way, and we know you will share with us in exclaiming to all and sundry that we have reached a point where we can say wholeheartedly, we have made a most momentous declaration! Expressing our views to the people of Earth in such a way, that will serve to initiate a new and vibrant understanding of all before us! We have entreated you to share with us in a new world of love, joy and peace, and we know with these good intentions, we are heralding in a new awareness, governed by the heart of a nation impressed to observe more regular contact with one another, sharing balance and harmony on all levels. We entreat you now to listen well to your own hearts and minds, for we are calling you to pastures new, and those who hearken to the call will experience a deep sense of joy and wonder that cannot be expressed in worldly terms!

26th November 2005 – We are now able to recover our sense of proprietary, enabling a sense of wellbeing, and wholeheartedly condoning our actions in this controversial, yet exceptional recording! We analyse what is given and purposefully endeavour to maintain a sense of direction. We have spoken in the past of various agencies that have taken control of proceedings; we now give full rein of approval for connection of services! We know there has been a misappropriation of energies that are not only excessive, but counterproductive to our needs at this time: we sense a growing apprehension and ask you to transcribe our words for the edification of those in need! We make examples of those who have instigated a tireless campaign of insubordination, and we exercise control in these areas, asking that you stand back and allow us through! Believe us when we say, we have never encountered such a vile and corrupt society, since the beginning of the Roman Empire! We have forgiven those of you who tread on the toes of a wanton society, and we beg you to reconsider all deals and pacts which are erroneous! We reconsider and justify what is necessary to mount a new campaign of joy and peace among men. We now take hold of an entirely new scenario and believe we have accepted the post of honorary adjudicator! It is not right to accept this post unless you fully understand the extent of your mission! We know this takes us to the bounds of incredulity, but suffice it to say that we have ventured into unknown territory and advise a certain sense of decorum! Attitudes have become perplexing to say the least, and we advise against any form of inappropriate action. We forgive you your trespasses and insist that you take back with you a fertile image of all that you have learned on this journey!

Please remind us of your true nature and we will allow you a tentative step in the right direction. A backward glance will allow you a last look at what you have left behind . . . a world of sadness and sorrow, irrespective of all that has been lavished upon her to retain that spark of love, hidden from the human race by their own greed for power! We alter the course of destination to bring you a little nearer to us, bringing you back on track. We invite you on this merry-go-round of intrigue, and defy the law of gravity to expound our theories. We have developed and grown at a vast rate, uncovering many views and opinions that have enabled us to make comparisons. We vouch now for your safety, and ask you to climb aboard the 'Marrakech Express'! We take you to the stars and beyond, delivering to you by hand all that is necessary for your journey. Abide with us and we will reclaim what is rightfully yours, a new life with new measures of understanding, governed only by love!

7th December 2005 – *I couldn't sleep and went downstairs to make some tea. Sitting quietly, I felt a blending of energies.* We become as one voice. There is a great need at this time to deliver ultimatums! It has become apparent of late, for the necessity of further directives in a government, so disposed to strategies of a devious nature, that we endow the population of Earth with the common sense to step forward and be counted! We have become a nation of rebel rousers, seeking not for truth, but to cultivate a breed with animalistic tendencies! We shine our light on certain discrepancies which are causing stagnation, and we now delve deeper to interpret a new stream of thought, which has become malleable in every sense. We superimpose our thoughts on yours to devise a new and prosperous alternative; action has been taken to address the situation we find ourselves in, and we believe we are responsible in being negligent to a degree! We have overridden and governed this new development, and ask that you bear with us while we examine what is necessary to overcome this complex scenario. We believe the time has come for a much more serviceable proposition to be made, and we have forecast this event as just over the horizon. We beckon you forward, and help you achieve the necessary formula to make this our worthiest cause yet. Please believe us when we say, that this has been the most rewarding encounter, and we believe we have encompassed a whole nation, captured in our mind's eye to develop further! We have access to a wide variety of data, and have held many conferences to undertake this mission of excellence. Be it known now in our two worlds, of a vast and growing sense of propriety that will give cause for celebration in the near future!

We have laid down rules and regulations to abide by, and receive in a certain Latin quarter, a most majestic approach to what was once ridiculed, now held in the highest esteem by those of you who have thrown down the gauntlet! We retrieve what is necessary to set you on your feet and protect you from afar. We welcome you here this night and detect a growing apprehension that will give cause for regret! We have been as truthful as we can over various projects, and feel that the time has come for our principles to be endorsed in one way or another, reflecting the new standards raised. We impel you to look closer at what is giving cause for concern, and we allow for a new strategy to develop as we proceed with an air of caution! We rely on you to upset negotiations of a dubious nature, and in this we must take our hat off to you! There is plenty to sing and dance about for this new knowledge will come pouring in from different directions, bringing with it a deep contentment and achievement of considerable worth! We allow you this moment to reflect on what has been a mammoth success, and tremendous spiritual growth in all directions. We understand the dilemma this puts you in, and ask that you relay our messages while participating with us, to a great extent, on a new level. We have become aware of a growing urge to rediscover what has been a most sensitive episode, and we would like to thank you for all your input! Remarkably, we have become accustomed to these wave patterns, making it extremely difficult to participate on other levels. We accept this energy pattern with extreme thankfulness, and appreciate this coming together. Our good wishes go with you this night, and we vow to uncover further truths, which we shall convey when the time is right! We assist you in your writings and venture to say, that we have incorporated a structure of love to be handed down to each generation, giving balance and harmony.

Chapter 5
Redemption

12th December 2005 – We have survived the holocaust and engulf you now in flames of redemption! Prepare yourselves . . . we come ready and armed with the tool of love for this shall vanquish, at a far greater rate, all hostilities encased in the bosom of mankind. We demand a heavy price to pay and we devolve a whole population that has given itself to the most pompous form of ridicule! We regard this kind of apoplexy, as being the most wanton form of disregard for human life! We take action and inspire you to take a new direction, which will bring you all closer to the heart of an entirely new perspective, one that has given us immense control over lower natures! We come armed with this new brand of eloquence to reinstate those of you, who have given us the utmost dedication and most heartfelt motives. Helping the population of this kindergarten on Earth, unfold to a revelation that has become second nature to us! We believe that we have led the population of Earth onto this roundabout of love, which has touched each and every one of us with the most moving expressions of a most bountiful love, unequalled anywhere in our universe!

This has become a most passionate and thought-provoking time for all, and we endeavour to save the most daring and challenging climax until last! We shall instigate a new boundary that will enable an even greater and more perplexing encounter, which we feel appropriate in the foreseeable future. There is a far greater need now to take on board this most exclusive framework, for we are considered by some to be the 'Master's of the Universe', amid speculation that we have agreed a most noble role in the education of mankind! We take this very seriously, speculating that in a year's time, we will have encouraged and nurtured many of you into new roles of extreme importance, gratifying a deep inner urge to resume our connections with one another, and devoting more and more time to encouraging one another in this next step forward! We propel you onward, endorsing all that has been given in glowing accuracy. We supply a new course of action to be taken in the next month or two, and ask that you now bear with us while we interpret our next step forward. This will be a most rewarding time for you all, but there is a great necessity to stand back and let us work with you, in whichever way is most suited to your needs!

We come to allow you this moment of self preservation that comes with the territory of developing a new civilisation. We bare our souls and ask you to share with us in a new future that will give each and every one of you, a most exclusive and powerful formula for initiating a growing mass of data recall! This will manipulate those centres within you, that are highly charged with information and recorded in the cells of your very being, and we heighten this awareness, allowing you to transmit back to us what is needed to recall you home! We have powerful transmitters that can interpret a wide range of elusive thought patterns, and with these we can detect what is needed to reconstitute a most prolific, and thought-provoking alternative to a growing, distressful time in mankind's evolution! We believe the time has come to forego pleasures of the flesh, and set course for a most monumental discovery of a new world, where all may live in peace and harmony!

We transcend all areas of transgression and obey the dictates of the heart, coming forward now to impel you to listen to our words. For we have seen with our own eyes the destruction of planet Earth, and we come in droves to evacuate the globe, taking you back with us to a new destination of invaluable success! We have grown extremely close to those of you, who have vanquished your doubts and fears as to our motives, for we are the most loving of companions who have always had your best interests at heart. We never believed for a moment that you would leave us to our fate, of becoming a race of people who would vanquish our dragons, only to be exposed to a macabre form of annihilation! We express our doubts and fears for a most obnoxious society, and reel in those of you who have expressed your concern for the majority of your planet. We know it will take time to manipulate your growth, and a new terminology that can express what is being achieved, even as we speak! We are compelled to understand this frequency, as being a new mode of transport that can alleviate suffering on a massive scale. We channel now a new, more positive energy to surpass all others, and we impel you to move closer and closer to that point of contact, which is being governed by the most natural force of love. We take the time and trouble to underpin all constructive thought forms with this most indelible, reconstitution of an entire population! For we are governed by our desires to reach each and every one of you, asking you to march with us, heralding in a new and loving connection between two worlds that have grown closer together in every way! We believe this time has given us greater insight into each and every one of you on the Earth plane, and we deliver to you now this ultimatum! Be prepared to forsake what was once your home, and let us lead you all into the sunset of a most rewarding completion!

13th December 2005 – *I have been asked to read out something at our spiritual group's candle service, but feel the content of the last message was not suitable.* We superimpose our thoughts on yours my friend to make amends, we have allowed certain material to be passed onto you, which we recommend to be used in a certain context only, for we have need of a more productive and volatile component to indulge the masses! We deliver to you now a most suitable essay that will allow us to proceed with a more appropriate study. We have exchanged places many times and we now proceed to take you along a certain highway that will govern a more purposeful strategy than we have encountered before. We feel the timing is right to declare certain practices, and we feel this will incorporate greater measures being taken to overcome this whole scenario. Please believe us when we say, that you have more than amply conveyed our thoughts and wishes, overcoming a complex state of mind to convey our words to your contempories! We believe we have overcome enormous barriers to take you on board, and we feel an overwhelming desire to carry forward with what is a necessary fusion of minds.

To be read out at tonight's meeting: There are many of you here tonight that have given your time to us, and without comparison, we would like to thank you all for the kindness and cheer that you have sent out to the world as a whole! Many of you have taken on board, what has been an extremely thought-provoking element of trust, we note that some of you have even obeyed narrative given, and forsaken a more conventional life to become one with us in your studies! We have taken on a whole nation of revellers, who have misjudged us on several occasions, only to be targeted for even more discussion! We have evolved from a single cell at a complete and utter disadvantage, but we remained on Earth to become known as 'Time Travellers' of great distinction! We have foraged our way through the universe, and are now residing in a place of outstanding beauty and gentleness of spirit. We ask you to join us in the not too distant future, and we are prime examples of how the human spirit can survive abominable disasters, for time after time we were subjected to abominations beyond all recollection of the human mind!

We superimpose our thoughts on yours to tell it straight, and we ask you now to superimpose your thoughts on ours, to allow a discussion of sorts, which will clarify points that need to be raised! We have for example, followed this being on many journeys and excursions into the unknown, and taken great delight in accompanying her on these trips! We have learned together what is necessary to save mankind from great despair, and we are here now for all of you – to maintain your life forms and to save your kind from total extinction!

We recollect that in the past, there have been many notorious eruptions, and these have given us grave concerns as to whether or not, you can overcome this most haphazard situation that you all find yourselves in! We need to prepare ourselves and those around us . . . to expect the unexpected! We never said it would be easy, and there are many roads to be walked before we can have a calming influence on those advocates, who will step into the foreground and show the way for others to follow! We subject you to the most powerful rays of love, and incorporate in all of this a most notable success, for we have ventured on this journey with love in our hearts for you all!

There is growing speculation on the horizon, that we may maintain this love a hundredfold, giving vent to our feelings that can never be expressed in just words alone. For we have vowed to God and all living things, that we have given our all to be with you here on Earth, and we justly comment on a few measures that need to be exercised, to make this endeavour the most fruitful account in man's history on Earth! We forgo certain measures that are in keeping with animosity, for we intend to take you all down a different pathway where we shall all have our say! We speak to you now in tones of love, generating this most powerful anecdote out into the universe, where it will be encapsulated and turned into the most magnificent kingdom that defies all expression! Suffice it to say that we will come together as one people, rejoicing in greatest measure for all that has been achieved. We believe that we have come together at exactly the right time in your history, to turn this most cataclysmic event into a joyous occasion that will turn you around to look us in the face! We shall become ourselves in the truest sense, and we know that around the corner is a most magnificent role for us all to play, which will enable this to happen on a grand scale!

Before retiring for the night I received a few more words. We have deliberately maintained an area of discretion over certain prospects looming on the horizon, and we now enable you to proceed at a more leisurely pace. Please allow yourself time to encapsulate what is needed to rectify conditions at home. We are looking forward to our time spent with you in your new arena, and will endeavour to show you what is necessary to target your concerns. *I'm starting my own spiritual group in the New Year, and feel comforted to know they will be around to help.*

16th December 2005 – *The moon is full tonight and right overhead. Before going to bed I went outside to see if I could spot the constellation of Pleiades, but there was too much cloud and I was not sure which direction to look in. I felt my friends with me straight away and knew that they needed to speak with me. We* have realised our true potential, pushing forward now on to new realms of delight. We negotiate further patterns of understanding, expressing ourselves with enormous scope! We transcend the inevitable – reaching new conclusions, governed only by an overwhelming desire to succeed! We discover new ways of healing the breach, alluding to this most difficult period of adjustment, and refocusing on what has become a total malfunction of attitudes and desires! We approve this new action, giving you clearance for a much desired course of action, and we endeavour to align you with us strategically, to allow for even more notification of what to expect in the next quarter. We have come at the very time when Earth is in greatest need, and we help you to overcome a malfunction of the highest and most important in man's history. We therefore endeavour to make this most worthwhile trip down memory lane, and exert some pressure on those of you who are here for the journey of a lifetime, in keeping with many notorious episodes that have led us to this moment in time! We do have for example, a most appropriate action to be taken, that will govern a broader understanding of what is expected of us in the days and weeks ahead. We shall by all means, access remedies that have not been taken for years, and we mean to move into a far more superior time warp than we have ever known before! This will bring with it a grander and more fortuitous expression of love divine, and we reclaim our rightful place among the stars!

Please present yourself to us in the highest state of grace and favour, for we are well armed for this exodus! We take you to great lengths, meting out what is necessary to achieve resounding success in all matters, and we extend you the courtesy of stepping out of yourselves, allowing you the opportunity to grow in all directions, surprising even yourself with glowing accuracy! We impel you to take heed of our words, and question your ability to set down, in true splendour, all that is required for this most splendid mission. We rely on one another to achieve optimum results, and wish you to take note of what we deem appropriate, for there is far greater need now to obey your instincts in all areas. Lurking on the horizon are many obstacles to stand in your way, but we shall make a stand and send them packing! Depend on us to forestall any arrangements that could cause stagnation, for we are bent on attaining our heart's desire and will not be led astray. We have come for the duration and will not be put off or cast aside! There is great need at this time to incorporate a deep sense of shame and ill ease, for what has been presented to us in the last few weeks or so, and we have taken on board a growing and decisive battle with, what was once considered, a most beleaguered generation of half-wits!

We shall endeavour to condense these recordings into a more compatible and energetic life form, so that we may resume communication in a livelier format, relaying our news more succinctly! We shall manifest greater control in proceedings that are giving cause for concern, and please believe us when we say; there has been a massive rendition of services that will allow us greater manifestation when the time is right! Be prepared to launch our greatest weapon of defence – an illustrious form of self control that will enable the masses to drink from the cup of love and kindness! We shall have our say and venture forth in all our glory to be with you and yours, incorporating a greater measure of trust and deepest respect. Please allow us to come forward and assist you in your new venture, for we shall permit a certain framework to be given that will compensate you for your lack of expertise in these matters! We superimpose our thoughts on yours and mean to forge ahead, and we now know that all is expected to take place in a month or two! We endeavour to show you what is needed, and a dedication of services is recommended that will lead to further discoveries. We impel you to listen more closely . . . we align ourselves with you to allow a deeper bonding, making this possibility a reality in every sense of the word! Please help us to reconnect at a new and vibrant level, helping us to achieve all in glowing efficacy!

Relentlessly we travel on into the future, regarding all we see with the utmost joy and conviction of a far greater and most rewarding advancement as we become one and the same! We travel forward together along this road and allow a far greater delivery, uncovering more and more information in an ever flowing stream of knowledge, feeding and nurturing the intellect, which in turn feeds the soul! We pass on this knowledge in small doses to be utilised at your convenience, enabling a more productive thought form to emerge as we travel together, towards our goal of greater understanding for all. We mean to impel you further underground, for we have many issues to resolve that need studying in greater detail, and in the future we can expect further activities coming to the fore, which may encumbrance your mind to a certain degree! We will need to be more careful in these areas and ask that you allow us to accompany you in these situations, as there is need of closer scrutiny to recognise what it is we are facing up to! These harsh realities are necessary to recover former identities, and we march you along to uncover them one by one! We believe that this mission will give us even wider scope to fulfil our main objectives, and we relate to you now all that is needed for you to grow in our love.

18th December 2005 – *I lay down to sleep after a long day and felt my friends draw very close, but I was so tired that I drifted off to sleep. An hour later I woke suddenly with words forming in my mind. As I sat ready for communication, I could sense an energy coming very close to mine in a loving and harmonious connection.* We are impelled to give you notice of further deliveries! We expose many of you on the Earth plane who develop and grow in our love; we have need of you now and amply provide you with enough information to proceed along this causeway of love. We have misread thoughts on certain ambiguities, and profoundly accept our resignation to a most disturbing proposition! We expel different notions and carefully assess the situation from afar. Let us take note of what is available to us – an extraordinary product of 'imagination', pronounced and as individual as we can plausibly accept within this short space of time! We endeavour to relive a short episode in our lives so that we may assess, with remarkable accuracy, what is necessary to maintain this era of grace and favour. We attempt to explain ourselves more fully to allow a rendition of services. We can expect to forestall an even bigger bout of industrial action, and we feel impelled at this time to multiply what is needed for further growth. We depend on one another to come forward, and allow you this time to actuate a reconstruction of all necessary items!

Please believe us when we say, that there has never before in all the annals of history, been such a momentous discovery, and we amplify this huge success to enable us to reach the boundaries of the universe! We bend to salute you, and ask that you take the time to execute this most noble role which we ask you to play! We revise certain conditions and maintain a certain grace and favour, allowing the proceedings to go more smoothly. We allow a further delay to ensure we get the message across more clearly, and we recognise the need for discretion while we change the format, stretching our boundaries to deliver the right accent on words. We need to assess the situation step by step, and ask you to put aside what is no longer required, to actuate this most moving account of all that has governed our manner of being. We do understand the need for further revelations, and ask that you keep silent on these issues until we have further feedback! There is a need to tread softly until we have initiated a contract, for we believe this will give us fuller advantage in obtaining our hearts desire. We treasure these moments and ask that you help us in our analysis, for we have governed this most prolific event to unravel and protect you from harm! We deliberately bypass this situation until we can rectify what is needed to grow in our love.

There will be times when we shall accomplish a coming together with greater revelations, and we take stock now of what is necessary to complete our deliverance. We obey all directives and ask that you surrender to our ultimatums, we are in no mood to accept anything but the best, and we impel you to take heed of all that is said! We now take our leave and ask that you will monitor our conversations, giving direction to an even greater display of talents worthy of your discretion, and with the certainty of greater displays in closer proximity to one another! We take the time to understand what is necessary for our further growth, and vow to you now, that we shall leave no stone unturned in our quest for truth and justice for all mankind! *I'm now being shown the older brother from a duo called 'Journey South', who were runners up in the X-Factor singing competition. He is dressed as a Roman soldier and is saluting me with a fist to his chest as he backs out of vision! I wondered why I was being shown this person and before making my way back to bed, I opened the window to look out at the stars. They were shining so brightly and to my amazement, high in the sky to the south was the cluster of stars I've been searching for called the Pleiades . . . my eyes were drawn to them immediately! I grabbed the binoculars and could see, quite clearly, six of the large white stars that are called the 'Seven Sisters'! In Greek mythology they represent the seven daughters of Atlas and Pleione who were pursued by Orion, and were turned into a constellation to escape him. I was as excited as a small child on Christmas Eve and couldn't sleep for ages! Thank you so much my friends for pointing out your home to me!*

20ᵗʰ December 2005 – We prepare for you an inventory of procedures, laid down to help you observe what is necessary for our restoration and harmonic convergence. We apply ourselves, surrendering to a greater, detailed analysis and we measure our achievements, knowing that in the end is a job well done! We have the power to uncover greater probabilities, and we know that you would want us to advocate the nurturing of this most, powerful anthology, which is deemed by our friends and neighbours, as the most nourishing theological discovery the world has ever known! We empower you now to take on board these sensitive issues, for there are outstanding measures to be taken that will give fortitude in the days ahead. We have accustomed ourselves to these measures being taken and deliberately ask you to stand back, allowing us to deliver, with greater accuracy, all that is needed for the completion of our book! We have certain principles that we must stand by, and we ask you to obey your thoughts and feelings on this subject closest to your heart. We desire you to proceed in all earnest and aptly require more attention to detail, asking you to relay our messages in such a way, that we can conquer over adversity on all levels. We require a course of action to be taken and impel you to take notice, with all your heart and soul, what it is we are offering to the people of Earth!

We are governed by our desires to help you to grow, and we achieve a most worthy form of governorship. We have not taken this offer of consolidation lightly and accept, on all levels, most humbly! We realise a new strength as our two worlds become one, blending and growing with divine ease and splendour. We have allowed this blending of energies to deliver greater accent on what is needed for a deep recovery, and maintenance of all we hold most dear! Reverently we step forward and make ourselves known . . . we come armed with love, a love so pure as to melt the hearts of all who approach, and we transcend our wildest dreams, handing ourselves over to the most sublime and greatest calling ever known! We have developed you to such a vast extent, that we have exceeded even our own boundaries, and we enclose you now in our love and joy at this Christmas time on Earth! We have obeyed our hearts in this, and come to envelop you in a cloak of safety, protecting you from the knocks and blows coming your way! We have allowed for reasonable access in our deliberations, and take you to that place of complete and utter sanctuary, giving you time to rest and recuperate! We have taken on board more than enough to give us the final seclusion that is warranted for those who have taken their final vows. We know you take these very seriously, and we impress on you now the need to sanctify these visits, so that we may better understand the need for seclusion!

We are able to deliver further revelations, for we have taken on board a new form of clinical trial to eradicate wastage, and we believe we have managed, to a lesser degree, to overcome our fears for the future! We have taken on board a growing mass of data which causes an overload on occasions, necessitating intervals of rest! We believe this action is necessary and back you up with an abundant stream of energy, being relayed even as we speak! We delve deeper and deeper into the maelstrom of events on the horizon, and take you to that place where we shall recover a most rewarding feedback of enormous proportions. We reinstate you and deliver the final remedy that will extinguish all doubts and fears, for we are at that critical stage of our journey, where we must endeavour to portray our friends in their true light, unmasking the future for all to see! We have spoken of this to many in your world, and we have taken on board numerous requests to visit our new destination!

22nd December 2005 – *I have been voicing the doubts that I know many people will have, as to the authenticity of these beings from other worlds, and to their having our best interests at heart!* We have developed an overactive stream of thought, and manipulate into order what is necessary to overcome this most extraordinary feat of imagination! We impel you further to reorganise patterns of thinking, so that we are better able to express ourselves most nobly. We allow this discourse to take place, so that we may incorporate our latest measures of achievement. We know this has been a most wonderful and powerful concept, and what is considered by some to be an over-zealous, but fruitful passage in the history of mankind! We accept that this has indeed, been the most powerful anecdote ever recorded, but we are also aware that greater trouble has been taken to fulfil the prophecy, of a far greater love than man has ever known! We proceed to take you down this pathway of love and light, enveloping all mankind in a most powerful glow of love divine, all love excelling . . . love from Heaven to Earth brought down!

We initiate new growth on Earth that will take man to that point – indescribable in physical terms! We light your pathway and take you to the top of the mount, surveying all before you, bathed in complete and utter dedication to the upliftment of all mankind! We raise you to the heights and intercept only to bring you news of further ramifications, for we are able to assist you in this new growth, and enlighten each and every one of you with the most rewarding and thought-provoking state of trance! We are able by the thought process, to envelop all mankind in this most powerful ray of divine love, and in so doing we are able to amply suppress thoughts of a lower nature! We are aware that there are many among you who have been exposed to thoughts of a dubious nature, and we rely now on all of you, to refrain from allowing this governing body to hold sway over your thoughts and emotions! We are gaining advantage every day in every way, and we allow you access to those points on Earth where we have installed greater and more productive motions of light, focusing on the heart centre to alleviate all mistrust and misappropriation of energy levels!

We allow you now an even broader discussion of events planned for the evolution of mankind. We express ourselves with the uncertainty that has governed us from the start, and we now deliver to you for the purpose of greater clarification, notions that have led us astray in previous encounters with the Earth plane! We have initiated further clandestine meetings to effect a reconstruction of thought forms, needed to allay suspicion of misrepresentation. We have therefore, decided to abandon all dedications of a less imperious nature, to allow through what is necessary at this time! We have allowed in all instances, a most delicate state of trance to alleviate all manner of stress. We have no wish to cause anxiety of any kind, but are aware that in the future, there will be far greater need to abolish, what may be considered by some to be, the most natural desire to stay on Earth!

We have superimposed our thoughts on yours, allowing this percolation of energies to manifest in greater strength, and we allow this reconditioning of energies to take place, presenting with greater accuracy our ideal theories for a new world! We impel you to take note of all that is given, and we empower you now for the journey ahead, taking you to that place that has so far eluded the majority of your planet! We instigate a trial period to ascertain political correctness, for there are functions that need to be performed before we can accurately take you to that place of astuteness. We have raised you up from your doom and gloom to prevent a most obnoxious form of degeneration and captivity of the mind! We prevent these tragedies from occurring in a world that has grown accustomed to malfunction at a raised level. We endow you now with gentleness of spirit, and pave the way for greater fortitude and inspiration of the highest intent. We allow our offspring to relieve us of our shortcomings, and envelop you in a most powerful formula of love that the world has ever known!

We submit ourselves to the most exquisite formula entitled to a race of people, and we enlighten you all, urging you to obey the dictates of your heart! We forecast emancipation for each and every one of you . . . a freeing of the soul from all encumbrances that cause friction and retardation! For we have evaluated the possibility of a new term of office, which regards even the mostly lowly of you, on a par with the most high! This reorganisation will be incorporated into every structure of civilisation, and we shall see in greater instances, reform being utilised in every sense. We vow to one and all, that we shall measure each and every function until we have displayed an inventory of all proceedings, manifesting a cooperation of all and sundry! We delay certain prospects that loom on the horizon, and ask that you cooperate with us at all times to increase the selection of desired outcomes. We manipulate your growth to coincide with a most fruitful episode, and we note your enthusiasm as we travel this highway of love. We have taken the time and trouble to evaluate our success, and propel you forward now to instigate a more powerful surge of regeneration. We know of no other way to express our love, and venture to say that we have experienced the most rewarding feedback from our adventures with the human race!

We allow now for further revelations as we stand in the way of future follies, which have been attributed to a lack of dedication and the governing of a less decorous mode of thinking! For example, we have regularly debated our thoughts on the subject of planetary union, but we have suppressed a more becoming attitude by preventing our genes from expressing, what is truly a most momentous discovery! We enlighten you all as to our whereabouts in the heavens, for we have obeyed our intellect in all things and we now come before you to compare notes. We have decided on this course of action, to allow all negativity to be dissolved in labyrinths full of deceit and lies! *At this point I was shown underground tunnels full of spider webs.* We have succumbed to many notions of ill health, but now instil in you the idea of life eternal! We depend on one another to get this message across, and we relay our thoughts to you now across the great divide, expressing ourselves in greatest wonderment and joy, obeying instructions down to the last letter!

We have approached this crossroads with extreme caution, and we are now able to express ourselves with greater eloquence, reconstituting to a greater part what is necessary to achieve victory on a grand scale. We realise that the scope of this has been immense, and we vow now to lay down a plan of action that will gain even greater victory over defeat, planning a course of action that will take us to the citadel and beyond! We take refuge in the fact that we have obeyed the law of the land, knowing we have greater powers of observation that will enable an accurate and more powerful resuscitation – delivering us from the brink! We have manifested in glowing colours, all that is necessary to save us from despair, and we will show you the way forward and onto the land of the living! We have supplied you with enough concrete evidence and inspire you now to take on the challenge of a lifetime. We proceed in all earnest to rectify conditions brought on by the stark realities we face. There has been constructive criticism which has led to an overpowering feeling of neglect, but we tell you now that this is not the case! We are here for the duration and we have greater understanding now, of measures to be taken, than at any other time in man's history on Earth!

We have foreclosed on what has become a most haphazard situation and we shield you from further involvement, allowing us access to new material that will shake the belief systems of the entire globe! We have known for centuries of this fusion, interpreting our hopes and dreams for a more passive paradox, and leading up to the most overpowering chain of events! We have expressed ourselves in a way that can be understood by all who venture outside to see for themselves, what is in the air. A glowing chariot of fire awaits you to take you to the heavens in all its splendour – a magnificent cage of light! Unrepentant we carry you into the night, developing greater assistance! We have forgone pleasures of the flesh to relay more accurately what is given, and we need now this incentive of love to drive us forwards! We feel compelled to deliver a more profound understanding than can be explained in a simple format, for we have uncovered what can only be described, as a tremendous surge of irrefutable love!

27th December 2005 – *Tonight we watched a film called 'The Minority Report' with Tom Cruise, where thought patterns were read by sensitives and passed onto officials, who then arrested the would-be murderers before the crimes were actually committed! I felt my friends with me very strongly during this film and later in the evening received the following information.* A reconnection of services is imminent, and we rely on each other to maintain a connection of the highest calibre. We surrender ourselves to the cause, and instigate measures whereby we have enough unadulterated resources to see us through a difficult period. We need to adjust our thought patterns accordingly and witness the next stage in our evolution, for we have governed from afar what is necessary to overcome a magnitude of indescribable horror! We have reclaimed what is rightfully ours, allowing no misconception as to the appropriate action to be taken. We have issued warrants for the arrest of those who have succumbed to the most wanton behaviour, and ask that you forestall even more inappropriate thought patterns from being released!

Prepare yourself for action, for there is every need to reconsider your next step forwards. We empower you for this journey and take you thirty leagues under the sea; here we will recover what has been lost! There is a need for absolution and we express ourselves most amicably, tending to one another's rhythms as we ignite the flame of love that has slumbered for so long! Please remember our times together on Earth long ago, for we have been of some consequence! Mistrusted and brought to further serve our term of imprisonment, we conducted ourselves in a manner that denied greater aspects of self control, witnessing the end of a long line of conquerors. We violated the laws of nature and found an extreme, and most formidable judgement was necessary to cleanse a long line of perpetrators! We have rectified this scenario and have need of further discussions. Allowing for a certain misjudgement of character, we devise a new role to be played out, offsetting the prejudices of those who come in torment . . . those in deeper need! We repent, and deliver to you now a more substantial request for mercy!

29th December 2005 – We have behaved impeccably in all things and propel you towards greater enlightenment. We navigate our way in space, allowing more beneficial studies of the human race, and we are endowed with enough information to help us proceed with the highest instruction. A masquerade of challenging thought patterns assail us, and we know that you have experienced a down pouring of anguish on all levels! This is a necessary adjustment that will mark the end of one phase and the beginning of another, we have matched like for like and issue new guidelines to achieve more revolutionary ideals. We postpone certain events so that we may monitor, in greater detail, all input and output of frequencies. We have reached a plateau of sorts and ask you to memorise, on a greater scale, all radical changes needed for battle to commence. We idealise a certain time framework where we can come together on the same level, executing very necessary procedures for a grand plan of action to recover what is rightfully ours! We implement certain procedures and allow a turning down of many other forms of contact, for we have allowed in this connection, a more natural study of your time spent on Earth. Please help us to protect our sense of values, for we come at a time of absolute power in a generation of mindless, sensation seekers! We develop a more sensitive and thought-provoking clairvoyance, for we are the unseen and we march forward now to claim our prize . . . the end of the human race as we know it, and the beginning of a new era of freedom for all!

We have been governed by a nation of halfwits, and we explore now a more positive future for all those of you, who aspire to a more dominant thought process! We propel you forward in the dead of night to overcome all misgivings, and to nurture that love that hovers within your very being. We will light your way, and we are inclined at this time to mention that we come armed with the greatest power of all . . . the power of love! We are known for our demonstrations of eloquence, and supervise now a new strength that will better help you to understand our motives. For we are 'Angels of Light', sent on a mission of mercy to forge a new and powerful collaboration with those on Earth! We are a 'Master Race' of beings of light, who have come to save mankind from despair, and we know with hindsight that we come prepared to take on this mammoth task, assisting the population of Earth in their recovery!

This operation was planned many light years ago, and we have forwarded onto your planet the necessary contacts which have enabled this discussion! We have sustained this species and have endeavoured, on all counts, to exercise control of the highest intent, enabling us to maintain a frequency that would allow us access to the heart of the population on Earth! We have maintained this frequency, and advise you now to take control of proceedings, allowing us to gain entry for a more provocative encounter of the 'third kind'! We have allowed this access to usher in a new awareness and we govern the proceedings from afar, asking you now to confirm your wishes to accept this position of responsibility! We ponder on these thoughts and wishes for an entire nation, and ask you now to consider your next move, for we are amply rewarded with your love. We retreat now and assist you for this grand connection!

31ˢᵗ December 2005 – *Today my husband helped clear out the spare bedroom to make space for my new spiritual group. I took down the curtains and blinds for cleaning, and reclaimed my meditation chairs that had been stored away. The room has taken on a new vibrancy, and I'm so looking forward to further revelations in 2006! At midnight, I looked out of the window and my gaze rested on the small cluster of stars where my friends reside. I felt a mixture of contentment and excitement for what is to come!*

1ˢᵗ January 2006 – We develop the thought processes necessary to bring action on a greater scale, and we have prepared a connection that will enable our thought processes to be actioned at a higher level. There are instances when we will be able to connect at a more vibrant level to bring you an even greater understanding, and we have augmented what is necessary to achieve production of a higher energy source! This has been recommended to alleviate pressure on all concerned, and we realise there is a far greater need at this time to measure our progress. We have alternative measures to fall back on, and this will release a new structure that can be incorporated into a new regime if so required. We have spoken before of more natural methods of reinstating family values, and we achieve, to some degree, a finer advancement in attitudes.

We have expressed ourselves in a way that has given us credence in higher circles, and we feel the pull of paranormal activity, displaying all we have experienced on this incredible journey! We have instructed new measures to be taken that will bring resounding success, and we alter the destination, allowing you more time. We devote ourselves to the cause, underlining what is necessary to maintain equilibrium, gaining advantage in every way! We have need of further action to be taken, and recommend drawing back in favour of a more beneficial strategy that will allow us greater expertise. We hereby declare that we shall have greater impact, and we advise most strongly, a turning back! *I feel this may refer to me withdrawing from my old spiritual group, which starts again in a week's time after the Christmas break! I have thoroughly enjoyed the time spent with them and feel disappointed that I must leave. However, I realise my friends have my best interests at heart and accept that now is the time to move on!*

2ⁿᵈ January 2006 – We compel you to stop and think, for we of supreme intellect come prepared and armed with love to take you to that place of complete and utter dedication! We express ourselves with the utmost joy to be working alongside you in this new venture, and ask you now to stand back

– for we deliver, in no uncertain terms, recollections of our time spent with you in other lands! We come at a time when all is made available to us, and we free you from all hindrances, allowing this new growth to supersede all other forms of enticement. The tenderest love awaits you in this 'Temple of Light', and we forsake no others to be here with you now, relaying our messages across the great divide. Please spend a little more of your time in reconnaissance, we also need greater discretion to precede our every move. We need to be able to look back and know that we have prepared a safe pathway for others to follow, and we need discretion also to maintain services of the highest calibre! It remains to be seen if we can accept all the challenges laid at our feet, but we have immeasurable strength to forge ahead, and deny you no access to frontiers before you. We have accessed deeper, darker avenues and have noted your worthiness, and talent for spotting what is necessary to overcome pleasures of the flesh!

We have vowed to one another our allegiance to the cause – time after time, battle after battle in ages past! We have conquered our demons and come forth now to multiply and grow in strength. The battle is not lost by any means, and we tread this pathway together to volunteer our services. Bravely and boldly we venture forth, for the crowning ceremony awaits us. We behold a new vision for the Children of Earth and we express ourselves in volumes! *I'm sensing a throng of knights gathered in a cathedral, their arms and swords raised high in the air, sending up a wondrous, musical cheer that is growing in intensity! I can see huge organ pipes reaching up high out of sight. The sound flies higher and higher in great crescendo, out into the cosmos as the sound travels on and on and on!!!* We recognise in ourselves this opportunity to grow, and we hold on strong and fast to that most cherished love. We hold you to our hearts and take you now to that place where Angels fear to tread – here we claim sanctuary for all those who have lingered on Earth! We reach out and touch the very heart of you, and we make this pact to take you on board, asking that you will convey our thoughts, expressing our desires to overcome the insurmountable! We have taken you to that very point of no return, and we accept that on our way, you have initiated a deep and lasting respect from those who have looked on, cheering from the sidelines! We express the difficulties that have assailed us, and we believe that in due course, we shall have mapped out a most extraordinary feat of dedication and love supreme.

3rd January 2006 – *I was awoken in the early hours this morning with the words of a song ringing in my ears . . . 'Suddenly I See'!* We resurrect you – blessings on you my child! We awake in you that light that has slumbered for so long, we awaken you to new probabilities and an ever increasing strength and vitality, shedding new light on circumstances that have come to our attention! There is a need to obey dictates of the heart and we allow a certain reverence to descend. Be prepared to take on board a structure that shall be complete in a matter of moments, for we have allowed access to a more demanding position, and strengthen you with clusters of energy that will relay the necessary requisites for a healthy two way connection! We rectify certain aspects of communication and ask that you put aside any grievances! For we are able to make these connections in a most perfect bond of friendship, delivering to you in no uncertain terms, a most delightful association of souls. We include those of you who have governed from afar, in what was a most necessary and deliberate form of association, and we impel you to strive for perfection in all things, asking you to take on board a most notorious plan of action!

We relish our times together and note that to a large extent, we will be able to appropriate the energy levels obtained to reach a most prominent position, we have allowed for certain unfathomable conditions but remain in all, calm and unruffled. Please remember we are with you at all times, and we note that in these endeavours you have been most purposeful. Elaborating, we suggest that you come armed with all the necessary requisites so that we may challenge you to a duel of sorts, sparring with one another! We recommend cool, calm thinking, obeying those aspects of yourself that reflect a massive change in perspective. We have been told of future successes and remarkably, we recover most nobly from our encounter. Please remember that we need to be more positive in our attitude, for there is a need to recover in principle, a more powerful formula to assist you in these matters. We have foreseen a going back in time to eradicate a poison, which has been given in the form of the most deadly of all substances! We retract and supply new evidence to give us a fighting chance, and we impel you now to move away from this scenario as we reinstate you in a more productive role. We have instigated a wide range of alternatives, and suppress further information until you are ready to take on this mammoth intrigue. Develop and grow in our love, and we will see a massive reflection of love beaming back at us from all angles of the universe, beckoning us toward our destiny!

We travel further and further afield, taking you to a place of immense destruction in your world today. We take you back to the sepulchre, back to the grave of Jesus Christ who saved the world from deep despair . . . to a time of the coming of our Lord! We reclaim that part of you that suffered at the hands of your countryman, and advise you now to proceed forward, obeying instructions down to the last letter in every aspect! We equip you with further wisdom and ask that you relay in great detail, our messages of love and joy for a world that has grown in our estimation. We propel you to this land of milk and honey, and ask you to remember our life together long ago, for we supersede a whole generation of star gazers and take you to that point of supreme ecstasy! Be prepared to hold in your hand the most awe-inspiring recipe for the destruction of Earth! We have maintained our allegiance to the cause and we unfold our plans to rectify this condition, taking you to a place of sanctuary and gaining free access to all necessary data. We record your progress and ask you to take forward a new understanding, allowing yourself the time to reflect on this new growth. We salute you and bid you farewell! *There was a feeling of great emotion as I received these words, and a sense of being one of Jesus' many disciples! Although I feel a great affinity and love for Jesus, I would like to say that in this life, I do not follow any particular religion, rather believing in the love and communion with Earth and all living creatures!*

6th January 2006 – I held my first spiritual awareness group at home this afternoon, and we all enjoyed blending together in peace and harmony. Later my friends drew close for another transmission. We are able to subtly change our awareness to such a degree, that manifestation can occur in a matter of moments. We have forecast certain measures to be adhered to, and we rely on you now to govern proceedings accurately and precisely. We are governed by our wishes to stay close to you at this time, and we know there have been recollections of the many times that our paths have crossed in the distant past! We amply gain access to that place of great beauty that awaits us, for we are the unseen and herald in a time of great happiness for one and all. Be prepared to take on board more constructive ways of dealing with these broader issues, that surface for examination under the microscope! We are able in this instance to prepare a more robust form of energy that will supply us with greater definition for the purpose in hand. We rely on you to discover new ways of delivering greater accent on words, and we are able in this manner to obey all directives. We have prepared for you a brief synopsis that we hope will cover all points raised, and we allow you a peep into this world of ours, which will give greater satisfaction for the way ahead.

We have tired of the endless array of antics that have been governed by a meaningless, desire to gain power and authority over others! There are many in your world who have overcome this charade and maintain, to all intents and purposes, a more definite and loving connection with one another. For we have reached that point in man's history where there will be a turning away from all that we hold most dear. Unrelentingly we push the button on a democracy that has led us astray! We are unable to assist you with these measures, until you have learned to control your feelings and emotions, in such a way that we can expect miracles to occur as a matter of fact! We enable the population of Earth to manifest a structure in time that will empower you all to take that mammoth leap into a new future. A new world awaits you where we can all become as one in mind, body and spirit, we can learn to fly in the truest sense of the word, taking on a vast and truly wonderful perspective on life! For life is for living to the full, and we experience now some of the most wonderful concepts with which to evaporate all misgivings. We have taken on board new measures that will instil in us greater self preservation, and we assess the situation from afar, asking that you will assist us to enable a co-joining, effectively to take place in the near future! We are able to make this assumption at a time when man has discovered for himself that he is not alone, evolution is the name of the game and we manifest for you now a greater control in your own destiny!

6th January 2006 – *Late evening* – We have need of your services! We impel you to strive for perfection in all things, and we unreservedly devote our time to accessing that port of call that beckons us forward! We take the time to execute demands placed before us, excusing what could become a most hazardous situation. We impel you to take care and invite you to rediscover yourself! Be aware that we have arranged for a meeting between those of you who are on this journey together. *I'm being shown a host of Arabs sitting astride their camels, jostling together as they make ready to start their journey!* We march you forward, taking care to rein in hostilities on the border. We have become suspicious of all we meet and do not accept, under any circumstances, any material that cannot hold water! We believe we have come across the most extraordinary feats of bravery, amid corruption of such proportions as to set the world upside down! Please be prepared to sacrifice your time to the devotion of further studies, for we have accessed many areas that need transcribing in greater detail.

We believe we have reached that point, where we can remain steadfastly engaged in matters that will stand the test of time. We take you to that spot that has caused great grief over centuries past, and we relay our actions to those of you who carry the banner of hope! We see greater sacrifices being taken to ensure a greater volume of success, and we mean to follow this up with a revolutionary control, mapping out those proceedings that give us greater advantage. We need to examine more carefully the data given, as there are fine details to be ironed out, and we need further measures in place to make this as harmonious as possible! We attend to details and supply a course of action that will allow for a certain quality to unfold. Operating on a new level we govern the proceedings with an air of sensibility, adjusting thought patterns accordingly and laying down a new measure of trust and respect. Embarking on this mission, we rely on our own resources to forge a new pattern of independence, allowing for additional points of view and a very rewarding outcome! We maintain this connection of services, and volunteer a new policy to intercept at each new level reached, enabling us to maintain contact and support.

10th January 2006 – Closer scrutiny is needed before we shall accomplish our main objectives, and we see greater advantage in being able to publish our own material. We suggest therefore, that you demonstrate your ability to grow, by being less concerned with what others may think, and more concerned with the complete package that we are offering! There is need for closer inspection, where we can iron out the creases and put this book to bed, we have made many discoveries about ourselves and we have shone forth a light of great magnitude! Please remember the necessary requirements for understanding our policies and procedures, for we have forecast a time of immense fortitude. We reckon on adjustments being made that will amply suit our requirements and we ask you to adjourn now, until we have enough time to clarify a few points raised! We feel this is necessary for us to overcome the traumas of the last few months, and we reckon on a year or two before we are prepared and ready to take on the world! We need this time to absorb new information and alter certain processes. We manipulate your growth to allow us greater impact; relaying messages to and fro across the universe, depending on one another to theme manage our accounts. *I'm now being shown Sayuri, my beautiful oriental guide.* We develop expertise in outstanding areas, asking you to play your part, and we allow for a certain display of those tendencies that are held in high esteem among the ranks. We have offended ourselves in respect to certain notions, that we must supply a course of action that is foreign to us! *I'm now being shown a Samurai, but he is not in full armour.* We suspend all arrogance and ask that you deny your right to centre stage until the timing is right, for we depend on one another to win through! *Now I'm being shown the American artist, John Rocha. I haven't had time to develop my artistic talents, and I know my friends were keen for me to start painting again. The book is using all of my free time but I'm determined to take up my brushes again once it is finished!*

12th January 2006 – *I woke around one o'clock in the morning with the full moon streaming through my window.* We obey our calling and come armed with love – developments have taken a turn for the worse and we are beholden to a wider audience to endorse new methods of communication! We succeed and revitalise proceedings, endeavouring to relay instructions down to the last letter. There has been an enormous uptake and we are all believed to be in line for promotion! We have reinstated family values and grown attached to certain disciplines that have led us to becoming more popular with those on Earth. On a more serious note, we amplify conditions all over the world, occupying a great extent of our time in revelations of a less grandiose nature. We are here to prepare a service for mankind and we err on the cautious, allowing a more natural progression for this enactment to take place. We have grown fond of our mortal counterparts, and feel the entrancement has allowed us to see for ourselves, what is necessary in overcoming the hideous malfunctions that have arisen, and growing wider even as we speak!

We feel that to a great extent, we have discovered a mortal race that has been overcome with a morbid fascination of death and disease! We have become a nation of child molesters, responding to bodily desires with no thought or consequence to others! We have instigated a vile and treacherous assumption that we are here entirely for our own gratification – and to hell with the rest! This is no way to behave! We have studied the human race and found them wanting on every count, except where there is love and sincerity of actions towards others. The population as a whole has become, to say the least, downgraded in every sense! We are appalled at the atrocities perpetrated, and we include a wide range of obscenities that have become second nature to many on Earth! We do however, defend those of you who display a sense of propriety, and acknowledge the fact that it has taken great courage and fortitude to live on as dense a planet as Earth!

We have relied on many of you to come forth, armed with the tool of love to shine your lights way out into the darkness of Earth, and we supply you now with more ammunition. We enable a deeper band of energy to envelop the Earth, and with enough rays to bombard her with a frequency that shall hold back a tidal wave of discontent! We come armed with love, most delicately and finely attuned, and governed from most high. We initiate a broader understanding and ask you to remember, that we have not always been this way, for we have been granted absolution and we maintain our frequency to be able to attain the necessary feedback. We govern our feelings and emotions, for we are a race of sensitive beings who are impelled to stand back, watching you grow and overseeing what is necessary for this grand connection! We rely on you now to maintain services, and supply you with a course of action that will take you to the highest boundaries. We oversee necessary inclusions, taking you to that point of discovery which shall hold you in the highest esteem, and we impel you to take heed of all before you as we venture into the unknown. Taking hands across the universe, we fly together on wings of love, taking for granted that we are protected and guarded at all times. We transcend all cares and worries to be here with you now, and extol your strength and fortitude. We deliberately take you to the abyss and beyond, knowing that we shall conquer and obey our hearts in all things!

14th January 2006 – On the 3rd October last year, my daughter's rescue dog became ill, and my star friends suggested that they help by using me as a channel for healing. Over the next week I sat with him quietly on several occasions, asking for healing to be directed where it was needed. It was as if he knew I was trying to help, letting out deep sighs and stretching out his body for easier access. At the end of the week my daughter was still concerned that he may be in some pain. A further consultation with the vet ended in an exploratory operation, which showed no reason for any discomfort. My daughter, however, is convinced that the operation may have dislodged any blockage there might have been, as her pet went on to recover completely. But I know in my heart it was the healing and change in diet that brought about a satisfactory result! We regret that certain actions have made it impossible to agree the respect we deserve, however, this does not mean that your efforts were in vain! We vouch for the fact that you have overcome a most destructive element that caused untold grief.

We amplify this connection and rendezvous with you on a higher level. We feel this encumbrance of the flesh has given you more wisdom than can be gained by standing on the sidelines. We applaud your endeavours and ask you not to fret, for we have outgrown various conditions and expel you for further studies! We accept this connection as valid and encroaching on new territory, we ably assist you in all matters of the heart. We impel you to understand the negativity of the situation ahead, and empower you to take on board a more constructive form of criticism. We take you to the point of delivery and have accounted for all persons present, revising conditions and spreading the news of further discrepancies. We have marched forward in full regalia and ask you to surrender to us, for we have adjusted our thought patterns accordingly and are determined to stand strong and true to the cause! We beam ahead, taking the challenge and setting down standards and regulations to be adhered to. Racing to the sidelines we cheer you on – we recommend straight talking and no nonsense for we are needed in the line of fire to overcome mortal conflict on all sides! Take care to adapt to all situations, and we shall see a rising of ideals and temperament. Please believe us when we forecast these measures . . . for we have a way of knowing what is just around the corner!

We take this next episode in our stride and very carefully step forward onto the horizon, taking with us the good wishes of all those here tonight. We have overcome many obstacles and on occasions been led astray . . . only to find our way back where we belong! We stand at the gateway and impel you to take a second look – before passing through that shroud of pain and sorrow! We recollect all that has been, and will be again, passing onto that state of perfect being that envelops us all as we step into the light of true understanding. We envelop you in our love and ask you to proceed in all earnest, for we are with you until the end of time, and the beginning of a new world of free expression, where 'Angels' are commonplace, and where we can all abide in a worthier state of existence! We maintain these thought forms, demonstrating our ability to grow in the light of love and passing on knowledge worthy of your attention. We supply the answers, encouraging you to ask the questions, and we nobly request an adjournment to regain status, rejecting any offers unworthy of the cause!

15th January 2006 – We are impelled to stand back and delay certain ulterior motives! We can understand the necessity for constructive criticism, but we must also be aware at this critical stage in our journey, of more than enough reorganisation taking place to rectify what is needed to maintain peace and harmony. We salute you at this time and respect your views, for we are in a decline and value these communications as a means to an end! We rely on you to step back and regain your composure – there is every need to forestall arrangements as discussed, for there is growing concern in an area of discontent! We feed you the right material to delay these thought processes from materialising too soon, and we believe we have amply conveyed our thoughts and feelings on this very subject, asking you now to remain in place, waiting for the command! *I'm being shown a flag and feel we are waiting for take off.* We attend to details and expressly forbid you to step over the line until the timing is right!

19th January 2006 – We are complacent in our dealings with one another, and ask that you take on board further new growth to expand our advantage. We have rectified certain procedures that were misleading, and we ask that you now obey instructions down to the last letter, for it is paramount that you deliver sequentially, all that is given! We have allowed for certain misrepresentation, which has occurred to allow a new pathway to unfold, but these measures in no way allude to a more serious proposition that awaits you on the horizon. We are impelled to stand back and watch you take off in a new direction, and we appeal to your more generous nature to allow the precipitation of a new and lasting bond of friendship! We have taken you to the ends of the Earth and brought about a bountiful harvest, believing in all honesty that we have prepared you for the moment of truth and justice for all, and we in no way spare you from delivering what is necessary to prepare mankind for the final assault!

We have managed our accounts in such a way to express our thoughts and feelings, and to summarise what is necessary to spare mankind from total annihilation! We have expressly forbidden this to happen – and we take you to that point of discovery that will allow you free access to all our hopes and dreams for a better way of life for the Children of Earth. We know with even further exhumation, we will uncover a multitude of pain and sorrow that shall be cleansed and purified, giving each and every one of you the choice to come with us to that point of reference that will bring you exquisite joy and peace forever more! We indulge your fantasies and exclaim that we have indeed brought you to that place of divine love, and we reclaim you and support you in overcoming what has been a most eventful time.

There is a need now to understand that we are in fact, a part of yourselves; we have taken on board a more salubrious time framework, and denounce all those who would deride us for our celebrity! We bring you an array of gifts that will satisfy you and enrich your lives – we come armed with love, a love that will bring you untold happiness and a way of expressing yourselves in the future. There has been a certain misunderstanding that we will rectify in due course, but we are impelled to state that we have functioned together through many ages, manipulating whole galaxies and taking our rightful place amongst the stars! We have grown together and cultivated a more natural ambience, giving total respect and admiration. We rely on other sources to influence a wide range of activities that are governed by a supreme control, and in this instance we have been able to sanctify certain procedures that have become second nature to us.

'Behold we bring you tidings of great joy – a child shall be born and we will call him by the name of Jesus. He shall be of lowly birth, and ye will know him by the sign in the sky that shall manifest before your eyes'! Reach out and touch that place that eludes you, strive for the best . . . the very best, for we rely on ammunition of this sort that sets the world ablaze! We achieve with glowing accuracy, a more positive and thought provoking alternative that will stretch the imagination with hypocrisy and all manner of innuendo! We have recovered what has been lost, and we supply you with even further news that will endow you all with courage and hope for the future of all mankind. We supply evidence that will lead to a going back to the 'old ways', and we rely on all of you now to obey the laws of the land! We have fulfilled our destiny and we wait now . . . for on the horizon, all is beckoning to bring us into alignment with a just cause that will free mankind from the manacles of sloth and discontent. We prepare for that place that brings us closer to God . . . for there is a God my friends – a God of love – a God of peace – a God of truth, and we indulge ourselves at this time, to make that connection that will bring us even closer to the truth! We have evaporated all misgivings and seen for ourselves what is necessary to overcome mammoth discrepancies. We reach that point of self discovery that will help us to expand and grow, allowing us access to those frequencies that have barred us in the past. And as we stand now at the brink, we bring with us great strength, courage and fortitude, for there lies before us a more radiant and perfect future that will dispel all fears!

Please believe us when we say, that we have found the people of Earth to be most welcome in our homeland, and we will encompass a wide range of prophecies that will incorporate a massive directive, given to undertaking a most magnificent spectrum of light that will bring us into total alignment! Here endeth the first chapter in our alliance – we have grown together and become accustomed to one another's thought waves, enabling a massive expansion on all levels! We have empowered you for this mission and thank you for supplying us with all the necessary criteria, we now take on board a more powerful union, isolating future instances of betrayal! We admit to becoming reluctant to leave, but know that we will be called upon to relay further evidence, producing a format that will project a wider understanding of our aspirations for a world of love and peace! We cement this friendship and ask that you allow us to manipulate your growth, attaining reasonable access and allowing our souls to entwine as one!

23rd January 2006 – We bring about a change of conditions, and we override as a necessary precaution to alleviate stresses and strains, remarking on the flamboyancy needed to restore conditions! We navigate our way across the universe, and we depend on you to maintain constancy while we negate certain behaviour patterns. We have exchanged thought waves and extract from you, more than enough information to draw lots on who will reach base first! We have screened our memory banks and speculate that we shall indeed recover our boundaries in the next month or so. We have divined what is necessary to achieve optimum results, and we forbid you from stepping out of line – as this would be counterproductive! We maintain our allegiance to the cause and beckon you to take heed of our words, for we are given to understand there will be a mammoth challenge ahead! *I'm being shown a huge spaceship moving slowly and quietly!* We believe this will cast a huge shadow over developments, holding us back and delaying our progress! We have examined data and recover thought processes to enhance a further capitulation. We challenge you to a duel of sorts, that will help you recognise where your talents lie, fundamentally recognising the leadership qualities that are an inherent gift we possess, and which will help us to maintain a certain advantage!

Chapter 6
Leap of Faith

24th January 2006 – We advise you to look back over the last twelve months and see how far you have come, however, this measurement can in no way compare to what is in store for you in the future! We have accepted that one pathway has come to an end – be prepared to move on, thanking those who have helped you along the way! We congratulate you on a job well done and shall manifest, at great length, what is needed to resurrect your career in helping others! We perform certain tasks to ingratiate ourselves with the populace, discovering new ways of making our peace felt amongst you all. Relatively speaking, we have come across a new structure for completing our journey; we have manoeuvred into place a retinue ready to indulge us, and have been given to understand there will be a reconditioning of services. We know this will lead you back to a place of immeasurable success, and we have taken on board what is needed to verify our actions. We have relayed our messages across the great divide, operating on a level that has been replaced with a higher energy source, and we replicate what is needed to bring about a stupendous recovery!

We respond to your needs, characteristically calling for greater support as this is necessary to maintain your motivation. We know for example, of certain malfunctions that have given cause for concern, we obey dictates of the heart and come to your side, knowing we can rely on you to take this to a higher level. There is just cause for concern, and we bring to your attention certain details that will bring about a reckoning! We deliberately forge a new alliance, developing greater advantage at a costly price. *I'm being shown a lady sitting side-saddle on a horse, she is wearing a long, russet riding habit and a little bowler hat, set at a jaunty angle!* We saddle up and ride out, organising ourselves we regain what is rightfully ours, suppositioning a whole new account of restoration. We delve deeper and deeper into the maelstrom of events on the horizon and note, with deep impact, that we shall receive news of grave concern! We regret a parting of the ways and deny all allegations of neglect!

30th January 2006 – *I've not been feeling well for the last week and have had to cancel my group.* We impel you to take heed! *I'm now being shown a nurse with red hair and a white cap; she looks very much like an aunt who died not long ago. I feel she is here to buck me up as she was a very bubbly character, always full of energy!* We infiltrate at a new level and assist you to recover your senses. We ask that you prepare the way for others to follow, illustrating what is necessary to recover and maintain our allegiance to the cause. We have known for some time now, of further measures that need to be seen to be taken, and we challenge you to this thought process that turns you around, albeit to face us head on! Mystified we challenge you again and again, until you accept the concept we are offering you, for we believe with all our heart that you have been able to sway the populace, interceding on our behalf to enable a coupling and docking of energies to take place!

We are extremely grateful for this association of souls; our only regret is that you have not been able to fully function on our level for longer periods of time! We have been able to assess the difficulty of approaching this level on your terms, and justify maintaining this process by accepting that we can co-exist together for short periods, maintaining thought waves in abundance! We have reached that place of final discovery, growing ever closer, entwined in an all powerful love as we resume our connection on a higher level. Transcend all cares and worries for we disclaim all thoughts of doom and gloom, expelling this bandwagon of love further and further into the unknown. We reclaim that part of you that is us, demonstrating our natural affinity with one another! A man for all seasons . . . we ejaculate our messages across the universe, and beckon you to share with us in a moment of your time! We have pencilled in a date and time and ask that you honour your commitment to us, for we take on board the necessary facts and figures that will give us access to a new dimension. Outnumbering the population by two to one, we call on you to help us with this fiasco on Earth; we reclaim our heritage and count ourselves lucky to be among you!

10th February 2006 – We interrupt your thoughts and salvage what is left of the day, we have promised in all sincerity to show you the way forward, and we welcome you aboard once more. *I had the feeling of being a small child, climbing up into the lap of a parent at story time!* We begin by expressing our heartfelt thanks for services rendered, and we initiate a trust and utmost joy for all that has been accomplished! We have taken on board more than enough to see us straight, and we vow to you now my sunbeam, that we shall accomplish even more as we vanquish our fears of failure! We have taken it upon ourselves to issue a request, and we deem it appropriate that you stand back and allow us to permeate your being with our presence. We impress upon you the importance of grounding yourself as we allow the tension to flow through and out, taking with it the stresses and strains of the day. We believe our main purpose now is to maintain a steady harmony, resonating to the sound of the universe.

I'm being shown cobbled streets and a horse-drawn carriage. I can hear the clatter of horse's hooves as they echo under an archway, finally coming to a stop. There is a figure of a man getting out of the carriage, he is dressed in uniform from the early 19th century, wearing white breeches and sporting a large naval hat. We spring into action penetrating your existence with our own, and we gain advantage by adjusting our thought patterns accordingly, realising the importance of staying focused. Initially we have made great sacrifices but we constantly seek new ways of alleviating pressures on those that serve us! We deny hostilities on the border and express our condolences for any interruptions this may cause. Be advised that we are constantly guarding you from outside influences, however, we do have some cause for concern as there has been a breach! We feel justly, that you have done your best to alleviate this state of conditions, and we in no way accept that this is the end of a more permanent relationship. We advise you to maintain your defences and venture to say, we are most perturbed! Shine some light on the subject and we shall see some progress made. We herald in a new awareness and speculate that in a month, we shall see feedback of a different nature. We allow a period of rapid expansion, and this will be followed by an enormous pressure to undergo a transformation … we insist that you take this seriously! We expel all doubts and fears, lifting you upon our shoulders in celebration of a job well done! We expressly forbid you to be downcast, asking only that you will serve with us on this adventure into the unknown. We deliberately take you down this road to set the record straight, discovering new facts about ourselves. Revelations are in store for you to explore further, and we shall be there by your side taking stock.

11th February 2006 – We reinstate values of great significance, pondering on further services. There is a constant need to check credentials, and we feel an overpowering urge to submit to promptings of the heart. We relay certain messages and hope you find a rewarding feedback in all instances. We are proud to call ourselves 'storytellers extraordinaire', and we recommend listening to a new and powerful tale that we have been told by our forebears! We insist on enlisting advocates with healthy hearts to by-pass airs and graces, that not only fall short but are demonstrating a world of loafers, who have no sense nor reason, other than to 'exist' in a world that feeds and clothes them! We have forsaken these temporary measures and curtail, in many instances, these patterns of thinking. We allow of course, on a more serious note, a studious approach that will govern a greater understanding of what we are about. We relay our messages across the great divide and examine certain ulterior motives, and we have registered and come to terms with, what can only be interpreted as being 'the end of the world'! We give you this opportunity to take on board this most natural ascension, and we believe that we can manipulate with ease, all those of you who wish to follow us to the ends of the Earth and on to new visions for the future of mankind. We have made examples of those of you who have led us astray, and we mean to evacuate the Earth by means of a voluntary execution of services, for we now have enough memorabilia to forge ahead and on to greater plateaus of existence!

We have travelled far to be with you here and now, and venture to say that we have regaled you with many divine aspirations, using this frequency to forecast many more applications. We have filed for divorce from this world, and wish to take on a new and powerful marriage that can initiate a grand connection of minds! We believe with all our heart and soul that we have reached that period in our history where we shall take you all to that point of delivery, allowing a mass exodus! We reel in those of you who hover on the sidelines and know you will all agree that this is a most hospitable gesture, as we reach out our hands to take you on board. We have devised a new framework where we are able to commit ourselves more fully, excavating in greater detail the methods to be used in our calculations for re-entry into a new dimension! We have freed the souls of many on your plane of existence, and we now obey our calling to take you all back home. Remember we have seen with our own eyes the destruction of your planet and, make no mistake, we are able to eliminate and extract the exact information to download what is necessary for this conjunction of minds!

Civil liberties expressly forbid us to take this approach, as anything other than the utmost importance, and we verify that we have found the whole procedure worthwhile! We back-track and offer you our condolences! We have been able to retrace our steps in time to examine data necessary for this transference, and we believe there has been great interest in our objectives. We know you will not take lightly what we are offering to you on a plate – a new lease of life in a framework that is hovering on the brink ready to receive her precious cargo! We believe with all our hearts that you will obey the criteria laid down before you to initialise these new requests. We dictate our letters to impress a large audience, captivating you with our charm and expertise. Rely on us to court you through this next stage, and we will supply further evidence of resurrecting a new foundation of love and trust among the people of Earth. We instigate a wider electorate that will push us all forward, and we invite you to sit with us and experience the dream!

12th February 2006 – We have accessed further information for you to take on board, and relay to you now what is expected of us. We rely on one another to take stock and prepare you for further advancement. There is a greater need to observe all before you, we have taken our rest and now instil in you a more productive stream of thought that will allow you to proceed in all earnest for the job ahead. We have allowed for certain discrepancies to stand in your way, this will allow for a challenging time and we devote ourselves to helping in these scenarios. We in no way begrudge you your dues, for we have manifested a growing desire to become more bold, and at each stage we shall recover our losses. We shall be there at your side, never deserting you, and we will stand firm in encouraging you not to lose faith! We explore new avenues and there in the distance we see, opening up before us, even more to conquer and explore new pathways that shall lead us to the land of plenty! We have foreseen a going back to the 'old ways' and we incorporate this in our new venture.

Please allow us to come through and analyse our next step forwards, we idealise a much sought after experience. We will show you how to conquer over your thoughts and emotions, and stemming the tide of tears, we promote you and yours to new realms of delight! We have promised to guard and guide you, and we believe in all sincerity that we shall shine down upon you the greatest gift of all, 'love from Heaven to Earth brought down'! We manifest a greater awareness, forecasting a time of immense fulfilment, and taking on board our main issue of the day, we inspire you now to take that leap of faith .. . to boldly go where no man has gone before! We plan ahead and ask that you will follow us on to the horizon where all is waiting as promised. We deliver you to a place of extreme advantage and we maintain our allegiance to the cause. We have supplemented our income and can now take advantage, we express our glee at being fortunate enough to recover our losses, and in this we shall be able to instigate an even wider pathway that will fulfil our ambitions for the future!

14th February 2006 – St.Valentine's Day. *I sat in meditation for help and guidance.* We believe in love – of that we have no doubt! We believe in strength of purpose as we tend to our siblings and ask them to bring forth all that is stored, all that is hidden! We have exchanged places many times in the past and recognise our true assets, we have come from past that framework that you call 'Heaven', and we believe we have accustomed ourselves to recognising the truth as we see it! We have behaved in a manner according to our station, and we deliver new and powerful anecdotes that will enable us to paint a different picture, one that can help you gain a greater understanding of what it is we offer to you all! We commend you for persevering with our words, for we come at a time when the utmost clarity is needed. We venture forth along this line of communication, and we vow to you all that we shall in no way cement our understanding of one another, unless we listen to our own hearts and minds, delivering the prowess to enable us to function as ordinary civilians! We have gained access to the hearts and minds of most of the country, and we devise new strategies for coming forward. There has been a banality of intrigues of a costly nature, which has given us the impetus to march forward, realising a grand connection of minds. We obey our calling and deliver to you now a sequential understanding of all that has arisen, and we notify each and every one of you of our vision for the future of mankind! We stretch the imagination and go on with lighter hearts, for we envisage a brighter future for all and we recommend now clear thinking.

A barrage of thought forms assails us, and we realise that it is hard for you to understand our motives . . . that we are driven by love for our own generation! We supply ample evidence for you to forge ahead onto greater structures of independence, and we vow to you my little one, that we shall in no way encumbrance you! We deliver to you now in all glory of excellence a most noble mission, and we transcend all cares and worries, enabling this exercise to bear fruit. We supply a different course of action for you to follow, and we allow you the prerogative of being the first to step onto that beam of light! We have no wish to arouse suspicion or entice you to a different framework, but we are governed by our feelings and emotions, and ask you to stand back from what is no longer required. There have been many that have stood in your place now, and we commend them to the highest degree! We allow only the best to pass through this corridor of fame, and we allow you this access at this moment, to accomplish our main objectives for a brighter future for mankind! We know you will allow us the freedom of speech in proclaiming to all and sundry, that we have given of our best, our very best, and we know you will take heart in knowing that we have transcended a most difficult framework of understanding! We have ventured far and wide to obtain the necessary resources given over to us, and we allow you access at this point to help us with our endeavours.

We come at a time of great joy for the people of Earth, and we transcend our boundaries to discover new ways of reaching that part of you which is us! We allow further access to those of you who obey dictates of the heart, allowing you further glimpses into our world of love, with the utmost benefit to mankind at this time of great turmoil where indignation is rife! There have been many recriminations and death defying obstacles that have stood in our way, but we have overcome them all, and we go on now to maintain this structure of peace and harmony, so that we may overcome all barriers that hold us back! Depend on us to come forward in times of trouble and intrigue, for we have given of ourselves in every respect, and allow you the grace and favour bestowed on you at this time. Remember we have come far along this pathway of self destruction, and we admit to being nonplussed at events that have driven us beyond the gates of Hell!

We rise up and taking your hand, we ask that you will obey your instincts in all things, for we are governed by our desire to help you and all those that stand with you. We admit to being suitably surprised as we govern from afar and ask you to obey our commands, for we expressly forbid any association with those that would hold you back from achieving greatness! We vow to you now that we have seen in the distance, coming towards us, a greater status than we could have ever hoped for or desired, and we mean to propel you forward on to this new vision that we may all learn from your example! We take you to that point of extreme love and devotion, and ask that you stand firm with us to conquer all doubts and fears as we venture into this realm of love. Help us to keep our act together, and we shall come through in glowing colours of every hue.

We have set our sights and inspire you to move forward along this spectrum of light, conquering our demons as we take you on board! We obey the laws of gravity and ask you to measure our success step by step, as we take you onto the maelstrom of events on the horizon. We deem it necessary to stand firm, and we ask that you impose our thoughts on the hearts and minds of those around you, for we have often visited them in their homes, taking advantage of all necessary contacts! We march together onto the horizon and ask that you will remember our words, for these will help you deliver all that is necessary to fulfil our ambitions. We develop you all and ask you to obey your hearts in all things, and as we proceed along this terrain, we ask that you magnify our love wherever possible!

15th February 2006 – *I sat at the computer ready for a day of editing and felt my friends draw close.* We are most impressed my dear, with your commitment!

We have taken it upon ourselves to monitor conditions more thoroughly, and we ask you to calculate a time for delivery. Preparation is underway and we have managed to manifest a golden opportunity on the horizon. We have taken it upon ourselves to resurrect a new awareness in mankind, and we take it to the limit, announcing in no uncertain terms that we have displayed great courage and fortitude! We have paved the way for you to join us, evaporating all misgivings as we take you into the light of true understanding. We ask that you obey our instructions down to the last letter, and we impel you forward now to do your duty. We reach into the realms of delight and we inform you of new measures to be taken, impelling you to strive for goodness in all things, knowing that you have taken on board many instances of vile treachery! We submit you to these revelations, so that you may know deep in your heart that we have found reasonable access in all areas. We have taken for granted that we shall excel in all aspects of our growth, and we know that you have taken this to the highest level to prepare our way forward. We negotiate a plan of action, and ask that you deliver this enterprise in the next year or so!

I'm being shown a lady in full Geisha costume. We expressly forbid a lessening of products, for we shall maintain our allegiance to the cause in this way! We depend on you now to bring this to the attention of those who can take this on board, and with agnomina we shall see ourselves on course for a greater display of love and affection! *After some research I found the word agnomina refers to a fourth name that was occasionally bestowed as an honour in ancient Rome.* We have grown together with great expertise, and we shall never forget our involvement with a most caring race! We have developed a new perspective and we come closer now to lift you up from your doom and gloom, for we are never far away and we shall deliver to you a greater understanding that will set you apart from those of lower natures. We appease that part of you that wishes to fly away with us, but we know that you must stay awhile and register our appeal for the human race!

16th February 2006 – *There is a full moon tonight and I feel compelled to leave my bed once more for communication.* We deliver to you now a most moving account of what we have come to expect from the Children of Earth. We have to say without a shadow of doubt that you have made us very happy! We can vouch for this happiness in the way that you have changed the lives of those around you, and we believe quite exceptionally! We have taken on board certain issues that have arisen, and develop further guidelines to express our new found freedom. We have reinstated a sense of purpose and empowered you for this mission, and as the time draws nearer we are reluctant to disclose our true feelings, for we are reticent in our dealings with others in connection with our work! We see this as a necessary exclusion at this time, for we know now more than ever, that we could free a deluge of uncertainty as we focus our attention on what is necessary to get through this period of unrest! We obey certain principles laid down by our Lord, and we mean to take this on board in a way that will rectify articles of war. We have discouraged those of you who have found this to be a main example of courage and faith, in a regime that shows neither its love nor commitment for any other than itself!

I was then given a short account of how two soldiers managed to survive the horrors of war, and what finally became of them! I believe I was given this anecdote to deter those who glorify war! "We have raised an army and remember, with great esteem, how we stood in ranks, holding ourselves erect . . . there was never a grander army!" "We drew on our reserves and marched through the night in a torrent of rain, unable to defend ourselves". "We sacrificed our talents, remaining in a world of make believe, which was necessary to help us through a most difficult period in our lives!" "We maintained a national talent for taking the rough with the smooth, and soon annihilated any form of treachery". "We were confined to barracks at any attempt to sabotage manoeuvres, and we fell foul on several occasions". "We have rooted out the company motto – Live and let live – damn or be damned!" "We believe these words do justice to what was considered by some, to be the most popular on campus, and we played our trump card one evening, when there were two of us on duties." "We had defied our sergeant major and forsaken our position as privates on a caper that was to cost us our lives!" "We were in jeopardy of becoming 'rat-arsed' and took no notice when relieving ourselves outside the officer's mess." "We were more than surprised when 'Jerry' delivered his bombshell – we had no other choice but to take our just desserts, and ended up being picked up in several pieces!" "We have delivered our tale of woe and ask that you pass on this ditty to those less fortunate than ourselves, for we are now in a place of great restraint, having time now to take tea and watch our p's and q's!" "We have deliberately sabotaged our mates here to recollect our times together when the grass was not so green!" *I asked their names and when this all happened?* Ted and Joe -1940!

17th February 2006 – *During meditation, I felt the presence of a nun wearing a large white, curling headpiece.* We have developed a new strategy that we would like you to keep to, and from now on we would like you to assess each situation on its own merit! We have come to the conclusion that there is only one way to win this battle, and that is through tireless discussion on the merits of each situation presented to us at any one time! We have taken these measures to ensure that all will benefit from our instructions, and we lay it on the line, asking you to bend over backwards to help us in this action. Be prepared to take on a more time consuming effort to stay in touch, for we are forever on the sidelines cheering you on! We have taken note of all that you have asked, and remind you of the need to focus more clearly, for there are many hurdles to overcome before we reach our goal. We know all is in readiness for our venture and we keep to the straight and narrow, declaring to all and sundry our wishes for a more demonstrative feedback.

We take on board all your efforts to relay our messages back to those on Earth, we have found this time to be one of immense pleasure, and would like to take the time out to thank you! We have displayed many agenda items and know deep within our hearts, that you yourself have forecast what is necessary to steam ahead in the right direction. We foretell what is necessary to alleviate all pain and suffering, and we amply explain our mission as being one of grave concern! There is a need to adjust our patterns of thinking and allow for a more sombre format. We have allowed for a certain subterfuge where we will encounter a more robust form of analysis, this may hold us back to a degree, but we are in no doubt as to where our allegiances lie! We understand your negativity at times when answering our call, but the pull must come from you. We allow no other to break the charms that bind us as one, and we rely on each other solely to extend our existence in this framework of time.

We allow now an opening that will govern our sense of performance, and we have noted that you express yourself in a way that will stretch our boundaries even further. Try to develop the knack of reaching out for that little bit extra, and we will strive together to make this work for longer periods of time! We have forsaken our structure of old and allow a new framework that beckons us forward on this rollercoaster of love. We deny certain action as being just a little too hard to bear, and we know it makes sense to stop and think before taking the plunge! However, we do feel you do justice to all we have given, and vow now to take a little more time out for ourselves. We reckon that in a years time we will have realised an enormous scope of energy, and ask you to retrace your steps to that place that has eluded us for so long!

We take you back to a time of immense pleasure and a love so impelling. We take you back to the altar and state our oath of allegiance to one and all, developing greater bonds of love! We welcome you here amongst us to take the vow of chastity and an end to living in a world of unrest. We save the souls of those in torment and beg you to understand our mission of love, for we have forsaken our duties of the flesh and submit you to the most uplifting connection of higher minds! We take you to that place of immeasurable strength and courage to help you on your journey, and we impel you to break with tradition, taking on trust that we have amply connected! We obey our higher minds in this initiative, and we pave the way for a brighter future, discovering new ways of reaching our goal. We maintain the discipline needed to rectify conditions, and take on board the need to observe any constructive criticism given more carefully! We have developed an outstanding quality of being able to reach out to make this connection, an achievement of the highest proportion, and one needed to carry us all forward and onto greater conquests!

I was awoken in the early hours of the morning for more transcription. We issue new guidelines for further restraint and we thoroughly recommend gaining advantage by allowing a more determined approach! We recommend this action to alleviate stresses and strains and vouch for a better way of life. We also maintain the freedom of a fast track approach on levies, and note the appropriate action will stand us in good stead in the days and weeks ahead. We are scrupulous in our dealings with one another, relaying our successes back and forth across the great divide! We allow these thought processes to manifest in a variety of ways and we have managed so far, to alienate those of you who deliver on a different frequency! This is perhaps unfortunate, but we realise that certain procedures unfolding will bring about a greater cleansing. Understanding is the key word, and we relinquish our hold on all that has gone before.

We suffer no interferences and would ask you to remember that we have been to hell and back! This time framework impels us to look more closely at what is needed, and we stay on course to deliver our final ultimatum! We relegate those of you who have no desire for a world of peace and harmony, safe in the knowledge that you will reap what you sow in this world and the next! We sublimely defer these matters and note with deliberate intention, we have forecast more appropriate measures for this interfacing of souls. We expect in all sincerity, that new measures will be taken to ensure a bigger output of energies, allowing for the condensing that is necessary at this stage of the game. There are discrepancies on the horizon that could lead to a closing down on a grand scale, but we believe these measures can in no way compensate for what is planned on a larger scale across the world! We depend on you now to come forward and be counted, and we gather our forces, marching together in unison. Be not put off by thoughts of a lower nature, for we will reign supreme in our efforts to get our message across. We are here to stay, and will not budge an inch, until we have obtained our heart's desire in realising a golden future for all mankind!

This is our manifesto, and we intend to bring to the people of Earth greater enlightenment, and a new perspective for focusing on issues that have determined a new approach! We believe a supreme effort will push this ahead, and we focus our power on what is necessary to achieve this grand plan of action. Please help us all by remembering that we are one and the same, we have gained advantage by reproducing ourselves at a level that will enhance our studies of the human race! We depend on you now to represent us in this race against time, for we have been cast into a cauldron of deceit and lies, and will allow no interferences from those who would put the lid on this! We now ask that you will supply us with a little more of your time by endorsing our methods of success. We amplify this connection to keep you on board a moment longer, for we feel it is necessary to alert you to a new format. We have delivered to you sequentially, all that is needed for your book, and note with much ardour that we confirm our decision to forge ahead with this endeavour!

Please note we are most pleased at the prospect of releasing our visions for a brighter future for mankind, and we deliver to you now a much, broader outlook that will keep you going in your hours of darkness! Please remember, we are with you until the end of time and the beginning of a new and vibrant dawn that will bring light into the hearts of all mankind. We retrace our steps and humbly beseech you to take stock, for we are here for the duration and will not leave you to carry this burden alone! We march forward onto the next conquest, keeping you in line and delivering a new referendum that will bring peace and joy to a world entrenched in darkness and despair! We deliver certain ultimatums and announce a grand connection of minds, followed by the necessary inclusion of a greater love than man has ever known! We have gained enormous impact in a world that reaches out to the farthest galaxy in an attempt to find other life forms . . . but we are here amongst you in flesh and blood, ready to make our connection!

18th February 2006 – *I was awoken in the early hours for transmission.* We reign supreme in our attempts to get our message across, and we know full well that we shall bring to the Children of Earth, a greater vision than at any other time in the history of mankind! We have obeyed our hearts in all things and we vow to you all now, that we shall leave no stone unturned in our search for the truth, for we shall have our say at any cost! We mean now to forge ahead and ascertain that we shall make that connection one week from now, and we will take it to the highest point, having reached that place of the utmost joy and conviction of a place beyond the stars! We recommend clear thinking for the time ahead, and associate ourselves with you to promote our plan of action. We need to remain calm at all times, and express ourselves with sadness at the passing away of all we hold most dear, moving on to a new mode of thinking and gaining greater expertise!

We reckon on the extraction of a certain understanding that will cement relationships, and have us bound for a world of hope and glory beyond all earthly measure, for we have seen this with our own eyes, and vouch to you now of its opulence and beauty beyond comparison! We express ourselves in a way that will open up greater vistas for us to achieve on a massive scale. We develop greater powers of observation, and encourage you to take on board all that is needed to maintain peace and harmony. We have allowed ourselves a certain respite in matters relating to art and creativity, but we shall see a massive expansion in this area, taking it upon ourselves to achieve with greater definition and self awareness! We have created a vision extraordinaire, and we welcome you on board now to execute what is needed to govern the unrest in your heart. We take it to the extreme and intercept to bring you a new field of vision, this will become our greatest venture yet, and we take on board our need to grow in all directions. We amplify this message to get across what is needed – for the courage to take that extra step forward and we believe we shall manage to stay ahead, strengthening our perception of growing together towards our goal of peace and harmony for all!

20th February 2006 – *Today while sitting in meditation, I recorded my journey. I'm walking up a mountain path lined with silver birch and pine trees, and can see mossy crags jutting out beneath me. There is a magnificent waterfall thundering down the rock face, catching the suns rays and creating a beautiful rainbow of colour. I carry on up the mountain, climbing higher and higher, the sky is a beautiful blue and I can hear an eagle calling, heralding my approach. I now see ahead of me the beautiful, golden gates of the garden of 'healing and remembrance'. They swing open for me to enter and I gasp at the sight of hundreds of African violets, beautiful violet petals with golden centres, lining the entrance to the garden. I walk on a little further and come to a magnificent, three tiered fountain, stopping for a while to watch the iridescent cascade of water making its way to a lower healing pool. Instead of my usual visit to the healing pool, I feel impelled to walk on further, following the pathway down a flight of six steps, counting them as I walk down.*

Reaching the bottom I see a gravel pathway leading to a maze of tall, dark hedges. There are several doorways cut into the hedge and it seems I must decide which one to go through. I walk further on, just over half the distance of the pathway and stop at one of the openings. Entering the passage I see a row of lanterns hanging to the left of me, tentatively I follow the hedge as it curves round to the right, it's very dark but now I can see a spiralling light drawing me towards it. There is a woman in a crinoline dress, wearing a white wig with long ringlets; she has her hand over her mouth, seemingly upset because she doesn't know where she is! I must admit to feeling a little lost myself, especially here in this maze. I'm plunged into darkness again and started to pray! Dear Father God, show me the way, please help me to find my way! Immediately I can see a pinprick of light, and now I'm feeling a pressure around my head as waves of lilac light bombard me. I started to repeat the words – I will succeed, I will succeed, I will succeed! I've come out of the maze now and am holding a lantern up in my left hand, which is very strange as I'm right handed. I retrace my way back along the pathway, up the six steps into the garden and past the fountain, making my way towards the gates. After this meditation I sat at the computer and asked for guidance from my friends.

We believe we have managed to date, a most enchanting form of contact, and allow you the grace and favour of becoming our most renowned champion! We deliberately request an even greater advantage to enable this contact to grow stronger in every way. We entreat you to listen to our grand plan of action, allowing for an even more salubrious encounter with our friends and neighbours who have given us their support! We relish these times spent with you my dear and allow a certain requisitioning of even further attributes. We take note that you are adjusting to our patterns of thinking, and we ably express our views in the forthcoming document, which we shall dictate at our leisure. We have known for some time now of new events taking place on the horizon, these have caused some dismay but we have relegated those who would stand in our way, knowing that just around the corner all is waiting! We have stored this in readiness for the next step forward, and are delighted in informing you that we have accomplished the last of our audit!

We have been mentioned in higher circles and know that you will bear with us in exclaiming, that we have 'never had it so good'! We deny all accusations of plagiarism, for we have accomplished this work entirely off our own backs, and wholeheartedly play our next trump card! We have initiated a new and daring plan of action that will encompass a wide range of objectives, enabling us to deliver a greater mass of evidence that is needed to win the hearts and minds of those across the globe. For we have been able to delay the action of thought processes in such a way, that we can reconstruct sentences in a matter of moments! *I felt tired and struggled to understand what they were trying to convey.* We blame ourselves in this instance for asking you to take too much on board, we ask that you recess for an interval of refreshment as we iron out the creases and put your mind at rest Be assured that all is being done to open up your vision!

I stopped for some lunch and went outside in the winter sunshine, it will soon be spring and I'm so looking forward to longer hours of daylight. I did some light weeding then went back to tune in once more. We have managed to come to grips with what is holding us back, and we take on board our new portfolio of excellence. We excel in all areas and take you to that place of extreme joy, beckoning you forwards and onwards. We take you aboard and have great pleasure in rewarding you with a most salubrious adventure. We feel you deserve this rest and we know that you have more than amply conveyed our thoughts and feelings on the subject of faith, and the surrendering of dual persona! We assist you now in conveying our heartfelt message to the population of Earth. We are here to set the record straight and to help you all achieve your destiny, for we vow to you now that we shall exceed ourselves in taking you to that point of no return! We empower you to deliver a message of great importance and we nobly ask you to take control of the proceedings more carefully. We recommend a turning back in instances of regret and remorse, for we have no other recourse than to obey our feelings in all matters of the heart. We have obeyed our own heart and note the reactions to our words on a more transcendental level.

We are compelled to move forward, and govern a more demanding role on the horizon. We shall amply explain ourselves and serve to rectify instances of regret. We feel we have taken on board a wide variety of issues that have been left unspoken, and we need now to endorse our thoughts and feelings on these very subjects closest to our heart! We recommend a period of socialising that will get us in the right frame of mind for dealing with issues on other levels, and we now take you to that point of no return, begging you to deliver our message loud and clear! We alleviate suffering on a grand scale, and welcome one and all in this race for freedom against tyranny. We have expressed ourselves in ways that perhaps, will cause unrest among parts of the population, but we remain totally unfazed by the prospect! We have developed a broader stream of narrative and convey our heartfelt message to the population of Earth, encouraging them to believe in themselves. We have stated the fact that we shall in no way blame the people of Earth, except for those few of you who have a complete disregard for human life! We take you to a land of love where there are no recriminations and we feel you move towards us step by step, day by day, growing ever closer! We send out our wave patterns of love to encourage a stature within you that knows no bounds, for we are created from love, and to love we will return, obeying our heart's desire in all things!

We deliver to you now a sequential understanding of what it is we are asking you to achieve. We have stated the facts and are offering you the choice . . . of coming aboard and joining us in a new and vibrant future, or staying behind and allowing yourself to be manipulated and governed by a rank and putrid form of government, which will never allow you the freedom of choice! We are governed by our thoughts and emotions, and we relay this message with a lump in our throats, for we know it will be hard for you to take that final leap into the unknown! *I'm feeling very tearful at this point.* We have transcended that time and place where you are now, and we too know the pull of Earth that was once our home; we had no choice in the matter, for we were expelled out into the universe through no fault of our own! We deliver to you now the consequences of staying behind, for we know you will live to regret this course of action! We take you to the brink and show you the hazards of staying on Earth, for we have inched our way across the universe and shown you what it was like long ago! We reclaimed that part of us – a single cell, and we designed ourselves in a new fashion, going on to even greater achievements, more than we could ever have imagined! We devoted ourselves to maintaining our life support systems, and we developed new means of elevating ourselves to a higher level of existence. We portray ourselves in this way so that we may get the message across loud and clear – that there will be no more life if we do not prepare ourselves for this great event on the horizon!!!

20th February 2006 afternoon. *I have only recently bucked up the courage to ask why we need to leave the planet Earth – I think I was afraid of the answer!* We have displayed great courage in changing our thought patterns in this way, and we reel in those of you who have made your choices. Believe us when we say that there has been a cataclysmic event, which will affect Earth in such a way as to send you reeling in all directions! We cannot give you an accurate description, for there is no way that we are allowed to convey this kind of carnage! Suffice it to say that there will be annihilation on a grand scale across the entire globe, and this will be felt as some great charge of electricity, accountable only in proportions as to that of nuclear warfare! We display our integrity in all things and ask you to show a sense of propriety, for we have forsaken our need to challenge you further, and we allow a turning back of the clock so that we may change the end result! We nurture you and bring you to your senses, for we can and will help you to reinstate yourselves on a new planet that will sustain all life forms! We have promised to honour your wishes and supply you all with your home comforts. We take you to a place of safety, safe in the knowledge that we have overcome all obstacles, and we stand on the brink, beckoning you to share with us a love divine! We have no need of paraphernalia, we greet you as we are and stand before you in our love. Please let us reinstate you in a place that will not hold you back from performing your daily rituals, for we believe we can integrate on a new level of understanding that will help us all to expand!

21st February 2006 – *I sat in my healing room in anguish, thinking of the beauty of Mother Earth and the sadness I felt to be leaving her! I know that in the world at this very moment, there are countless people being murdered for nothing more than a mobile phone! We constantly hear of the taking of innocent lives because of greed and jealousy, or just simply for power over the weak and vulnerable! Life is precious . . . this beautiful world we live in is precious, but we just take it for granted, sucking every last ounce of energy from her! A cloud of sorrow settled upon me and I sat in prayer, asking for the cleansing and transmuting of all negativity energies for Earth and all mankind. I then took myself off in meditation to a beach where the sand is white and the sea is blue. On a previous visit to this shore I had felt carefree, walking along the sands with an African, father figure. I had seen myself as a little child holding my father's hand as we paddled in the sea, laughing with joy as we jumped over the white, bubbly waves. He had swung me high on his shoulders and we watched a red, paper kite flying high in the sky. It was the most wonderful feeling being carried along that beautiful beach, I had felt so happy and without a care in the world! This time though, the feelings were very different. I still saw myself as a little girl, but this time I was being carried off the beach, crying no, no, no!!! I picked up my recorder and spoke.*

We cleanse a long line of perpetrators and bring them to justice! We allow a disruption of services as we navigate our way across the universe, taking on board new measures that have been incorporated into our plan of action. We know this has come as a huge shock to you, but we know also that we must make amends, and we take this to the top! Although we beg to differ over various points of view, we have grown together and recognise the challenges ahead. We make available what has been given to us on trust, and we shed some light on the proceedings that will enable us to take on board this news. We have been overwhelmed, and we suffer you now to come and kneel before us as we comfort you! We have registered the displeasure of those who give cause for concern, and we rectify these issues by taking on board as many of you as we can muster to alleviate sorrow of this kind! We have propelled you forward and onto greater distinction to help others, we know that you will give us the utmost dedication, and we have expelled from our thought streams a greater wealth of knowledge!

I'm getting a huge shiver over the whole of my body, and I can feel a current of energy around the left side of my head! I drifted off into meditation and felt I was getting into some kind of round, metal construction, shaped like a deep sea, diving bell. There were others with me and a large, round door was closed and locked into position after we were all safely inside. We call you to attention and ask that you come with us, for we have managed to convey our respects. We venture forth with great uncertainty in our hearts and minds, and we know you will find it extremely hard to accept the purpose of this news, for every country in the world must rally round as we govern proceedings from afar! We know you will find this a most sombre act of disconnection, but we allow you this discourse to enable you to come to your own conclusions, as to how we shall defend ourselves in our hour of need!

22nd February 2006 – We have undoubtedly suffered the doubts and insecurities that come with accepting these new thought patterns. We have undergone enormous pressure and we are able now to some extent, unfold a new horizon that beckons us to safety. We feel impelled to allow you this time to recover your senses, for we know it has been hard to accept these final measures that have been laid down for the purpose of self discovery! We are able now to turn back the clock, and insist on a finer tuning to alleviate any discomfort caused. We justify our actions by taking on board a more nonchalant retrieval of records that have been put at our disposal; we have allowed for certain discrepancies but appreciate the need for greater deliverance. We have allowed ourselves recourse to set the record straight, and we deem it advisable to take on board a more conclusive pattern of thinking to alleviate any mistrust. We have vouched for your safety, and deliver a higher and more definitive programme that will enable us to retrieve you at a moment's notice. We are incapable of supplying you with further evidence at this time, but mean to take you on board at all costs! We will never allow you to postpone what is inevitable, for we take you to the brink and deliver you to a world of joy and ecstasy beyond compare! Here we will attend to your needs and desires, for we are able to encompass you with all that is needed to sustain you on every level.

We depend on you to console us in our hour of need, and we believe you will do justice to all that is meted out for our success in this project. We have walked many roads together and we now come to a crossroads . . . we make our choices and congratulate you on the fact that we have come this far! We deliver to you now another course of action, which will delay to some extent, practices that have become second nature to us. We relay certain conditions that have given cause for concern, believing in all honesty that the contact we have made has become necessary for one purpose only – the reclamation of all those on Earth! We have made a final demand and impose heavy penalties on those who do not listen to our words. We have extracted from our memory banks, certain conditions that remain a viable, core part of who we really are, and we suffer no interferences from those who would cast us into the flames! We have become dependent on all those who make this initiative their own, and we come to rescue you and take you to that place of love, truth and understanding.

We tell you now, with our hands on our heart, that we have never felt so overwhelmed with joy and admiration as with our time spent with the Children of Earth! We embrace you, and lay down no laws that you cannot examine for yourselves and see their true worth. For we are a nation of star gazers, and we vouch for the fact that we have come a long way in time to be here with you now, foretelling your destiny! We come flanked by those from other star systems, who have an interest in how this all pans out! We know that you will see this in a new light as you examine the data we have retrieved for your perusal. We only come to take you all back home where you belong, and we beckon you now to hasten your footsteps along this highway of love. There is no time to dawdle, for we have much to achieve in a relatively short space of time, all must be ready when the trumpet calls to take you home! Make haste little ones, we enfold you in our love and ask you to take care of yourselves and your offspring. We make a place ready to receive each and every one of you, and take great pleasure in ushering in a time of immense joy and pleasure for one and all. We set the record straight and deliver a new venture for mankind!

23rd February 2006 – We lurch from place to place unable to find that connection, but deep within your heart you know that we are here to help and guide you. We state the obvious and wrap you in our love to protect you from harm. Prevarication has given way to a form of anguish, and we know that you will allow us to approach you, meticulously obeying dictates of the heart! We know in this instance you have given of your very best, and we allow you now to stop and recuperate. We bear in mind that you have more than enough on your plate at this time, and we excel in all we do! Be prepared to take a mammoth leap into the unknown, for we know you will bear witness to all that has been given as we venture forth in all our glory, armed and ready to take on the world. We grow together with great expertise and emphasise the need to rest!!! We reinvent ourselves and move forward, there are certain procedures that need to be followed and we recommend a more demonstrative participation. There are certain aspects that need monitoring, and we put it to you that there is every need to obey us down to the last letter! We feel the encumbrance of certain elements, and ask only that you obey dictates of the heart in this, for we allow this time framework to bend backwards in anticipation of events on the horizon.

We have need of you now to rectify complaints, and these will come rumbling in across the universe asking to be healed! We know this is justifiably a tall order, but we need those like you who have some experience of these issues. We allow a certain refuge in the fact, that we have obeyed all criteria, remaining steadfast and true to the cause. We delight in telling you that there have been further discoveries that give weight to our arguments, and we are notably impressed to find that we have delivered on time our résumé! We coax you to come forward and be counted, for we have gathered for the naming ceremony, given to those who have completed their mission! We take it upon ourselves to impose this final honour, and we ask you to accept the honorary name of Carpelia. *I hoped I had got the pronunciation right and asked for an interpretation, I was told the name signified a flower of virtue and felt very touched! I was given the word 'agnomina' on the 15th February and found it was a Roman honour occasionally bestowed as a fourth name. I already have three names and am very honoured to accept this fourth one!*

24th February 2006 – *I'm sitting in my healing sanctuary waiting for a friend from my spiritual group to join me. The others all have family commitments and are unable to attend this afternoon. My star friends joined me instead and I started transcribing their words.* We impel you to take care and remember that the framework we come from divides its time in two, to represent you here on Earth! We need to congratulate you on this forthcoming acquisition, for we are now prepared to venture forth in all our glory, displaying our talents! We beckon you forward to take on your role of guardian, for we vouch to you now that we have acquired a greater standing in the archives. We present in all honesty, a most prolific avenue of thought, allowing a more productive flow that is necessary to achieve our aims and objectives. We bow before you, bringing gifts that are most exclusive, reaching out and bringing forth all that is stored and hidden away from the world of men. We deliver to you now in greater eloquence, for we have seized this opportunity to grow with both hands, and we venture forth now displaying our talents, persevering with all that is given in great measure. We take on board a most ample description of what is necessary to obtain our heart's desire, and although the time is not yet right, we know that you will succeed in bringing forth greater knowledge for the dedication of others.

We kneel before you my child, to access that part of you that reminds us of ourselves long ago, and we now take the time to alleviate all pain and suffering that is stored in the heart of mankind, instilling in them a greater trust! We are restored and given impetus to forge ahead! *The telephone rang and I had to break off the connection to answer the call, which turned out to be the remaining member unable to make the class. I went back to resume my communication, apologising for the disruption!* We deliver to you further proof of what is needed to rectify the situation we find ourselves in, and we need to amputate services until there are enough of us to take on board what is paramount! We delay our action until you can represent us, and we feel these services will be open to negotiation at the beginning of spring. We correlate our actions to coincide with a more advantageous production of energy, needed to sustain us in the forthcoming weeks and months ahead.

Please prepare yourself for this conjunction, for we have every need of your services so that we may forge ahead in our endeavours. We believe this course of action will allow us to maintain further services, and render you speechless at times! We rationalise what is given and deliberately set you back to allow for a modicum of stability. We feel the agenda has given some cause for concern, but we will alleviate any form of mistrust that may sabotage what is our only form of recourse! We allow a certain subtlety to creep in, and forgive you your trespasses in disconnecting us earlier. We rely on one another to keep this discourse going, and refrain from answering calls of a less imperious nature, for we feel these times are imperative to us. We relay further information and ask you to take on board what is necessary to gain the utmost respect in all circles. We maintain a certain harmony within this group and derive great pleasure from your company, for you have all been handpicked to accelerate your growth, and we mean to access all that is needed to help you associate yourselves with the fact of deliverance! We participate in your lives to extract certain information, which will lead to a greater dedication of services, and we impel you now to take on board these new leadership qualities!

We descend upon you in great numbers and access the population at every given opportunity. We have made startling discoveries, and have known for some time now that these events will take you all by surprise! *I'm being shown people with their eyes popping out on stalks!* We delicately suggest that you manufacture a certain decorum when adjusting to this phenomenon. We accelerate all thought forms to adjust wherever necessary, and we take this to an incredible pitch, relaying information back and forth in an endless stream of repartee! We proclaim to one and all that we shall vanquish, at a growing rate, all avenues of neglect and abuse, and we will show the world that there is more to life than listening to idle gossip, or forecasting a 'win on the pools'! We bring a much, more salubrious framework of existence, and we tell you now that we have circumferenced the globe in our attempts to dispel the barrage of negative thought forms assailing Earth!

We reach a level of self destruction, suppressing unknown glutinous debris that carries with it a most obnoxious gas! We supply you with these details so that you may know the harm you do to your world, encased in a putrid film of layer upon layer of chemical by-products, rising up through Earth's atmosphere! We reckon it will take only a few more years before this chemical imbalance will have a dire reaction, with an elixir of poisonous gases waiting to implode! We have infiltrated at new levels to bring about the desired effect of neutralising this elixir of death and despair. We vouch to end this destruction on a massive level and achieve equilibrium, restoring Earth to her former glory! In this way we can maintain balance in the universe, defying all obstacles and creating an atmosphere that will produce new life. Bringing about a healing to the Earth so that she may be used to propagate new forms of life, extracting herself from harm and mutilation on a grand scale! We reconnect on a larger scale and ask you to keep faith, for we have accessed at great length the necessary protocol to take you on board, and we allow now a reconditioning of energies to take place before this can be accomplished! Please bear in mind that we have examined all criteria, and are notably impressed with all that has been accomplished so far.

Late evening – We have published a new account of what we can come to expect, for there are mammoth challenges ahead and we can expect further growth in all areas. There has come to our attention the constant need to review conditions, and we see a new field of vision opening up quite soon. We enable a channelling of excellence, revealing a frequency that will enable us to progress much further at a faster rate! We know you have worked hard to achieve this, and allow a moment's respite before challenging you further. In our defence, we have foreseen on the horizon, issues that need to be redressed. We speak of events not far off, and we impeach you to carry your role of ambassador to those who are bound to make this exchange a bountiful and natural progression! We deliver a wide range of alternatives, and beg you to consider each and every one before making your choices, and we endeavour to show you by hook or by crook, the best way forward! Believe us when we say we have not come to gloat, but to encourage you to spend your time more constructively, deepening the bond that draws us together. We tether you to us and simplify this connection; remain constant to our needs and we will exemplify your every move. We recommend a deep cleansing to alert the body and mind!

25th February 2006 – *I sat in the sunshine to meditate, but a chill wind had me scuttling into our rickety old summer house. I could feel the warmth of the sun on my face and at last relaxed, asking my friends to draw near.* We supply a course of action which will allow us to exonerate all those on board, and we rectify disturbances as and when necessary, forging ahead onto to further conquests. We relay information back and forth, enlightening you as to our progress, and we take it upon ourselves to acknowledge certain discrepancies that persist! We refrain from embarking on this mission without suitable feedback from our friends, who are guiding us step by step of the way. We have acknowledged their releasing you, for the purpose of helping us to achieve greater feedback, and we know we can count on you to help us in every way. Please guard against intrusion of any kind, for we are now at that critical stage of completion! We rendezvous with you to allow a reconditioning of energies, and we realign where necessary to complete this circle of love. We reinforce our desire to steam ahead, and know that you will deliver with complete and utter dedication to the cause.

We remain on board to give you a helping hand, setting ourselves on course for a new world. We amplify this connection and take it to the extreme, sublimely manifesting a most natural illumination. We take the next chapter in our stride and maintain perfect harmony, reaching out and taking on board a creditable production of services. *I'm now being shown a lady sitting in her boudoir; she is wearing a long, red gown that is layered with frills. There seems to be a clearing out, there are curtains are coming down and I can see a butler wearing a white wig, who is running to and fro, helping to make a start on a big spring clean!* You are entitled to a good deal more, but there have been instances in the past where we have not been able to follow through and bring you back! We are preparing a place for you, and now allow you easier access. We are making way for you to receive in a few months' time, news that will bring you the utmost joy! We keep this a secret and keep you in a state of anticipation, acknowledging that your gifts are rewards for obeying our instructions down to the last letter!

26th February 2006 – *I woke in the night to words forming in my mind.* We illustrate the fact that it is sometimes better to govern one's feelings and emotions, and we access parental control to take on board finer measures that need observing! We are in a state of grace and favour, and recognise in each other the need to push forward. There have been instances of self loathing, and we realise there has been a mammoth undertaking to rule over self doubt! Presentation of integrity and self esteem, have taught us that we must maintain our sense of dignity and value of life above all other pursuits. We are able to assist you in these measures, and we intervene to bring your attention to certain discrepancies that are causing concern. We are able to forgive ourselves many things, but there are certain aspects that are holding us back from making further revelations! We are reliant to a certain extent on what we are told, and realise this growth has been stupendous in recovery, but we know you harbour secret doubts as to your abilities and we would like to set your mind at rest on this issue!

We have seen with our own eyes what you have achieved in your own right, and we are amply impressed with your perseverance in all matters. We supply a further course of evidence that will allow you to understand your part in all of this, and we portray you as justly as we can, developing greater awareness of each other's needs. We amplify this connection and draw you closer for further discussion, rectifying your needs and monitoring your growth daily. We have greater need of assistance in the time ahead, and believe we will amply portray what is needed to alleviate conditions on Earth. We demand reasonable access and allow no morbid assumptions as to our motives, for we take you on board for one reason only . . . to prevent a calamity of enormous proportions! Please accept our apologies for allowing this to happen in the first place! We realise the emotional pressure this has placed on you, and remind you that we have found this contact to be exemplary. We point out the need to relay your thoughts and feelings on the subject so that we may lay your fears to rest.

Please allow us to register our displeasure at certain notions that we are as, 'men from Mars', for we have encountered a much more reliant account of our sobriety! We are deemed as being 'apparitions of light' and we manifest from time to time, a countenance that is more fitting for the occasion! We have allowed a lifting of the veil to reveal ourselves on numerous occasions, and are delighted to inform you that we will grant you the opportunity to see us in our true light! This time will be most auspicious for us also, and we decline to be interviewed until we can ascertain what level is needed to amplify this connection. We are well aware that all is being prepared, even as we speak, and we ask you to take courage for we shall express ourselves most admirably! We take it upon ourselves to manipulate your growth, to such an extent that we will have no other recourse but to speak our mind! We adjust levels accordingly and take you to that point of extreme ecstasy, knowing in reality that we have obeyed that very aspect of ourselves, which has been restored in all sense but one. We assist you in these proceedings and tempt you with our words, delivering a broader current of frequency needed to govern proceedings. We request a time of perfect precision, and we see further need of reconnaissance to adjust thought patterns. Delving deeper and deeper into the maelstrom, we invite you to take a closer look. We regale you with even further discoveries about yourselves, and we know you mean to follow us down this route of self discovery, so that we may analyse what took us to the brink and beyond! To make a finer point we registered our appeal, kicking up a storm . . . but we failed to gain support . . . and the rest is history!

27th February 2006 – We call you to attention, allowing the impart of our words to bring you strength! We realise there has been an enormous and significant rise in the number of participants in our recovery process. There are many of you who are prepared to take up the banner and allegiance to the cause, and we are well noted for our attempts to portray our friendship with those of you on Earth who have hearkened to our call! We have measured our success and gained respect in many avenues, relying on one another to get our message across. We never said it would be easy, but we know this mammoth undertaking will ensure that each and every one of you can rise to the challenge! We are expected to make way for a time of complete and utter dedication that will light the way for others to follow. We have opened your eyes to bring you the success you deserve, and we empower you now for this journey that will bring great rewards in Heaven and on Earth! We vouch for the safety of the little ones, and know you will allow us to come much nearer to them, as we issue new guidelines to intercept at a level that will bear fruit. We have adjusted many thought patterns, and express ourselves with the utmost joy to have registered and encapsulated such a remarkable recovery!

We take this to the point of no return and address other issues that have taken precedence. We are now able to remove ourselves from what could be considered by some, to be a madcap scenario, and we are able to alleviate this condition by expressing our desire to move on! We have obtained notoriety, and believe our success is partly down to a constant monitoring of services. We convey our heartfelt thanks to one and all, for the love and devotion that has been poured on the gaping wound of humanity!

We prepare ourselves for action and know that on the horizon, we have adjusted ourselves to the fact of a complete and utter cleansing, this has been the hardest choice to make, and we deliver to you now this ultimatum to follow your hearts! Do not hold back with floodgates, that which threatens your very existence, for it is in this we shall reach our salvation! We impart the need to understand our motives in this, and we reach a new formula for ascertaining the precautions necessary to make this disembarkation, a most natural recovery operation! We have allowed an assessment programme to precede our every move, and we relay certain measures to be taken by the Children of Earth that will enable this recovery to be completed in the blink of an eye! This process may only take a matter of nanoseconds, but we realise their true import as we rationalise what it is we are actually achieving! There will be no flash of blinding light, but we will assist you all to make this recovery genetically speaking, in a time framework that will give you ample opportunity to grow in a finer existence, and one of extreme and utter dedication to the service of others! We recommend a delay of certain elements that will need to be summoned forth more strategically on a higher level, and encompassed at a later stage in developments. We do however, take the time to nurture each and every one of you to grow in our love! This will necessitate further boundaries to be pushed back, and we know you will give us the choice of being reinstated as part of your family, for we have achieved salvation in a way that warrants our future as citizens of a new domain!

The words seem to becoming fast and furious just lately, and I was again awakened from sleep for a further transcription. We take it upon ourselves to usher in a light ... so profound as to illuminate the whole globe with the intensity of our love! We express ourselves with a resilience that knows no bounds, and we intervene to express our fortitude, making way for a far superior framework of existence. We have mentioned in the past of certain ulterior motives that have come into play, and we realise that this may seem to be nothing more, than a simple display of unrequited love! We therefore have decided that for us to get along, we must make a supreme effort to understand our different points of view. We accept that this has been a mammoth undertaking, and we have been taken to task for expecting too much in any one moment of your time! We have obeyed our heart in all matters, and are justifiably pleased to learn that you have already passed the test of a lifetime! We have examined data and prepare now a submission of our work, we intend to allow further studies so that we may assess the script more carefully, before we raise up our hand to be heard! Please investigate the possibility of taking this even further, for we feel a growing awareness of politics will be beneficial in these circumstances. We know you will allow us to make the necessary articles and deliver them with increasing speed. Please accept our resignation to the fact that we have become accustomed to your sleight of hand! *I feel they may refer to me sometimes transcribing incorrectly, as at times my mind jumps in to finish a sentence and we have to correct it afterwards.*

We feel impelled at this time to scrutinise in greater depth, what is necessary to claim our inheritance, and we broadcast that we bear witness to the fact that we were here on Earth long ago, long before the dinosaurs! We beamed aboard your planet in an age when men were no longer deemed a viable life form, and yet we took what little we could find, and initiated a seed that grew with such strength that we were able to manipulate its growth, forecasting the re-birthing of mankind! We have resurrected you now so that we may take on that format of long ago, resurrecting our hopes and dreams of a new nation. It has taken this final surge of growth to pull us through in all directions, and we now utilise this growth to restructure our alliance, depending on one another to forge a new identity! We have the ability to gain strength from each situation, expanding our theories to take on board the illusion of youth. We have known for some time of the fiasco on Earth, and we take you to task for allowing such indiscriminate acts of violence, in a society which has set such store on a mere 'golden globe' award, rather than focusing its attention on bringing to justice all those who display acts of terrorism towards their fellow man! We have found this to be a time of immense hatred that cannot be tolerated on any level, and we focus now on the heart centre to bring you a far greater love than man has ever known!

We resume our connection to bring you up to date. We have focused on what is necessary to bring about the release of certain prisoners, and we venture to say that we have compiled a list of suspects, who have displayed a dubious connection to those in charge! We implement a certain structure of defence that will allow a surrendering of all military personnel, this will decrease the violence displayed so vehemently in the Middle East! We regret there has been certain patronage that has caused great unrest, and we take it upon ourselves to release those who no longer are a threat to society! There have been instances of great regret, and our new policies will realign us to a new dimension of peace and purpose. We examine data and notify our friends and contemporaries of certain malfunctions that have arisen; we align ourselves with you and stop what could be a potentially harmful situation! We now reckon a month from now that you will have the necessary feedback to push forward, allowing us a greater renewal of services, and we broadcast to one and all what is necessary to save mankind from destruction! Prepare yourselves for delivery of more material that will enlighten you as to our whereabouts in the heavens, for we have instigated further retrieval of data stored, and will allow this template of love to be broadcast at a higher density for greater coverage! We have accepted our part on this journey and know you will take great delight in accompanying us. We push back the boundaries even further and ask you to take control of a situation that looms on the horizon, this will allow a replenishing of energies and we need this to be done quite urgently! We take our leave and wish you goodnight!

28th February 2006 – We have cause to celebrate, and we would like to bring to your attention a subject worthy of your time and commitment! We superimpose our thoughts on yours so that we may monitor what is fast approaching. There have been certain aspects of our discourse that have prepared us for this, and we maintain prior knowledge of events on the horizon. We deliver to the world a most comprehensive study for the future of mankind, and we join together in exclaiming that we have appreciated your company and input, delivering to us the data necessary to achieve this on such a vast scale! We thank also those from the higher realms who have passed on information, allowing a more natural format! We have become very aware that there are those of you who have forsaken your homes and children to be more constant to our needs, and we ask you now to join with us, exclaiming to one and all that we are here to lead you onto that land of milk and honey!

We close the gap that keeps us apart and allow you a closer look at our connection; we feel that you do justice to our words and impel you to believe in yourself. We recommend a course of action that will take you to further heights, and we lay our cards on the table, expressing our wishes for greater fortitude and a duty of care to those around you. We impel you to grant our wishes and with greater distinction, take on a more salubrious undertaking. We have monitored your success and allow you the pleasure of accompanying us to greater heights, we believe that all is in readiness for us to appreciate this next step forward, and we impel you to take great care in all you do! We mention no names but rejoice in the fact that one more lamb has been returned to the fold! *We have recently invited a new member to join our meditation group, who has added a certain vibrancy to discussions, and I'm very pleased that our star friends approve.*

We believe we can measure our success in two ways, by a deeper understanding of ourselves and by supplementing further growth with greater initiative, pushing forward our demonstration of love! We allow you a certain time framework to manipulate proceedings with a more potent management. We allow the formulation of certain ideas and substitute greater access with delivery of finer proportions, we are then able to realise a tighter framework where we can reach one another simultaneously, improving our accent on words. We make this a most simple format, and carry with it a formidable account of each moment spent on Earth! Volunteering our services, we recognise in each other the need to grow, and we bestow upon you a curriculum based on integrity and self esteem, completing the process of surrender in the fullest sense. We subject you to further rays, allowing you to take on a mission of excellence – hence the need for you to understand our motives! We clarify a few points, recommending that you step back in certain areas of mischief making, for we are not allowed to intercept! *I had been thinking of sending healing to a friend's husband to enable a more loving connection between them, but it seems I must not interfere!*

1st March 2006 – *Working at the computer, I gradually became aware of a strong energy drawing close and blending with me. I started to type the words that came into my head, but they were so fast that I had to stop and speak into my recorder instead!* We target different areas and take refuge in the fact that we have known for some time now of this recovery process. We have been mealy mouthed in expressing ourselves, and we perform for you now in a way that will bear witness to our needs and desires for a better world! We take on board a much more salubrious role in proceedings, and draw close to show you what we are about. We recognise the need to grow in areas of expertise, and we rally round now to give you the support that you need! We register the fact that there are many who are here listening to our words, and we superimpose our ideals and theories to take you further and further unto the brink. We have denied access to those of you who feel the need to express yourselves, in a way that bears witness to the trials and tribulations of a lower nature. We have forbidden those of you who take this one step further, and we vow to you now that we will in no way allow these measures to take place!

We have forbidden, in all instances, these taboos from interfering with our thought forms, and we ably assist you to take back these thoughts and ideas of a less imperious nature!

We remember well our times spent with you on Earth, and we deny no access to those of you who we welcome aboard with open arms. We shall measure our success in the fact that you have grown in our love, and our time spent with you has brought us the utmost joy and conviction of a better life for all! We remember those areas of contest and self discipline, where we were able to come among you and broadcast our news. We believe it has taken us further and further into a world of mismanagement, lies and deceit, and we have noticed that there are many of you, who have taken us to task over what is given! We depend on you now to come forward and help us in our initiative, and we have involved as many of you as we can muster for their services. We simply bend and whisper in your ear a most impressive, imaginative stream of thoughts and ideas that avail you at every given opportunity! We measure the time spent with you, overcoming obstacles that stand in our way, for we are governed by a mightier source! We can instigate changes as easily as this! *I can now see my guide, Sayuri, clicking her fingers!* We obey our commands and ask that you do the same, so that we may relay these messages across the great divide.

We have welcomed this moment to be here with you now, expressing our hopes and our wishes for a grand recovery! We have expressed our needs and desires to be with you my child, and it is our pleasure and utmost joy to be here with you now! Please also express our wishes of goodwill to those who work with you, and we look forward to their company in the time ahead. Be prepared to devote your time and freedom to the cause, for we know you will do your utmost to bring us nearer. *I'm seeing Sayuri again among beautiful clouds of purple.* We take it upon ourselves to usher in a new control, and we depend on you to set the record straight, allowing us the freedom to initiate these sessions as and when the opportunity arises, for we take this to the highest level! We instruct our courtiers to extend a welcome, and we know you will take on board what is necessary as we approach this crossroads with our eyes wide open. There is an abundant opportunity that should be grabbed with both hands, and we extend our good wishes and heartfelt thanks for services rendered! We programme events to coincide with a delicate operation of skill and expertise, and we rely also on methods of adjustment, allowing a greater display of subservience to the cause. Operations are underway and we believe you do us justice, uttering each and every word and syllable with perfect ease. We adjust our thought patterns accordingly and take on an exuberant note, we impel you to strive for perfection and we accelerate our gift, preparing the way forward. We take a bow and deliver to you, in all her glory, a most handsome carriage that awaits your edification! We are alerted to a tampering of services and take on board a rescue that will outfox attempts at sabotage, engineering a supreme effort to take on the world in significant numbers! We attempt a coup de grace and invite all to come aboard, experiencing for themselves what is manifesting right before their eyes . . . a majestic monument of undying love!

A supreme and conscious effort is being made to reclaim the people of Earth, setting them on their feet in a new world of ample proportions. This will allow us to recover and govern a new existence in a format that will encompass the people of Earth in a warm and loving glow. We allow you to settle down and reclaim your identity while we manage accounts, bringing you all back on track! We believe this can be achieved, and will associate ourselves with this splendid mission that faces us head on. We do believe that we have encompassed every foreseeable cause for concern, and we alleviate all forms of mistrust as we relinquish our hold on the old and make way for the new. We have surprised ourselves in this endeavour, and we conclude by thanking one and all for their help in this programme; please extend our wishes of good health and happiness to all, and especially to those who have dedicated their lives to pushing this movement forward and along to its final conclusion! We are supremely aware that this challenge has given us all food for thought, and we take it one step further and congratulate you on a job well done! *I'm aware of a crowd of people lined up and clapping!* We summon the desire to have one last word, and submit a most worthwhile rendition of 'Land of Hope and Glory'!

We tend to our offspring and coax you now to leave behind all you hold most dear, as we venture into the unknown, literally taking a leap of faith into the universe and beyond your wildest dreams! Please accept our apologies for causing dismay . . . but as you allow these thoughts to percolate, you will come to realise that it is futile to stay in a world that has become sterile, where there is no love or promise of a future of any substance, only the remains of a world that forgets its true purpose . . . to procreate the species and to live in peace and harmony! We amplify this connection to bring you new hope and the promise of a far greater happiness, and we give this gift to you all wrapped up and ready to go! You have only to answer the call . . . to stand up and be counted and to climb aboard for the ride of your life, for we promise this will be the greatest journey ever recorded in the annals of time immemorial! We celebrate this coming together of two worlds where we shall grow together in peace and harmony, maintaining our structure of independence and living on a planet of outstanding beauty, one of immense privilege for us all! We recalibrate what is necessary to maintain our life forms, and declare to one and all that we shall remain in a state of total and utter dedication to our brothers and sisters of light. Amen!

We have taken upon ourselves the task of establishing a more productive role, and we summon now an army to bring forth this golden opportunity of freedom from oppression, silencing the tongues of those who would pour scorn on the afflicted! We venture forth onto further challenges, and take with us a sense of propriety in the knowledge of a job well done. We implore you now to prepare yourselves for the coming of our Lord, Jesus Christ, a man for all peoples! This will bring great sorrow to those of little faith but we believe, in all earnest that the gates of salvation will never close on those of you, whatever race or creed, or any soul who honours his brother! We forbid any association with the harbouring of greed or retrospectively, any form of monopoly over another. For in our domain we shall accomplish the impossible . . . to live the impossible dream and to fulfil our destiny of reaching the stars! We have taken time out to exemplify those of you who have risen to the occasion and obeyed the calling of your hearts, for you are most welcome in our world! For those of you who deny our very existence . . . we say unto you, that we shall not rest until you see with your own eyes that we are one and the same! We have seen a massive expansion of minds on all levels and we take you to that point of no return, developing you in a way that bears credence to our words. We move you forward on a beam of light, and take it upon ourselves to issue a direct promise to the people of Earth . . . to keep them safe from harm!

Chapter 7
Stairway to the Stars

7th March 2006 – We accept our pathway, forgiving those who would cause us harm, and we infiltrate at a new level to bring greater awareness, drawing to a close our last mission on Earth! We rectify what has given cause for concern, and know that you will bear witness to what is to be our greatest achievement yet! We have remained on board to take you to that point of no return, but we must now relinquish our hold on you so that you may initialise our plan of action for the future. We obey our calling and take you further along this highway of love; we reclaim what is rightfully ours and pass you on into capable hands! We take it upon ourselves to issue you with new guidelines, and express our sadness at losing that part of you which has grown alongside us! *I felt very tearful at this point.* We discuss rudimentary deals and pacts and come up with a more lucrative contract. We obey our calling and remain on track, casting our veil across a wide area and scanning for evidence that will prove to be rewarding in every detail. It is necessary at this time to stay focused, and we participate in a grand reunion, interpenetrating on a level that will allow us to connect at a new frequency more becoming to our status! We recommend a clearing out of the old and making way for the new, for this structure will help us to appreciate and maintain resources available to us. Please ask yourself this question . . . do we obey the dictates of the heart in all things? If the answer is no – then we are letting the side down! Please remain on track at all times for we need constancy in the times ahead. We believe there is a purpose behind every judgement, and we know it makes sense to follow your heart. Take it from us, we have been there and got the T-shirt!

We invest in a frequency that will maintain harmony, and allowing for discrepancies, we vouch for a more fruitful episode on the horizon. Be prepared for storms of a density that will cloud your mind to a degree! We are offering you hope and salvation; we state our integrity and know with increasing abundance, you will divine a greater wealth of knowledge. We betray our emotions with a tear or two as we help you to accept the inevitable, enveloping you in our love and maintaining the necessary structure to alleviate discomfort! We remain by your side, issuing you with new guidelines, and we take it upon ourselves to warrant this connection with a promise of outstanding beauty and grace, a remarkable assignation that will bear witness to what has become a momentous exodus! Betrothed to an idea that will bring a greater legacy for one and all, we deliver a new strain of thought, underlining in greater detail those requisitions required to make this work. We govern proceedings from afar and take it to the next level, we are well aware of the constancy needed and recommend prior to taking your rest that you assist us with your presence!

6th March 2006 – We impel you to take heed – remember that we take you to the brink to overcome a disaster of enormous proportions! We regale you with as much information as we can muster at this time, and ask you to feel assured that all is being done to help you. We are convinced of a need for further measures to be taken before we concur on what is necessary to maintain peace and harmony on a grand scale. We accelerate this condition to enable a fact finding operation that will guide us nearer to the truth, displaying agenda items that are needed to maintain constancy. We reply to questions that have been directed to us and ask you to monitor, in greater depth, all we have requested. There is a constant need to operate on a level that is achievable, and we require you to understand the necessity to apply yourself in all directions! We govern proceedings with an air of authority, asking you to accept each and every item for recalibration, for we have assisted you in this new growth and allow you to connect at a level which will support and nourish you. We apply for new jurisdiction over matters that have become second nature to us, and we succeed in bringing forth a greater volume of success!

We attend to details and iron out the creases to bring you aboard. Once more unto the brink dear friends . . . we challenge you further and request an enlisting that will bring about great changes! *We have ventured forth and sailed into harbour's view. I can see men in a boat – one has a loud hailer and is calling out!* We recommend taking action and impel you to come aboard, there are many of us here and we welcome you most warmly, assisting you in making a full recovery! We assume the role of adjudicator and accept there have been instances, regrettably, where there has been a malformation of certain attitudes. We impress you to take stock, and ask for a surrendering of services until we can maintain peace and harmony in all directions. We take the time to amplify what is needed to rectify conditions abroad, superimposing our thoughts on yours to get the message across loudly and clearly. Do not, in any circumstances, bend to the whims of those who would betray you with a cursory glance! We have noticed a certain reticence in dealing with those who have cost you your growth, on more than one occasion, and we impel you to make a stand for yourself and for those who cannot hold their own! We have denied action to those of you, who we feel have implicated themselves in matters that do not concern them, but we shall extricate those who have showed themselves to be entirely at a loss for words, mesmerised by events taking place at this time! We exemplify all who have taken on board what is necessary to sustain life and we allow you to govern proceedings, however, we take you to task for not displaying more agenda items!

We take great delight in enthralling a nation with our repartee, and we believe this will all make sense in a month or two when we have dispelled all thoughts and fears of events taking place! Please believe us when we tell you that this is all in your best interests, for we have no way of knowing how this will unfold in a pre-history scenario! We are therefore, greatly indebted to your expertise in allowing us to experiment with your prior consent, this will allow us to come forward at a much earlier time scale! We introduce you to a more salubrious time line, and allow you access to our data banks, for this will help you to achieve a growing volume of success. We allow you to manipulate your structure so that we may be seen through your eyes as one and the same; we believe this will enable us to accept one another on the same frequency! We viably connect and allow an intermingling of races, encompassing a new structure of interdependence that will weigh heavily on the success of those who have gone before. We participate in this new venture, allowing a certain reticence in areas where respect is due; we foresee this new venture as bordering on the extreme, and we take you to that point of complete and utter control! We guard the proceedings and watch over you, making sure that all is above board. Regrettably there are time constraints that make it impossible to give full rein, however, we shall be able to amply display all necessary criteria and vouch for a committed study of interests.

We rely on the grace and favour of those around you to accept their part in proceedings, acquiring the perfect partnership in this assemblage. We register our disapproval by forestalling any advantage from neighbouring activists. We suppress and delay countless forms of reproduction. *I think this may refer to cloning.* We have also registered numerous claims of neo Satanism – to be avoided at all costs! We do not tolerate any detrimental references to Judaism or any dysfunctional racial discrimination, and we set the record straight by ironing out the differences in beliefs and cultures! We have justly denied any references to the 'Third Reich', and we also abolish references pertaining to terminations of pregnancy! <u>We decree most absolutely that there can never be any consequence that is too great to forgive, and we ask</u>

you now to look at your lives and ask for redemption! We display motions that are open to debate, and we rely on you to come forward and isolate the anguish within you, releasing that part of you which is hurt so that it may be expelled and healed in all senses! We believe there is a part of you that is like a little child who is lost, and we come now to enfold you in our loving care. As we take you into our arms and hold you . . . let out those sighs and frustrations with life . . . we come to take away your pain, to reduce your fear factor and to make you whole! We will tend to your irritations, helping you see they were all worthwhile, and together we shall gain contentment! We have justly been called 'Jesuits' and yet we come from a time where all men served God. We most nobly decree that we stand before God in all our splendour, calling upon Him to usher in a new awareness that will wreak havoc on Earth! We say unto you now that we shall in no way be deceived by man's desires, for we have conquered over the lower nature of mankind, guided and betrothed to a higher source and reclaiming our right to sit at the feet of the redeemed!

7th March 2006 – We are on a soul journey that will lead us to discovering for ourselves, what is necessary to maintain peace and harmony. We have recovered and reclaimed our heritage and we hark back to those times on Earth, when we were renowned for having taken that most difficult step of reaching out and touching that part of us which is God! We grapple with defence systems purporting to be under our control, and we measure our success by enrolling in further studies. We reserve our frequency and put on ice until needed, and obeying the laws of gravity, we descend in great numbers to help you achieve your destiny! We feel an incredible struggle taking place on all levels, and we are rewarded with an ample display of acoustics as your voices gather momentum, singing the praises of our Lord, Jesus Christ! We unfold what is not known, allowing the suffering which has taken place to fall away and be replaced with love, a love so divine as to awaken in each and every one of you, the inspiration that will take you to the heights of ecstasy and beyond! We are reminded of that time on Earth when we gathered together to pay our tributes and respects, remembering how we suffered our loss and the pain we felt at losing our beloved Master! A chapter closed on our lives when he was taken from us, but we believe in all honesty . . . that the day our Lord gave up his life . . . was the day we vanquished over evil! For it is written that he who cometh into the world and redeems himself, will reap a greater harvest than his brother who forsakes his neighbour to save his own skin!

We rely heavily on these anecdotes to persuade a nation of revellers to listen to that voice which beckons within them, for we have taken our own values and principles to stake our claim of eternal life! We prepare a way to take those on board who have examined in great detail what is necessary to sustain our advantage, and we recommend a clearing out of all that has held us back from delivering a finer frequency! We have allowed for certain drawbacks but deliver to you now the words our Master spoke to us at the 'Sermon on the Mount'! We have prepared a way forward so that you shall see with your own eyes all that is before you, and we tremble with fear at the pain and suffering of mankind, cast down into the fires of hell of their own making! For we shall be raised up into the land of the living where the waters of everlasting life pour freely! We strengthen that part of you that abides with us and we wish to take you now to that place of immeasurable love, and dedication beyond the bounds of duty. Be uplifted in your endeavours as we take this to the point of supreme and utter joy!

We welcome you into the fold my little one, and tend to your needs . . . we hasten to add that we are overcome with joy at receiving you, enfolding you in our hearts and minds! We take delivery of a new point of reference and intercept to bring you news – we have powerfully recommended a bringing to the fore of talents not yet recovered. We identify the need to grow and delight in informing you that we shall greatly benefit from this next chapter in our lives! There has been a massive expansion of minds, which necessitate further powerful studies as we realise the potential of our words, and we recognise the need to forge ahead, developing our work of extreme importance! We take it upon ourselves to notify those of you here listening, that we shall behave in an exemplary manner at all times, recognising the fact that we shall make a mockery of all that is held sacrosanct! We have ignited a nation bent on war into achieving a greater vision, one that will encompass the hearts and minds of all those who strive for peace and harmony in a world of chaos, which has reduced the masses to tears of pain and frustration!

We bow down before you and offer you salvation as a means forward, we ask you to love one another, protecting each other from harm! Supporting each other through trials and tribulations so that you may come to love those that hate you and trample upon you, for they are as children who have lost their way! <u>Love will transmute all pain and suffering – we cannot emphasise that enough</u> and take it one step further! We redeem those who will recant on their lives of jealousy and mistrust, overpowering them with a sense of justice and of a better world to come, so that we may all stand in the eyes of God and be counted! *At this point I'm feeling so emotional that my eyes are welling up with tears!* We are supreme in our connection to Heaven and relay our messages of hope to the Children of Earth – to make a special commitment in helping them achieve their highest, divine right – a place with God in Heaven. Amen! This is your divine right, each and every one of you, and we help you attain what is rightfully yours to complete the journey of a lifetime, and to take that final step that will bring you to that 'Stairway to the Stars'!

9th March 2006 – We shine light on a clouded issue and ask you to remember that we are able at this time to realise our ambitions of a future paved with good intentions, we apply ourselves and resurrect a dream! We wish you well and know that we are bound for that place of utmost joy, and resignation to the fact that we are one and the same. Be prepared for more of the same as we extract even more information to be passed onto the Children of Earth! We have examined your motives and note that you are incredibly possessed of those qualities we find most endearing, we take you to task though in assuming that we have the God given right of exposure! Do not limit yourself in this way, as we see greater sacrifices being taken to forge that bond of love and respect. We impel you to take a firm stand in your endeavours for we are concerned in an area that shall hold you back, and we push you on to further advantage. Please instigate a new line of support, and we shall encourage you to fly in all sense of the word on to new challenges. We ask you to bear witness to what has been a time of increasing joy and happiness for us, your friends on the other side! We empower you now to take a stand for us and all mankind, uplifting the hearts of all those who have come to expect the unexpected. We take you to new heights and wish you all the success in this world and the next!

11th March 2006 – We continue our avalanche of success with further discoveries, taking the time to analyse and surrendering ourselves to the dream of a better world. We visualise a time of peace and prosperity and are compelled to look at certain issues more closely. We ask that you take care in respect to a clearing that has manifested in an area of karma! We ask you to look closely at what is needed, and we impel you to take more care with your energy levels. There is greater need to forecast attitudes that have arisen, and we take you to task for allowing this pressure to increase at a time of unrest! We relish a season of goodwill among men, rectifying disturbances that have led others astray; we march for freedom of the people and know we have manifested a greater interest in Earth and all those on her. We rectify this programme that has taken us far and wide – our destination is Earth and we realise greater measures are in place to allow us the pleasure of your company! We believe it will be only a matter of moments before we make contact, and ask you to initialise this bonding of energies, giving us access to your dimension. We have taken great delight in your company and assist a new awakening in the community as a whole; please assist us in this passage of time for we are able to make a greater impact at this level of communication!

We feel an immeasurable tie and bond with those on Earth, knowing our time here has borne fruit, and we persist in bringing to the fore even more knowledge, permeating its way into the hearts and minds of mankind! We are indebted to you at this time for alleviating the stresses and strains of every day life, and we leave it to your imagination as to how and when we shall make our comeback! This has been our greatest adventure yet and we will not spoil what will be a most hospitable encounter – by allowing negative feedback to stand in our way! We have manufactured enough energy to take you on board and notify you of any changes made before the event in question. We allow a certain manipulation of energy levels to pronounce you as one of us and we take it to the extreme, announcing our credentials appertaining to our state of existence! We regulate each meeting at a moments notice, supplying you with enough information to enable a crossing over of fundamental and basic instincts. We have taken our time in recovering what will probably be our greatest mission yet, and we would like to thank you for cooperating with us to bring about this complete recovery! We depend on you to take this every step of the way, and we know too, that you will allow us to beam ahead of you in making this mission a complete success!

We inspire a nation to take that next step forwards, and we vow to one and all that this new growth will stretch the imagination to such a degree, that we will see an increasingly, greater advantage in our manoeuvrability to merge the hearts and minds of mankind, steering them away from what is holding them back, and turning them around to face us head on! We come from a time frame that will give easier access and are constantly orbiting the globe watching over you, supplying you with new challenges and overcoming obstacles that prevent us from delivering on time. We appreciate at this time that you have a great deal to process, and we make our study a concentrated effort of focussing more clearly on issues outstanding! We believe that this next episode in your life will bring with it a feeling of wonderment and joy, and we are beholden to you in our measurement of success. We propel you gently down the stream. *I'm now hearing the song 'row, row, row your boat gently down the stream.*

12ᵗʰ March 2006 – We are inclined to believe in freedom of speech, and we recognise in each other the need to move on, to stand up and be counted in this time frame. We juggle with our thoughts, surrendering with complete and utter dedication – a sweet surrender. We constantly examine motives and satisfy our questioning of ideals, asking you now to be prepared to take on what will probably come to be known, as the greatest adventure of all time! We forecast a massive explosion of services right across the world, all taking on this objective and carrying it forward! We empower the people of Earth to support our regime, scrutinising every possible defect, registering any disapprovals and helping us to make the right decisions at the appropriate time! Hiroshima and Nagasaki amplified what man is capable of . . . and we decline a repeat of that scenario! We have magnified our resources and expect you to make further discoveries in due course. We have demonstrated the ability to fly, and we know you will take this to the top of your priorities, overseeing what is necessary to make this as painless as possible! We take on board what is necessary for a *coup de grace*, and recognise the fact that we are similar in nature, expounding our theories on the universe, and delaying action until we are sure we have the right components to make this a roaring success! We develop a mainstream advantage by preparing, in great detail, a constant stream of chatter at a more leisurely pace. In this way we are able to define each other's views on policies and procedures at every stage of the game plan!

We envisage that in the next few years we shall have lift off, and this will bring about an immense learning curve on both sides! *How many years are there to go before we have – 'lift off'?* We make an analysis of between five and six years! We feel the advantage is on our side, and we shall endeavour to take over at a time that is compatible with resources. We beam ahead of you and light your pathway, taking you to that place of immense beauty, unparalleled anywhere in your universe! We enable this co-joining to take place between our two states of existence, to enhance both of our life lines; we expect miracles to happen as a matter of fact, and insist on a soft landing! We experience a setback in certain conditions that are left to the imagination, depending on the structure of each home to be compatible with thought forms. We realise this may seem bizarre, but this is the way we conduct ourselves, for everything is manifested by thought, and we allow no subterranean thoughts to mar the presence of perfection! We recommend a short break! *Mulling over these last few words, I came to the conclusion that using the power of thought to build our homes, may not be as easy as we think if you'll pardon the pun. I guess there may be some strange looking homes until we have got the hang of things!*

After a rest I carried on transcribing. We recognise true talent when we see it, and we recognise in you – tact and diplomacy! We take on a new vision that will alleviate stresses and strains, embarking on a grand plan of action of the highest intent. We relish constancy but recognise the flaws that lead us astray, and we ask you to be prepared to sacrifice more of your time into governing issues of a clandestine nature! We foreclose on attitudes that are obsessed with melodramatic and insidious discrepancies, vile innuendos that have no truth or substance, other than to feed the minds of the sanctimonious! *I have finally had to confront someone who has maligned many of my acquaintances and caused me a serious draining of energies! I have now stepped back from them, sending out love and healing instead!* We retrace our steps and proceed to take down all paraphernalia that now has no part in our lives. We relinquish our hold on a barbaric society, venturing forth in all our glory and supplying a connection which illustrates the final measures to be taken. We hearken back to a time where we reigned supreme in our endeavours to forge a new alliance, we governed a nation entrenched in war and we behaved mercilessly with our brethren! We took our punishment and forged a greater bond of self reliance, becoming soldiers of great resilience and standing in a world that was rent in two! *I can feel tears stinging my eyes, as I'm shown warriors fighting with great swords; they look as if they come from around the time of Genghis Khan!*

We empower you now to hold onto that place in your heart that belongs to us, we relay the action needed and impel you to stand firm! We understand your tears my child, and exude control to win through this time of discord. We segregate those of you who have administered, to much acclaim, a most powerful episode and we take you to further heights, enabling an expansion of minds that will deliver further proof, that we are here among the population of Earth to earn the gratitude and respect that is due to us! We reprogram you to start your mission in earnest, taking on a more salubrious role in the upkeep of a nation bent on war! We supplement a meaningful desire to overcome the lower thoughts and nature of mankind, and to impose a stricter regime of maturity and grace! We impel you to listen to our words as they get through the clutter of thoughts, igniting in you that peer pressure that will supply you with enough encouragement to forge ahead! *I'm now seeing a priest wearing a long robe and little black hat.* We are with you all the way, for we associate ourselves with a God of love and do all within our power to lead you in the right direction, giving sustenance to your mind, body and spirit.

We have caused you to come among us and be counted, and we shall not rest until you bring your true identity into the light! We have grown accustomed to this barrage of thoughts that assail us from every angle across the universe, and we give full rein to what is considered, by some, to be an over active imagination! We can vouch for the fact that you have given us ample opportunity to express ourselves with clarity, and we take you now on a mission of much importance. We allow our stream of thought to give way to a more advantageous expansion of ideas, formulating in our minds and ready for the world to take on board! We have violated no laws to be here with you and express ourselves most eloquently, enabling a flashback of past events to surface and be remembered in greater detail! We forecast this flotilla of events to take place at a time in the near future, where we will be eligible to accommodate a larger audience, and we will take a superficial role in presenting a series of events that have caused consternation – a catalogue of disasters that happened long ago! We remember, with extreme dismay, events that took place which gave vent to, what can only be described as, the most ludicrous attempt to sabotage and destroy our world!

We have regaled you with tales from the past, and bring you now to that place where it all began! We have opened our hearts and minds to one another, retrieving what was necessary to obey the laws of our structure, and we relay our messages back and forth across the great divide, enabling a connection that will give us form! We terminate a frequency that is no longer required on this level, taking on a framework more suited to our needs, and we rely on you to take on board these agenda items, forecasting a greater reserve of energy. We look back on our times spent together with great respect, thanking you for all your endeavours, and we now impel you to make a stand so that we may grow together with greater expertise! We allow a reconditioning of energies to enable this growth to expand, and we take on board certain resolutions that will enable the population of Earth to be expelled and brought into alignment, with a surge of energy that will propel all into a new awareness!

We take this time to monitor in greater detail what is necessary for our evolution; we work our way through any teething problems and associate ourselves with a greater broadband of energy. We take action as and when necessary, taking this to a newer level of expediency, and we depend on you to allow broader issues to be resolved! We recognise the ability to grow in a role that has held back many, and we believe it is necessary, at this time, to develop further measures that can be taken to adjust the situation at present. We prepare you to stand your ground and be counted; there are numerous possibilities ahead and we vouch for your safety, backing up with a grand plan of action that will allow a coordination of services in the near future. We develop further measures that will stand us in good stead, and allow these proceedings to take a certain twist! We return the lamb to the fold, announcing in no uncertain terms that we shall reign supreme in our actions. We deliberately refrain from making too much of an issue with identification processes, these will be maintained and brought up to date as and when needed. We have broader issues to concentrate on and in the meantime, enable you to supply us with the facts and figures necessary for our evolution, for we have refined your growth, activating in you what is needed to maintain harmony!

18th March 2006 – *While sending out absent healing, I received the following transmission.* There is a nation wide disaster taking place, regrettably with loss of life! *I'm being shown a group of surgeons with masks over their faces in an operating theatre.* We are able to claim back those who are bound on a course of destruction, and feel that mammoth blunders have given way to formidable distress! *I can now see waves of energy like the ripples on a pond and sense there will be repercussions.* We initiate a raw understanding of credentials necessary and proceed along this pathway of light, instigating measures needed to bring about complete success! We open up the pathway to enable a massive expansion of minds and develop a broader understanding of what is needed to relay these facts and figures. We put it to you that there is a constant need to check and maintain this frequency, allowing us the scope necessary to portray our ideals and theories for a better world. We unveil and present to you certain feedback pertaining to the production of services across the globe, and we allow ourselves a moment's respite, gathering information that will enable a massive co-operative of voices to be heard! We encourage a positive stream of thought to deliver greater advantage, and we foresee on the horizon a greater need to follow your heart in all things.

Vanquishing our demons, we stride purposefully forward, full steam ahead; we multiply in strength, gathering forces, and ask you to regulate these meetings to give us greater impact. We forecast a growing expenditure of energy and proceed to take you down an avenue of thought that will bring great rewards. We attend to minor details that have led us astray, triggering greater delivery, and we broadcast to the nation changing our frequency to a higher level. There is new evidence that has given further cause for concern, and we bring to the fore a rapid expansion of plans to alleviate tension brewing on the Earth plane! We deliver our record of assumptions and lay them at your feet, reconciling differences of opinion and realising our strengths and weaknesses. We send packing all negative feedback, ensuring a greater production of services on the horizon. Raising ourselves up, we pick our way through the debris accumulated over many years, dusting off the cobwebs and relying on each other to pull through a hazardous situation! We interlope and bring you further news, we have the power to back this up with greater reserves and we hover on the brink, ready to bring the necessary requisites into the bargaining process. We are indebted to those of you who have maintained their silence, and we know it has been hard to maintain this structure while chomping at the bit, ready to spur you on! We entice you forward and utilise a requisitioning of energies necessary for our next encounter; we maintain our success and take you one step further.

Do not underestimate our power, for we are seen as a 'super race', contracted to regulate proceedings and take you to that furthest point, bringing sweet success! We are prone at times to monitor your growth with an aptitude of grace and favour, for we have found our time spent with you to be most worthwhile. We sanitize those areas that are infected and delay repercussions on the horizon, feeling extreme measures are in place for a full recovery. We have taken to task those of you, who interpret our wishes as being beholden to a race of introverts and pen pushers, and we instil in you the strength of purpose needed to push forward our plan of action! We note that you are most beleaguered with our requests of redundancy for the human race in its present state! We have malfunctioned at an alarming rate, posturing and proclaiming innocence in a world that has simply 'lost its marbles', where we have lost all sense of purpose and grown old before our time! Relinquish now your hold on a democracy that has bent over backwards to lead you astray, governed only by greed and despair of a fortune misspent! We take this to a summit of enquiries, and develop a mainstream authority that will allow us access to deliver our messages on an even keel to all and sundry. We have displayed integrity and self control in areas well beyond our boundaries, pushing back the deadline on a variety of issues outstanding. We give precedence to those points of view that remind us of who we are, and we help you assimilate memory recall that will satisfy your curiosity as to our intelligence, developing a broader understanding and concept of our heritage and clansmanship! We deliver a broader spectrum of intuitive sensing, enabling the population of Earth to bond with us on a level necessary to make contact. We allow this bonding to reconstitute a reformation of hearts and minds, which will enable us to make that mammoth leap into a new dimension. We batten down the hatches, and take it upon ourselves to offer our condolences to those of you who have felt the full force of negativity on Earth!

20ᵗʰ March 2006 – *I was very tired this evening and went to bed early, but was awoken a couple of hours later with words buzzing round my head. We* raise you up from your doom and gloom and push forward our incentive. Be not afraid – we instil in you greater fortitude as we power our way forward, and we take this to a higher level, instigating new methods with which to adequately prepare our messages. We maintain a network that will gain control across the universe, putting in place a grand connection of minds, and forecasting extreme measures to be taken in our search for an ideal world! We have taken on board more than enough research, and we forecast the necessity of greater measures before we have input of the highest calibre. We depend on you now to put aside any quibbles you may have, and concentrate on that which is most becoming to our cause. We aim for justice on each and every level, guaranteeing wider speculation and a sense of purpose, ratified on this occasion by the need to observe a greater connection of minds!

We forecast a clarity of understanding that will give way to an enchantment beyond all comprehension, and we allow you a peep into this forbidden world of ours, relaying messages that will give greater access in daylight hours! We have conditioned ourselves to remain on board, and forecast certain measures to be taken that will enhance our connection. We rely on you to analyse each and every thought process until you have honed, with complete satisfaction, each and every detail right down to the last letter! We beam you aboard now to amplify what is most necessary, and we access that place which has led us astray, forecasting measures necessary to enable a swift enterprise of energies needed to take this on board. We prompt you and deliver our anthology, giving reasons for our great distress on this momentous occasion! We feel the rapid expansion of minds on the horizon, and forbid any entry that has not given us complete satisfaction, trusting in each other in a way that will bring complete success!

We take you to the brink and bring back as many as we can, allowing for a downturn of frequency on a level that can be manipulated, and given impetus to forge a new alliance. We recommend at this stage of proceedings, a further uncovering of statistics necessary to indulge ourselves, displaying agenda items not covered previously! We recommend a clearing out of all clutter no longer required, and detoxify a situation that has warranted further amplification. We terrorise a nation bent on destruction of your own free will, and we allow you now the choice . . . to obey your heart . . . or prepare to face thy doom! We reckon on the average measurement of distance required to retrace our footsteps will take until the end of time, and we propose to take you along a difficult pathway that will bring about a change in man's history! In the blink of an eye we will resurrect a world of people who will no longer rely on one another to march for freedom, for we have annihilated treachery and deceit, giving full vent to our feelings in a new society where all men stand together in the eyes of God!

We incubate our measure of expertise to initialise a bonding of energies, and as we reach our destination we allow you the privilege of unravelling your heritage! It gives us great pleasure to instil in you the necessary requisites to enable this encoding, and we know from our peers that you have more than amply rectified any differences we had, drawing together in greater harmony and allegiance to the cause! Be not dismayed my child, for we have divulged secrets ready to be expelled and given to a world in dire need. We relegate thoughts of a lower nature, tearing them aside to make way for a grand connection of minds, and we forecast greater respect for advances made in areas of expertise. We know it makes sense to betray a tear or two, in the making of this fine example of an outpost at the furthest reach, on the edge of an empire built of hopes and dreams! It beggars belief that you would stoop so low as to change horses at this point in the proceedings; we bear witness to the fact that you have led us astray on numerous occasions, and we defy new action that will take us further into the maelstrom!

Please deliver our manuscript and take it to the top, supplying greater evidence than ever before of a nuclear reaction of enormous probabilities, that will have catastrophic expectations in a world that has remained unchanged by events taking place all around the globe! We need this interchanging of energies to reconstitute a new programme where death and dereliction have no means of expression! We accumulate a vast knowledge of proceedings, taken to alleviate malfunctions of this nature, and claim you back to live among us in peace and seclusion of the highest network of minds! We forecast greater absolution and prepare the way ahead for you to follow; we maintain sources available to us and evoke further discoveries that will lead us to a place of divine aspirations. We release our hold on you now and detach from this connection, please accept our heartfelt thanks for services rendered!

We beseech you to stay on board a moment longer, and ask you to portray our good wishes to those of you who have amplified this connection! We feel we have amply displayed what is necessary to release each and every one of you, taking measures to expel an entire population and initialising a new connection of minds. We forecast growth on each and every level of commitment, and we vow to you now my little ones, that we will leave no stone unturned until we have recovered each and every one of you! We fulfil our promise to the Children of Earth that we shall reclaim what is rightfully yours, setting you on course for a new world of utmost joy! Be in readiness little ones, and listen to our words for we have given you ample opportunity to grow in our love. We redeem all of you and allow a reconditioning of minds to allow you access to this port of call. We negotiate a new infrastructure that will release you all from old patterns of thinking, enlivening each and every one of you into becoming a race of people, who have taken to the stars, leaving behind a world of sadness and sorrow that has no hold over you, other than to release your fear and negativity born of self indulgence! We forecast that new measures will be in place at a time convenient to our usage, and we will dedicate our services to allow a joining of hearts and minds, becoming one voice. We dedicate our services to the cause and welcome you aboard, reclaiming our heritage and rightful position among the stars! We initialise a regrouping of energies and counterbalance any negative feedback, welcoming further discussions on a material level. We now have enough information to allow a further channelling, and this shall discharge energies needed for our catalogue of expressions! We empower you now to take this to the highest point and watch over you to enhance this connection of services. We impel you to take care – there is a need to relinquish our hold on certain items appertaining to the constitution of material success; we will devise new measures that will allow for a more constructive validation!

21st March 2006 – *Once more I was woken in the early hours with words buzzing round my head.* We develop and maintain this connection to bring us back on track; there have been certain impediments that have caused us to stray and we realise this puts a strain on all concerned. We now have to maintain our allegiance to the cause and this undoubtedly puts further strain on resources, it is therefore highly unlikely that we will be able to maintain this connection in the foreseeable future! Consequently we depend entirely on the resources of those who come to mock; there is a need in these circumstances to refrain from taking control, until we know for certain of patronage that will make history! We take this to a level of undisputed harmony, and we materialise for you now in great doses, future episodes of denial! We reclaim that part of you that has given cause for concern, helping you adjust those levels that need constant support.

Dear friend, we rely on you to maintain harmony and your perception of free will is guaranteed, only for so long as you are able to fill the gap that we have come to expect! We supply the means to an end and we deny you no access to this point of reference, vouching for your honesty and purest intent. We take you down an avenue of thought and portray your self-esteem to be bulked up to a higher level than ever before. We know this will enable future growth and we depend on you now to pull this off! Please endeavour with all your heart and soul to realise this connection, grow with ease along this highway of love for we have reclaimed you and put you back on track. We develop new measures to alleviate a deep sense of loss, and we will take you with us into the valley of death, enabling a soul searching that will give us a viable connection with the unseen!

We depend on you now to give vent to your thoughts and feelings and take this to the top, we are able to assist you with this, and ask only that you will give us your constant support. Unveiling these thought processes will to some, seem the epitome of further consternation, but we know they are in your best interests! We research our subject and allow you to reconcile your differences with a world that has wracked and ruined, what was once a place of immense peace and beauty of spirit. We come to save the world from deep despair, and forecast a growing concern with all we hold most dear. The time has come to foreclose on a population that has brought doom and gloom in every nook and cranny, causing untold heartache and misery! We undoubtedly express ourselves with great reserve, and deliver to you now the final measures needed to win back your affections. Please allow us to stroke and soothe your brow, initialising a new strength that will enable us to take you on a journey of the highest calibre.

We bend over backwards to make this a painless experience, allowing you free access to our dimension and giving you full rein to initialise a new future for all mankind. We take it upon ourselves to reconstruct what will become your home, and we ask you to accept our humble blessings as we invest in a new future together! We respectfully request a time of thanksgiving, and donate to you now a more lucrative role in reconditioning an entire galaxy! We reinvent ourselves and set our sights on higher issues, the like of which have never been seen before! We take this now to its final conclusion, and let us be done with innuendo, for we renegotiate our plan of action and ask that you represent us in this race against time! We represent a people who have come together at a moment's notice, and epitomize a nation that has given their consent in a time of struggle and ill ease. We forecast the necessary measures to put this book to bed, and take it upon ourselves to wish you the utmost joy, and expectancy of even greater deliveries as we recreate an atmosphere of light, reconnecting you to a higher sphere of existence!

22nd March 2006 – *I sat meditating before retiring to bed and was shown a tall, slim lady, who looked very much like the late, Princess Dianna of Wales.*

She wore a long, white dress and a lovely, large-brimmed hat, decorated with the same yellow flowers that were in the bouquet she carried. Behind her there was a long pathway that led to a large white building. Destructive elements of fear and mistrust take hold of a nation, developing egocentricities that, to a large extent, are brought upon themselves! We hasten to add that we have accomplished a mammoth fact finding operation, which will allow us to sample some home truths! We have discovered a new way of analysing data, bringing to your attention the considerable success in monitoring our growth and accessing boundaries previously closed to us.

We now have ample feedback and welcome you to come among us, we are delighted in your company and retrace our programme to analyse certain data that has become muddled! *I'm now being shown a film star from the 1920's who I think is Mae West – or is it Mary Pickford – I'm not sure!* There are instances when corrections are necessary, and we have gained great scope and energy from our dealings with the general public. We assist in these proceedings to bring you a lighter hearted look at what has become a society of goons and morons, for we fail to see the question that is on everybody's lips, and yet has never been spoken! This is because of a desire to hold back the floodgates on what may be considered unpalatable – and yes we do understand your cause for concern! However, the time is drawing nearer and nearer for us to call a halt to proceedings, informing the world of a trial and error scenario where we shall expand our boundaries, calling upon another frequency to enhance our standing! *I'm now being shown the English comedian, Norman Wisdom.* We have a basic knowledge of what we can expect from the human race, and are delighted to accompany you on this journey of a lifetime!

We deliver a broader, sequential understanding of what is to come in the near future, and we put it to you that miracles do occur! Further growth is needed on many levels before we have the necessary feedback, this will take until the year 2012, and we forecast further difficulties if we do not have this in place! We are prepared to give as much help as needed, waiting until each of you is ready for this demonstration of love to be complete. We take on board a resurrection of the most high, enveloping each and every one of you in our love – to be redeemed and given impetus to forge ahead. These structures will be put into place in a year's time, and we shall have even further feedback that will enable a recovery of the highest order. Please allow yourself more time to reconstitute what is necessary for these procedures! We claim back our inheritance, and deny you no access to this highway of love and devotion to the cause. We superimpose our thoughts on yours to get the message across loud and clear, for we believe you have the right to life eternal, and we empower you to carry the flame of love in your hearts, developing further action needed to take this to the highest point! We regard you as being most able for this cause and salute you!

I settled down for the night but two hours later felt the call for more communication. These promptings come from within your heart and enable us to make headway! We remember a season of goodwill and joy for all men, and we prepare you now for a season of the utmost tranquillity. We strive for that place of deep contentment, exclusive of trials and tribulations, and we offer this to you on a plate, being given ample time to grow in our love. There is cause to celebrate, and we take it upon ourselves to congratulate you on a job well done! We empower you for the journey ahead and ask that you take care; there is every need to be cautious for there are connections that would lead you astray! We are here to take your hand and guide you through the holocaust onto a different pathway, one that will lighten your steps, depending on a certain magic to take you on board! We grow together in our love, and develop ways of reaching out and touching that very part of you that has grown beyond recognition. We are most proud of your achievements and wish to develop you further to lighten up your days! Beyond is a pathway not yet tried, and we realise the scope that is necessary could become a burden to you if your heart is not in it one hundred percent! We are most indebted to you at this time, and envelop you in a mantle of strength and joy, enabling this passage of time to flow more easily.

We prepare you for an awakening on a grand scale and we treat you with 'kid gloves', to awaken in you that sense of purpose necessary for the journey ahead. We allow you the refuge of remaining in a state of perplexity, until we have reached that point of no return, in this way we save you from anxiety! There has been a massive shift in perceptions, transcending the enormous difficulties of maintaining equilibrium, and manifesting in a most enjoyable rendition of services across the globe! We see these activities taking place as highly commendable, and instruct you with further measures to be taken to ensure greater fortitude. We are empowered to give you short notice of impending details, and we know you will allow us to further manipulate your mind in readiness for what lies ahead. Success! We need to remind you that there have been further issues presented to us, which allow for no mistakes, and we propel you forward to usher in a new awareness for mankind, taking us all to a new level of understanding! It is within this framework that we will have a better chance of making that commitment, and we regulate this mission, allowing a connection of the highest. We recollect our times spent together, and transcend our boundaries, on course for the stars and beyond where all is waiting! *I thought about my eldest daughter and how I missed her, wishing she could live closer.* We impel you to stand back and watch closely, we are forbidden to access these quarters! We rely on you to summon forth that growth that will assist us on this pathway, and are indebted to your tireless campaign to help us fulfil our destiny. Keep on track and we will reclaim our rightful place in the hearts of those we love.

25th March 2006 – We manifest a greater glory for mankind, and infiltrating at new levels we make this as honest as we can. There are ways and means of healing the breach and we deem it advisable at this time to maintain your common sense! We are divided on certain issues and these we can adjust when the timing is right. Do not be downcast or dismayed at events taking place, for we have deemed it our responsibility to take you in hand and show you the way forward! We believe there has been a certain anguish that has given cause for concern, and we maintain our connection to give you the strength that is needed to take us all forward together. Be it known in our two worlds of a redemption that will reclassify areas of dedication. We feel a going back to the 'old ways' will amplify this connection, and bring the people of Earth closer to their final destination! It is with great reluctance that we surrender our principles on self gratification, for we are personally responsible in all areas of neglect, and we feel the timing is not yet right for a mass recouping of souls! We are governed by our hearts and take on board the consequences of having too ideal an approach.

We navigate our way across the stars and contemplate our next move! We are most indebted to you, and venture to say we have acquired a most valuable lesson, discovering new ways and methods of coming to terms with a new-age experience and connection! We believe we have had unparalleled success in bringing this to the attention of the masses, this will achieve more than we could have ever hoped or dreamed of, and we take it upon ourselves to heartily thank you for services rendered! We are extremely pleased and ask that you take this time to understand our connectedness. We are aware that there has been a violation of certain perimeters that cannot be tolerated at these times, and we undertake a massive expansion programme to get back on track!

26th March 2006 – *Mother's Day – After lunch, we settled down to watch 'Hitch Hikers Guide to the Galaxy'. I was amazed when I saw their space craft – it was almost identical to the pod I'd been shown during a meditation last month! It never ceases to amaze me that our friends also have a sense of humour! I feel that I've been on a long journey, gathering material from different species from other star systems. All who have an input in the future of mankind, as the knock-on effect of Earth's destruction would have dire consequences for our unseen neighbours!* We experience a growing need to register and apply ourselves at this time, and we listen to your innermost thoughts, relying on you now to help us maintain equilibrium. There is every need to take care, and we manipulate your senses to expel those notions that will take us far. On the horizon all is waiting as promised, and we mean to stretch the imagination with an alarming honesty! We foreclose on what is no longer required and ask you now to surrender yourself to us alone. We have vanquished over our darkest thoughts and taken you to higher realms, and we deliver now with great strength of purpose, all that is needed to keep the peace. We initialise a beam of light to envelop you at this time, releasing greater reserves of energy. Please prepare yourself for this campaign, for we are at that most crucial point in your history where mankind will take a massive step into the unknown! We implore you to utilise all at your feet, taking on board with you the power and knowledge that will satisfactorily reclaim your heritage! We have spoken of this before and know that it comes as no surprise, challenging each and every word has become second nature to us, and we deliver to you now an even more salubrious tale.

We will begin by telling you of further accounts that have led to our annihilation, and we take it to the extreme by rewarding you with our undivided attention in respect to where our allegiances lie! We are by no means entitled to accept this barrage of thoughts that assail us, as we have no comparison to vouchsafe our safe arrival on this planet. However, we do have more information flying at us from every angle of the universe, relaying messages of sympathy at our plight, and we have instigated new measures to be fathomed out and displayed for all to see! We have recommended a going back into time – to delay the prospect of an untimely explosion that causes great destruction to planet Earth! We forego the pleasures of the flesh, and delight in telling you that we have at last come to our senses, regaling you with our exploits in a new kingdom that will knock spots off your existence on Earth! We have known for some time now that you would constitute a final demand on us to display our affections, and we make this timely connection to witness at first hand, what is necessary to sustain a whole colony of folk who have your best interests at heart!

We believe we can make this leap of faith, whatever you want to call it, and ask you to take a chance on us! It is as simple as stepping off the pavement and walking across the road; we have no traffic lights to intercept us, just the sheer power of magical illumination! We share our sense of humour with you and develop new ways of growing closer together. Believe us when we say that this will be a supreme challenge to you all, and we know that it will come hard to many of you, making this mammoth change to your energy circuits that will in initialise in you that trust to thrust yourselves forward into a new dimension! Some say it will be as easy as falling off a log, but we like to epitomise it in a way that sounds more regal, such as sailing on the river or venturing down the stream. We cause ourselves great humiliation by not understanding, what for many is a difficult concept to accept! This time period will be used widely to convey our thoughts and feelings on this very subject, to allay all fears and mistrust of the situation at hand. Be prepared to accept a broad understanding of the capabilities of mankind, and finalising what will come to be accepted and given credence in all avenues! We have the greatest pleasure in announcing a new energy circuit that will bring about an incredulous transformation on all levels! We feel this will enable a greater understanding of what we offer you, the people of Earth, and we tremulously wait with bated breath for your answer!

Later in the evening I received a few more words. We take a very necessary step in mankind's evolution, paving the way for a joyous communion of minds, and we congratulate ourselves on the fact that we have come this far, preparing to take on further studies of the human race and all her idiosyncrasies! We supply you with enough material to further develop our allegiances and display our agenda items. *I'm now being shown figures from around the 18th century. In particular there is one gentleman who stands out as a very jovial chap, wearing a long coat and large hat, reminding me of a 'town crier'!* We make a mammoth effort in regards to the regaining of our composure, we require that you stand your ground and take all in your stride! Venturing into the realms of sheer fantasy, we stand at your side, and looking from left to right, we survey what is needed to rectify disturbances! There are many who call to us exercising their right to control their destiny, and we supply you all with enough information to make your choices, depending on common sense to prevail! There are isolated cases where we are unable to make contact, and to no avail, we knock at the door repeatedly in an attempt to alleviate the misery inside! In these circumstances we can only send out the love that is needed, and hope for a full recovery nearer the time. We reinstate those of you who follow our advice and show others through example. We depend on accuracy to maintain our structure, and allow you the nicety of developing stronger bonds with those you love. Beware in instances of betrayal – where you will come unstuck! We delight in informing you that our rescue attempt has released some new patterns of behaviour, and we believe, to some extent, we have made progress, for we have powered our way through negative thought forms and conquered over indescribable terror! We propel you now through this minefield of events, and catapult you into a new scenario, forecasting greater tolerance and a desire to do your best come what may!

28th March 2006 – We believe entirely in free speech, and deliver to you now a more eloquent study. We are reminded of times gone past, of a great hue and cry where we were dependent on monitoring our growth on a daily basis! There is now, however, a greater understanding that all will be achieved on a massive scale, and this development will help us to advance on a level that will give us greater impetus to forge ahead. We develop an initiative that will give us boundless energy, and we regret not being able to take on board more of you at this time! We feel this development will give us greater access to the minds, feelings and emotions of mankind, and we give greater access to those of you who have taken our instructions to heart. We obey our deeper instincts, allowing us the freedom to move and grow in each others love. We depend on you to access this connection at every level and we depend, in extreme circumstances, on a governing of forces that will enable us to function on a lower level! We relieve ourselves of any encumbrances that hold us back and push forward with greater resolve, maintaining independence of character. We feel this movement will help us to empower you all with our services, and we reckon on a year before we will have ample feedback of enormous proportions. We are able now to access those areas that have so far been denied, allowing us to connect you to a higher frequency!

We delve deeper and deeper into the maelstrom, resuming our connections to win through all that is troubling the nation as a whole in regards to pleasures of the flesh. We insist on rejuvenation and feel the need to aspire to higher levels. We curtail the need to fly beyond our orbit and we pull you back, enabling you to grow alongside us. There have been added instances of repression that have required us to cope with further instances of denial, and this has led to a massive reconnection of services that will stand us in good stead. We propel you forwards now and we take you to the 'Bay of Serenity' to motivate you further! A connection of minds has taken place and we invoke a response that will enable us to move forward together. We propel you to that place of indomitable love, and resume our connection with a stronger understanding of what we are about. We accept the vulnerability of your exposure, and will take you to that place of deep acceptance. We need a connection on a finer level to bring you closer, taking us to that frequency that can be controlled effortlessly, and we beam ahead of you to light your pathway, enabling this transmission to take place!

30ᵗʰ March 2006 – We follow the pathway, expressing our need to grow alongside one another and we fathom the destructibility that has given us cause for concern! We monitor our growth and suppress a growing curiosity that has enabled us to function momentarily at a higher level. We oppose action that has led to repercussions, and we know it makes sense to stop – and listen – before making that connection! We allow an incoming flux of energy to manifest greater control, enabling us to conquer over those issues that are forthcoming. We impel you to be more careful, there are certain aspects of behaviour that need challenging, and we are prepared to accept responsibility for our own actions. Needless to say this will be a most prominent time for all, and we delight in informing you that we are prepared and ready to go – full steam ahead!

We sanction this visit and ask that you take on board a deep sense of fulfilment and connection of the highest. There is a need to instil greater wisdom and we measure appropriately what is needed for this conquest over fears growing in the East! We manifest for you now a greater introduction that will manage our accounts in such a way, as to posthumously accept, without ridicule, our namesake! We go on from here with firmer ideals and principles, managing a network of promotions that will enable us to push forward. We enable a quickening to expand our prerogatives, forging ahead and growing stronger and wiser with each passing day. We manifest a super indulgence for what is necessary to perform our tasks, and we believe you will bring this to the highest attention, enabling us to take on board a more definitive role in proceedings. We forecast the need of certain measures to be taken, which will exemplify the necessity to stand back and listen! We indulge ourselves at this time in a corporate sense, to overcome misgivings of enormous proportions, and we indulge ourselves even further to take on board what is necessary to fulfil our ambitions!

We make this announcement at a time when all men will listen . . . and listen well, for we come to entice a nation that will allow us to demonstrate all that is necessary to relieve mankind of his shortcomings! It is with great regret we inform you, and we have spoken of this in the past, of preventative measures necessary to overcome destruction of the planet Earth! We have duly accepted our fate, and realise greater instincts of self preservation that have come to the fore. We visualise a year from now, and we take you to that point of the utmost clarity and respect, for issues that have surfaced for all to see! We make no exceptions and deliver our messages, superimposing our thoughts on all those who have the necessary aptitude to help us in our cause for freedom for all. We relay our messages to those of you who listen intently, and we obey our heart in expressing our humility. We express the ways and means of delivering our ultimatum, and we know you listen keenly to all we say, envisaging a new future for mankind so that we may we all grow and prosper as one kind!

We have taken this to heart in every aspect, opening up new ways to seek and explore all that has been given freely, and with great love. We are determined to make a success of this, and announce in no uncertain terms that we are here to stay! Our band of followers grows daily across the globe, a free enterprise giving greater access to those who struggle to make sense of the world in which we live! We have come far along this pathway, and we know you have delivered to us a most wonderful record of your pursuits on Earth. We reclaim that part of you which has grown alongside us, and we levitate to higher realms to access that place waiting in the wings! We believe we have match cased an opportunity of outstanding charisma, and we take on board new measures to undertake your existence on our planet! We isolate a moment in time and bring it to your attention that with our facts and figures, we have discovered a trilateral reference which will activate a surge of energy for our growth! We replenish our batteries and take you further, for we need to resurrect that part which will enable us to maintain this structure of excellence!

31st March 2006 – We move forward in glowing colours, taking with us what is necessary for the completion of our journey. We forecast greater measures being taken to overcome certain obstacles, and we relentlessly pursue what is necessary to reinstate our boundaries. We have no other course than to act with the utmost clarity of thought, and we enable now a dawn chorus to revive our sense of purpose. We enable a gathering of the clan, and supervise for you a reckoning of intent! We are bound on a course for the stars and enable you to re-enact this life and death scenario, giving full vent to our feelings and passions, for we have discovered a far better way of reaching out and touching that part of you that is us! We reclaim our heritage, and reach a place of unconditional love, on a frequency that everyone can understand and abide by. We take this great event as being the most powerful in history, and advise a strengthening of boundaries to regulate conditions, maintaining a source for negotiations. We rectify disturbances that have seen many grovelling in the mire, and we pay particular attention to the needs and desires of those who battle in our defence! We subscribe to a more affluent society, bringing back on track those of you, who have manipulated your way into the hearts and affections of your brothers and sisters on Earth.

We are prepared now to look back on our success and feel completely at ease with the situation, bearing in mind that we have taken on board a most notorious approach. We deliver a mainstream application of thoughts and ask you to lift your sights higher, for we mean to access a frequency that will give us far greater access to the hearts and minds of mankind! We deliver to you now a grand reckoning, and ask you to instigate a renewal of services, so that we may render the population of Earth on a par with ourselves! This coalition will be spontaneous, and we regard each and every one of you as our brother and sister, infiltrating at that level needed to pull you through – from this dimension of existence – to a much finer and harmonious level! We can reach this place of harmony by attending to the finer details in life, helping one another to get through the stresses and strains of everyday life. We have a tendency to run away with ourselves, and we believe that it is in your best interests to 'lay low' at this time!

We recoup our energies and let you into a little secret . . . we are bound for 'Heaven', and we believe, in all earnest that we have displayed the tendencies of a saint! There are certain instances, however, where we have fallen from grace, and we know that it grieves you to hear us say this, but we do at times, have to stop ourselves from laughing at your antics! Bearing in mind that you have adjusted yourself to a situation that many would be unable to handle, we are most proud of your achievements, and beckon you forward to obtain your just desserts! We have foreseen great success and propel you forward to accept your prize. *I'm now seeing myself up on stage accepting an award.* We take the patronage of our friends very seriously, and accept a final demand to be played out at our expense! We operate on a level that has won over the population of Earth and depend on you now to accept our advice on all levels. We maintain our services and welcome you aboard, please accept a reconditioning that will take us into a framework of the highest order! We maintain our success by regulating thought patterns in abundance, and we know that you will allow us to intercept those thoughts of a dubious nature! We pay particular attention to detail when the need arises, and we manifest for you now an incredible structure that will depend entirely on the imagination!

1st April 2006 – Figuratively speaking we come at a time of great repression, and although we deem it advisable to live by the laws of the land, we infiltrate at a level where bygones are bygones! We retrieve the data necessary to forge a new alliance and we relate to you by means of a telepathic condition. This vandalises to the extreme, corporate reductions of services and we know it makes sense to alleviate pressure of this sort! *There have been reports in the news of threats of many redundancies.* We analyse our thoughts and fears, putting it to you loud and clear, we aim to please and consider the nature of our adventure to be materialistically based. This enables a greater cross section to be coordinated, and we feel it our duty to point out to the people of Earth that we have made vast discoveries of enormous proportions, putting it to you that life on Earth has become second nature to us! We maintain our system and support you through your challenges, urging you not to lose faith! We have great regard for those of you who triumph over regret and remorse, for we shall not be weighed down by innuendos of a passionate nature. We recommend taking a step back and looking with fresh eyes at a situation staring us in the face! We have been compromised on several occasions and we need this to be as perfect as we can make it. Don't doubt your capabilities for we have all taken a leaf out of our own book, describing in nature what is apparent to us all! We reflect on our growth, making startling discoveries about ourselves, for we have been born into a new dimension of time and space!

We know you will give us this opportunity of thanking you, along with tens of millions of other folk, for this great quest of fulfilling our hopes and dreams, and materialising our words in book form for the Children of Earth, so that they may sit up and listen to what we have to say! A grand reunion of souls and minds has led us on this mission and we have forecast many ideal theories to be taken on board, but in the end it all boils down to the fact that we shall need to help one another in this crisis, which approaches with alarming speed! A necessary precaution to enable 'Mother Earth' a long term prognosis, for we mean to save her from total annihilation to be reborn in a new format, assisting us in our quest for evolution! We take the initiative in asking you to follow us to the shore, where we can evaluate our growth and come up with the necessary adjustments to enable a solution, which will rectify mistakes made in the past! We shudder to think what impact this would have had on a planet of lesser morals!

2nd April 2006 – We propose a toast . . . good health and happiness to one and all! We have cause for celebration and would ask you to accept on our behalf, a most welcoming formulation of ideas, which will enable us to grow and prosper as one and the same! We relinquish all doubts and fears, and tend to the needs of those who draw close to us. We embellish a certain ambiguity over the prospect of taking on board, what is the most natural progression of events to have surfaced for a very long time! We maintain an ecstasy that will govern proceedings for this eventuality and we elaborate, purposefully displaying our needs and desires to move forward on this beam of light. We are extremely rewarded with your persistence in having maintained our allegiance to the cause, accepting that your part has been one of most consequence, forming an alliance with the most noble of participants! We indulge ourselves by referring to these grand statesmen by name as we venture into the realms of light, dismissing the fact we are overcome with emotion at this grand reunion! On this occasion we are joined by those of you, who have impeccably given your allegiance, developing tolerant attitudes against the murmurings of discontent, in a parliament that has undertaken to uplift the people of the world! We have recognised in you the grace and favour bestowed upon the esteemed, and we welcome you here amongst us in retrospect, causing the utmost disruption of services as we march towards the same consequence! We materialise for you now a most potent address, to be sanctified and given expression in the execution of services, imparting our message loud and clear! We prepare a way for the legions on Earth so that we may govern with a sure hand, just and true!

3rd April 2006 – *Last night I dreamt of two bats, one seemed to be mummified but the other was alive and raring to go. To me this symbolises rebirth, the letting go of the old to make way for the vibrant and new. While checking my work I received a news flash from my friends!* We interject to bring you news . . . there is on the horizon a more fulfilling role, which will enable us to grow even closer together as one true voice! We shall update you as and when relevant news filters through!

4th April 2006 – *In the early hours my cat woke me, wanting to go downstairs. I sat with her awhile and felt my friends draw closer.* We bargain on further disturbances and notify you of what is required. We rally you to action, depending as always for you to maintain a sense of decorum in proceedings. Thought forms of every conceivable nature assail each waking moment, and we examine most carefully; there are mammoth challenges ahead with aspects of denial resurfacing for a final display of magnitude! We prepare for what will be our finest moment, and realise our hopes and dreams of a better world with coping mechanisms that extend our boundaries, forecasting greater reserve in our dalliance on Earth! We propel you along instigating further measures of atunement, and we need to discover for ourselves what is necessary to achieve the greatest heights of self awareness. We have grown together with alarming speed and request a recapturing of our glory days! Capitulating, we have taken you to that place of immeasurable beauty, trading places with the esteemed and venturing into unknown territory. We make massive changes in our ability to conduct ourselves with grace and favour, and we shall see further action as and when necessary, appertaining to our desire to overcome a neglected frame of mind. We are incapacitated to a degree, striving to maintain order of sorts, while succumbing to a barrage of futile gestures that lead us astray! Remain strong and true to our pathway together, for our mission is of the highest calibre and we will recover our senses in full to re-evaluate our needs and desires!

Be it known now in our world of joy and peace, for the need of further seclusion of the highest nature. We are bound on a course of the utmost importance, taking it upon ourselves to manifest all that is waiting on the horizon and begging to be looked at with closer scrutiny! We beg to differ on occasions and we see this as a necessary inclusion, allowing for all that has been permitted and occasioned, reminding you that we shall see this through until the final curtain! We display certain tendencies to erupt at a moment's notice; this is because we are becoming a trifle too involved in pursuits, other than allocated! We sacrifice our time spent with you to bring about further discoveries, relaying to you as much information as possible to make headway, and we can expect to be happily surprised at outcomes hovering on the brink! We take this time out to call upon you, giving strength and sustenance; we betray a tear or two in the proceedings and ask you to lean on us for preservation! We are given the respect we deserve and take this to a higher level, maintaining constancy and an overwhelming desire to succeed. We are grateful for your persistence, and envelop you in rays of understanding that will see you through this mission. We receive bombardment on a level unreached by neither man nor beast, and this will enable us all to reinitialise our growth even further, developing a greater span of attention in all directions!

We enable this cross section of services to manipulate your DNA in such a way that we may develop closer scrutiny in our friends and neighbours. We are forever in your debt and ask you to survey our memorandum in greater detail! We deliver in essence a final message, conveying our respects to all those of you who listen to our words, and we ask that you take upon yourselves the responsibility of carrying our thoughts to those around you, who can carry this burden of light! We manifest for you all far greater control in your own destiny, and find it most worthwhile to incorporate a sense of pride in the way we have conducted ourselves here on Earth! Now is the time of reckoning, and we shall look back at our time on Earth in great awe for what has been accomplished! A growing epitaph of fear and destruction shall be replaced by a glorious account of the day mankind lifted their sights to the stars and beyond, overcoming the greatest hurdle of all – death and destruction! We have overcome this scenario and take you forward on a beam of light, radiating our love in all directions and delivering the will-power to live and love one another! This is our destiny and we supply a course of action that will develop greater reserves of energy, asking you to watch your step!

7th April 2006 – We develop a connection with the unseen and venture on our journey into the unknown, we relish these times spent with you and congratulate you on further improvements made! This has enabled us to make contact for longer periods and we are delighted with events thus far. We initialise a new connection that will allow you further breathing space, for we realise that the time is imminent for a grand reclamation of souls. We divine greater knowledge for the time ahead and prepare the opening of another time framework, which will enable us to grow further into the realms of light. This mammoth change in identity will enhance our connection, and we will become truly ourselves! We take this initiative very seriously and recommend a time delay that will encourage further growth of the population. We are able in this way to comfort the bereaved, and allow a change of identity with greater formation and accuracy! We enable these proceedings to take place in a time lock mechanism, regulated and watched over by 'Time Sentinels'! These 'Beings of Light' have transcended our structure and are empowered to watch over us, bringing harmony and reflection to one and all. We recommend at this time an anchoring of services and take it upon ourselves to rectify disturbances of spirit, for we have inclined to incorporate into our energy fields a less than satisfactory turbulence, which has caused havoc to our energy systems! We betray our solar system into thinking it has outgrown our structure, but we realise in this time of chaos that we have been flung into a major catastrophe of ever increasing circles! This can cause in itself greater destruction, and we take it upon ourselves to supplant this natural creation of energies with a much more defiant attitude, one of respect for the suffering this has caused on a large scale! We realise the impact of this scenario has caused wide anger among the echelons, and we declare ourselves 'non compos mentis'! We have reached agreement on terms and conditions and superimpose our thoughts on yours to intercept at this stage of play.

We command respect and a most loyal following, depending on

a stratosphere of love and understanding to reach our final destination. Consequently we believe that all our goodbyes are hellos in reality, and we reach out now to forge a pathway of light that will take us to that place of constancy! We supply you with enough courage and take you to a place of safe harbour and sanctuary. We are able to withstand the torrent of abuse laid at your door and we prepare you for action, bringing you to a place of tranquillity where we shall connect you to a higher level. We impress you with our terminology and defy action that could cause distress; we believe you will assist us in these gatherings and ask that you keep us a place by your side in the near future! We rectify disturbances and put to shame those of you who defy us, for we are not about to let go in any way, shape or form! We are tied to Earth by bonds of love and reclaim what is rightfully ours, a chance to live and breathe in a world undefiled! We experience a setback, pledging our allegiance to get back on track with a variety of issues that need addressing. We are prepared to make a stand and set the record straight; we will need to abolish all designs of a less scrupulous nature, and we see a growing reservation on the horizon for issues unresolved!

We shall 'bite the bullet' and take a course of least resistance, which will in effect bring us to exactly the same point of reference! We exchange particles of mistrust and replace with a sense of foreboding, this is because of unforeseen circumstances that have led us astray, and we apologise for the interference caused! We now take upon our shoulders greater responsibility and enquire after your health! In all of this we have taken on a most noble mission and are delighted with the consequences of our actions. We feel extremely rewarded with your warmth and animation of spirit, taking on board, in large amounts, a perfect grounding of energies that will help us to reach a state of equilibrium! We define a course of action that will reinstate our self worth and we take these issues, broadcasting to the nation all that is needed to bring about a reformation, which will enlighten each and every one of you! We reprogram a course of events that will lead to the ultimate connectiveness to the source, and we will truly recover ourselves in this moment of time! A grand reclamation of souls that will take us back a million light years, and give us the grounding we deserve! This we will accomplish with your help, and we tend now to the Children of Earth, empowering you to join us and reinstate the values that have been, to all intents and purposes, lost in a world besotted by technology!

We perpetuate a race that has been brought to justice, and we take it upon ourselves to allow you the privilege of standing alongside us in our quest for everlasting life! We shatter the illusions of those who come to mock, and feel a sense of pride in those who have stood firm and tended to our needs! We believe we have conquered over the most difficult time on Earth and we retain those of you, who have allowed us to penetrate their existence with our own! On this most auspicious occasion, we sanctify and bless the population of Earth, taking them on a pathway to the stars and beyond, to share in our dream of peace and harmony among all nationalities, gender and creed! We ask now that you close this file and dedicate it to the 'Children of Earth' in the hope that one day, we will all come together to be as one, a grand reunion of souls on a plateau of existence that will push back the barriers of disbelief – enabling a rebirth!

After Word

We have reigned supreme in our attempts to get our message across, and we know that you will manage our accounts in such a way that will bring great pleasure to those of us here in Elysium! We decorate your hearts and minds with a fragrant reminder of all that we have achieved, and ask that you bear witness to a most death defying ordeal that has ever been our misfortune to experience! We have accomplished more than we could have ever imagined, and we take you to that point of total and utter dedication, safe in the knowledge that we have accomplished in our main areas of disbelief. We have regaled you with stories from the past and taken you to that place of unimaginable horror, portraying our need to invest in a new future where we shall make more sense of the human race!

Karma

We are part of a collective consciousness sometimes referred to as God
Born as sparks from this eternal flame we are then released – some to
the Earth plane
We come to learn our lessons to improve our souls and minds
Some come as guides and teachers sent to help us and all mankind
To lift the Earth's vibrations and save her from despair
When all around is chaos and a total lack of care
Life is a continuous circle there is no death of the soul
We re-emerge on a different plane of existence – that is all
Why is it so hard for man to understand this plan
When God has promised this to every woman child and man
His house has many mansions there's room enough to share
If we look to one another and show a little care
His patience is deep and boundless long centuries he'll wait
Knowing each and everyone of us can never escape our fate
Love will draw us like a magnet back to the central force
Asking for forgiveness full of tears and remorse
We all will be shown as children a love so fierce and strong
And forgiveness will be given no matter how bad the wrong
We'll meet those who have gone before us family friends and guides
Those who have loved and encouraged us and never left our side
Gently we will be counselled and shown the life that we have led
With no recriminations for blood that has been shed
No man will stand to judge us for crimes that have occurred
But our hearts will weigh so heavy when the victims voice is heard
A plan will be drawn up of how we can compensate
This age old law of Karma is everybody's fate
No matter how long it takes you or how many lives you live
From the one that you have taken one day you'll have to give
When mankind can understand life doesn't end with death
His soul will strive to make amends until his final breath

Eileen Coleman

Printed in the United Kingdom by
Lightning Source UK Ltd., Milton Keynes
140328UK00001B/45/P